Litigation Support Department

Mark Lieb

Litigation Support Department
©2005 Ad Litem Consulting, Inc.

ISBN Number - 0-9774267-0-X
ISBN-13 Number - 9780977426706

Library of Congress Control Number (LCCN): 2005909508

Ad Litem Consulting, Inc.
PO 124873
San Diego, CA 92112-4873
http://www.AdLitem.com

Dedication

For my family -

Sam & Anne,
Saul & Adele,
Michael & Roslyn,
Larry, Kate, Nick & Annie
Jeff, Louise, Evan, Matt & Diana

Acknowledgements

There are many people who I would like to acknowledge for their help, whether technical, editorial, advisory or philosophical. If I forget someone, there is always the next edition.

- Barberio, Greg
- Brown, Ed
- Campbell, Ian
- Cheung, Terence
- Hanahan, Barbara
- Jaycox, Don
- Jensen, Dave
- JosephLynch, Jason
- Kennedy, David
- Krehel, Greg
- Lambert Jr., Dennis
- Leib, Jay*
- Marean III, Browning
- Mercereau, Beau
- Petrie, Scott
- Raugust, Alex
- Rosenwein, Thomas D.
- Tominna, Michael
- Utsler, Joe
- Weber, Rick
- While, L David
- Williams, Cindy
- Young, Frank, Ken & Joan
- Young, Steve, Carolyn, Jake & Ashley

* A special thanks to Jay Leib who introduced me to Litigation Support. He and Rick Weber offered me a position and stake in a startup company called "Advocate Solutions." At the time, Jay and Rick were creating a new product called "Discovery Cracker". Jay indicated that a new development, "electronic discovery," was going to be big. He also suggested that Litigation Support was an industry where one could make a good career. Just exiting from a startup, I passed on the full-time position and ownership. I did, however, take his advice and a consulting position. I spend the next years learning everything I could about the industry. He was right, this is a good industry. Thanks, Jay.

Table of Contents

Preface

Every law firm has its own personality and culture, often with people who have been there for ten, twenty or more years. In this sort of environment, instituting a new system can be difficult, if not impossible. However, the current state of Litigation Support in most law firms could do with a complete overhaul in order to deal with the various documentation needs demanded by the average case. Attorneys do not have the time or interest in distinguishing between single page .TIFs versus multi-page .TIFs: they simply want to start looking at those images. Who can take ownership of this type of technical consideration, thereby leaving attorneys and paralegals to the law? That is the purpose of this book.

The system described here offers a set of tools to assist law firms in setting up a Litigation Support Department, dedicated to provide clear procedures that will bring order to the currently chaotic world of Litigation Support. Ultimately, the procedures and methods described in this book give the vendor and support staff a common frame of reference. Litigation Support gains the trust of the legal team and gains technical project management responsibility for all forms of discovery.

The real issues in Litigation Support work are work flow and delegating authority. Litigation Support manages all the discovery projects, database administration and data analysis work; often, this work is done in an ad-hoc manner, and has no real defined procedures or methodology. That type of "system" is management by abdication, not delegation.

Whether there are ten litigators or a thousand, a law firm must implement a unified strategy to Litigation Support or drown in the very data its clients generate. It used to be that one lawyer could literally swamp another in paper and thereby push for a settlement. Today, the recipient of one banker box of electronic discovery can spend years looking through documents and categorizing them -- assuming that the client can afford to turn that discovery into a reviewable database.

This book explicitly outlines how to organize everything for cases, departments, and the firm. It also covers strategy such as knowing what and when to outsource work. Cost recovery is a major issue for every firm. Services such as computer forensics and database creation may run into serious money for an individual case. Should the firm bring certain services "in-house"? All firms, regardless of size, must address many considerations having to do with mitigating risk, cost recovery and creation of a litigation technology plan.

This book attempts to outline how to run the department as a business. It shows how to organize the data and people so that your department can accommodate a growing volume or work. The book also includes operating procedures for supporting a case, from pleading to trial all from a litigation technology perspective.

This book is intended to provide a firm with the knowledge necessary to implement its own Litigation Support Department, run as a business, and thus able to save and indeed make money for the law firm that it supports.

About Mark Lieb

Ad Litem Consulting, Inc.

PO 124873
San Diego, CA 92112-4873

Phone - 866-477-4523

mark@adlitem.com

Mr. Lieb has provided Litigation Support to legal teams for cases ranging from small collections to multi-national, multi-firm litigation, involving millions of pages of discovery. He currently consults with firms, service bureaus and software companies on litigation technology and standards.

Mr. Lieb is the co-founder and technical hand behind the Litigation Support Vendors Association. The LSVA, a not-for-profit organization, provides online forums and discussions moderated by industry experts and representatives from major software companies, and covering topics from computer forensics and electronic discovery to best practices and standards.

"Mr. Lieb's expertise focuses on the full range of modern electronic discovery. He has been instrumental in creating a robust infrastructure for providing electronic discovery services within the firm. In addition, he was the principal author of Gray Cary Ware & Freidenrich's *Litigation Support Technical Standards*. This document has done much to enhance communications between vendors and end users".
- Browning Marean, III, Partner, DLA Piper Rudnick Gray Cary US LLP.

In March of 2004, Gray Cary Ware & Freidenrich generously made *Litigation Support Technical Standards* public to help the industry formulate standards and best practices. Mr. Lieb continues to update the document; as of March, 2005, the document has been downloaded over 1,000 times by a wide range of vendors and law firms.

Litigation Support Department, Mr. Lieb's most recent book, outlines both how to run the Litigation Support Department, organized as a business, and how to use technology to support and help win the case. The text discusses how the Litigation Support Department can provide a consistent product and experience for the legal team, vendors and associated parties. The book includes discussions and diagrams of case life-cycle, work-flow, budget, strategies, tactics, check-lists, roles, responsibilities, and more. Also included is a Litigation Budget spreadsheet file, among others. Establish standards in your firm and enjoy the benefit of consistency.

Mr. Lieb also provides consulting services for individual cases and implementing best practices for the Litigation Support Department and firm.

Author's Note

Special thanks to Gray Cary Ware & Freidenrich, which was instrumental in allowing me to organize and run their Litigation Support Department according to many of the ideas and strategies outlined in this book. The end result provides Gray Cary Ware & Freidenrich with many options regarding review and production costs not available to the majority of firms, many of which might prove profitable for other firms if they should choose to employ them. That being said, the systems and procedures discussed in this book may or may not coincide with how Gray Cary Ware & Freidenrich, now DLA Piper Rudnick Gray Cary US LLP, currently operates.

Throughout the text I may reference proprietary marks of other companies, such as CaseSoft's CaseMap®, Dataflight's Concordance®, Summation's iBlaze® and Microsoft's Word®. These are trademarked terms and readers should check their sites for their respective terms about their trademarks and use information.

To Litigation Support Professionals

In most law firms, an argument between attorney and support staff will always end in favor of the attorney, and the dispute will probably not be mediated by the managing committee. The question is not how to win these disputes; it is how to get both the firm and the firm's attorneys to delegate certain authority to Litigation Support, and then to support that delegation by providing enforcement of procedures.

Many people comment about how different from a corporation it is to work in a law firm, where the commodities being provided are billable hours, legal advice and filings. Despite this, a law firm is a business—and like any other business, a firm will take actions that make business sense.

This book enables one to build the case for resources, standards and firm-wide compliance. Several methods of institutionalizing the procedures recommended by this manual are as follows:

1. Have the Accounting Department use cost codes to track all vended litigation technology goods and services, such as ediscovery processing;
2. Bill clients as any vendor, attorney or paralegal would;
3. Move all discovery vending through Litigation Support;
4. Institute a Firm Standards document; and
5. Understand case lifecycle.

Cost Codes

A cost code is how a company (law firm or any other) tracks where it spends money. Accounting keeps track of how much a company spends on every category of business, from supplies to legal research, in order to identify spending trends and other numbers necessary to usefully allocate financial resources.

With regards to Litigation Support, assigning cost codes to items such as discovery and litigation technology is a fundamental first step in tracking the contributions and value of a Litigation Support Department. By assigning cost codes and having the Accounting Department track these items, Litigation Support can:

- Spot cases where teams are vending discovery on their own;
- Determine future firm or departmental resource needs;
- Build a case for bringing types of work "in-house";
- Identify what types of litigation technology services are growing or shrinking;
- Argue for better rates with vendors; and
- Identify how much Litigation Support billable time is "written off."

If "electronic discovery" shares a cost code with "legal research", then management receives a skewed financial picture. This book has the Litigation Support Department work with the vendors to have them incorporate the appropriate cost code into their invoices. The Accounting Department would normally have to look up this code every time an invoice arrives. Incorporating cost codes saves the firm time and can help the vendor get paid more quickly.

More information about "cost codes" is available in the Cost Codes section of the text.

Billing

In a firm that does not bill Litigation Support's time, the point of cost coding is to get Litigation Support Department goods and services on the Accounting Department books. Don't be too disappointed if attorneys decide to "write off" the bill, because at the end of the month, quarter, or year, Accounting can present the total potential income to the firm—both the total billed and also the total written off. At that time, the firm will be able to see what kind of revenues the Litigation Support Department can generate. Then, presumably, partners will talk to the "write off" attorneys.

These accounting reports are the tools that your department can use to make the business case for additional staff. When a department member bills $150,000 a year (1,000 hours at $150 per hour), the decision and ability to add staff, supported by accounting reports, is much simpler.

Remember, if a vendor would bill for the work, Litigation Support should too. The question of rates is one for each firm and the marketplace to decide.

Centralize Vending

There are definite advantages to having one department handle the vending of all electronic and paper discovery; that department can get better rates and spend time finding the best vendors. Paralegals and attorneys do not have the time.

Further, when the Litigation Support Department administers all litigation technology for the firm, the Department can work directly with the vendor, explaining technical requirements.

The Litigation Support Department can also concentrate on project management. For large cases and "rolling" productions, the Department can provide weekly reports and make certain each attorney understands key issues along with budget and deadline updates.

The final advantage for the Litigation Support Department is that vendors deliver a higher quality product that matches internal technical needs. The attorneys and paralegals get quicker turnaround times coupled with lower bills from the vendor and Department.

Institute a Firm Standard

The greatest problems for Litigation Support today stem from technical details. Sample considerations include any firm preferences for file format, which metadata fields the vendor should capture, database field names and field order. These answers are not case specific. They are firm specific. The same answers should apply irrespective of client, matter or attorney. A document that outlines all the possible specifications will operate as a template, and when these specifications are not met, the Litigation Support Department must make appropriate adjustments. Often it is more expedient to correct the vendor delivery than to have the vendor attempt another potentially incorrect product. If Litigation Support bills this time to the client, the client is essentially "double-billed."

Through institution of a firm-wide standard, all incoming product will match the firm's technical standards, or "template." The Litigation Support Department can then pre-qualify vendors. Any vendor who can match the firm template is thereby qualified to perform that service for all firm cases. Litigation Support can point to the firm's technical standards when any vendor product does meet the firm specifications.

This template, *Litigation Support Technical Standards*, is available as a free download from the Ad Litem Consulting site, http://www.eDiscovery.org. It is also included at the end of this book.

Understand Case Lifecycle

Everyone must understand the litigation case lifecycle but for different reasons. The attorneys and the paralegals need to understand how to use technology at every phase of litigation to win the case. They must also understand how to use software options to strategic advantage. Through such means, a very large collection of materials may become much smaller. However, strategy must extend beyond the collection, review and production phases.

The Litigation Support Department and the legal team must understand technology will enable the team to identify useful documents, and use them as exhibits. As every case lifecycle is the same, so the technology and considerations are the same. Only the legal team cares about the document content. Consistent approaches to technology for all cases means a minimal learning curve for the legal team member and the Litigation Support industry professional.

Litigation Support professionals need to understand how the legal team uses the content of the database to win their case. If technicians understand the larger picture, they can perform a better job. When technicians understand how technology applies to the business for the entire case lifecycle, they can help the team.

To Attorneys and Paralegals

It is my hope that attorneys and paralegals can see how to leverage their Litigation Support Departments to their advantage, allowing for quicker turnaround and lowered internal and vendor costs.

This book does not limit the attorney's ability to litigate as they see fit; rather, it is intended to show an attorney how to use software and hardware to support their litigation efforts.

For example, in electronic discovery, attorneys may wish to forgo the creation of accompanying images in their database due to the high up-front costs, thereby forcing the reviewers to base their opinions only upon the database record text and not how the document would appear if printed. This makes review a slower process. At the end of discovery, with production looming, they then pay to get the database "tiffed." This is akin to fixing up your home just in time to sell it, and is just as stressful; having the TIF images from the beginning would have made review a lot easier, and review must be stopped in order to allow the vendor to create the images and cds, and ship them for firm quality control (or "QC"). If the images had been generated at the start of the case, there would have been more time for review and less stress for all involved.

When the legal team identifies all potential sources of discovery for a case and how it will be used, Litigation Support can create an appropriate technology plan. The more quickly Litigation Support and the attorney communicate, the easier discovery is to manage. This type of procedural approach minimizes both errors and stress. Every case can benefit from the use of technical standards.

At the start of the case, the attorney should come to an agreement with opposing counsel as to production format and other technical considerations. Without such an agreement, one may have to pay a vendor large amounts of money to convert the production to a format the firm can use. This agreement should be made with the involvement of Litigation Support personnel on both sides. These issues can mean the difference between immediate access and access that takes days. Delays have a compounding effect.

This book will also show how to store information such as transcripts and CaseMap files on the server in an organized format. This type of simple folder-naming scheme makes life easier for users and support staff. If attorneys store their work in random fashion on servers, how will anyone else find those files? The use of client matter number folders has a few other benefits, including income generation, which are covered in more detail later in this text.

I. Hierarchy

Some would argue that because every law firm is different, there cannot be one correct way to organize and operate the Litigation Support Department. Some firms put the Litigation Support Department under the Information Technology ("IT") Department head count, while others put Litigation Support under the paralegal department. Other firms may decide to make the Litigation Support Department a separate group unto itself with its own budget. The real concern should not be how the department fits into the official firm hierarchy; rather, what are the internal operations of the department and how it interacts with its customers: firm legal and support staff, outside vendors, and outside counsel. The system outlined in this book helps ensure the department provides the same experience and quality product, irrespective of firmwide organization or department size and from case to case.

However, the firm hierarchy can benefit the existing Litigation Support Department: for the department to run as a business, it must be organized as one, with an internal hierarchy that matches a typical business hierarchy, with managerial, accounting, and technical roles. Irrespective of a specific person, these roles and their associated responsibilities are always the same. Therefore a change in staff size is a matter of assigning roles in order to balance work load. These roles ensure the person knows not only their appropriate responsibilities, but how to achieve them.

Soap Box:

As the nature of the work is technical, not legal, it is the author's opinion that the Litigation Support Department should reside in the IT department. The term "Litigation Support Department" is a misnomer. It should be more accurately called the "Litigation Technology Department". Allow the paralegals to concentrate on the law and the Litigation Support staff to concentrate on the technology choices and direction.

Fortunately, by the adoption and application of standard operating procedures, the person filling the management role for Litigation Support does not need an IT background. The technical requirements are already outlined for the person performing the technical work. The managerial role makes certain the resulting product matches the firm technical requirements.

Your firm may decide to use Litigation Support purely for project management and technical guidance. Your firm may decide to bring electronic discovery in-house. The hierarchy approach should accommodate all of these strategies.

1. Traditional Business Hierarchy

Every business—and in this book, Litigation Support is viewed as a business-- needs a hierarchy. If your department includes just one or two people, then each person may need to fill multiple roles, covering all aspects of the business.

For example, let's look at accounting roles. Your law firm has an Accounting Department or at least a CPA firm on contract. They are responsible for tracking finances on both case and firm levels. The Litigation Support accounting role makes certain everything billable, and potentially billable, goes into the accounting books. If the department created 200 CDs in January, the person filling the finance role makes certain the $5,000 charged for media creation appears in the firm's accounting books. The Accounting Department provides the Litigation Support Department and firm with reports charting spending and other trends. This information is an important index of your Litigation Support Department and Litigation Group activity. Even more important, the best way for Litigation Support to get the firm to spend money on additional people, hardware, and software is to use accounting numbers as the basis for business decisions.

It is interesting to note that, in the chat below, the top position in the hierarchy is traditionally the "shareholders." As the lawyers are the only "shareholders" in the firm, this is not so far from the truth. Partners are lawyers who are shareholders. Associates are attorneys who aspire to become shareholders. As such all attorneys appreciate a department which helps them win their cases while reducing and recovering costs for both the client and the firm.

Let's take a look at the traditional business hierarchy and see how it applies to the Litigation Support Department.

2. Chart – Traditional Business

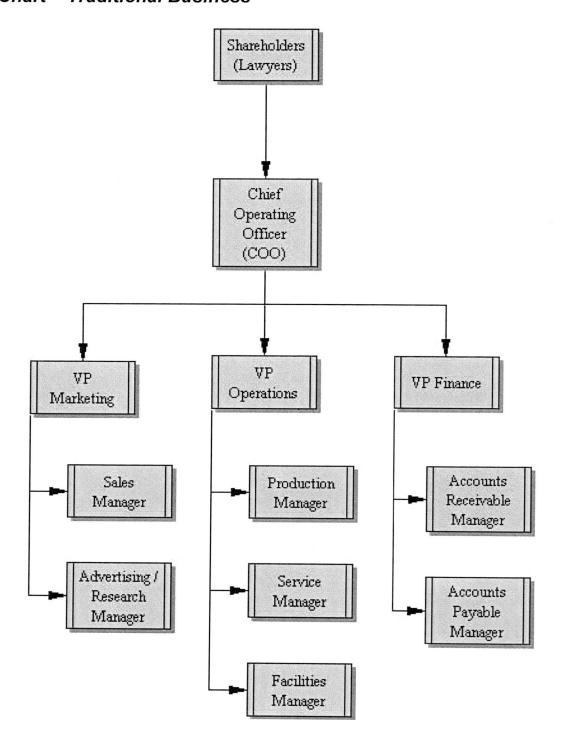

3. Chart – Litigation Support

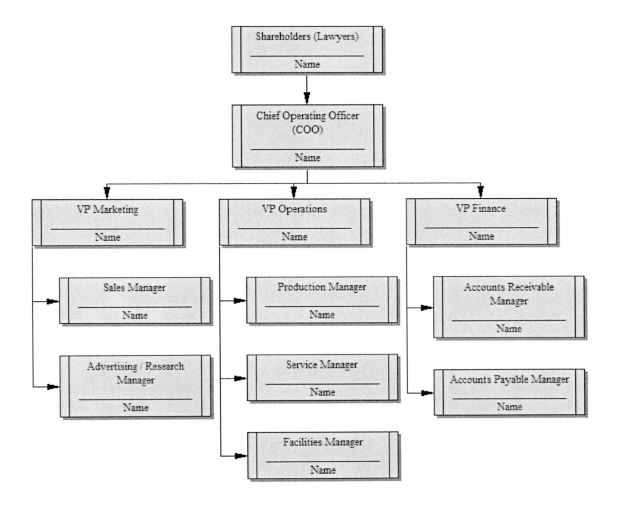

Although most departments will have fewer people than the number of roles in this chart, the department needs each of these major and minor roles to be fulfilled by one or more individuals to provide appropriate support. When the law firm out-sources work, they are delegating the responsibility for these roles to another company.

In a smaller firm where the Litigation Support Department is one person, it makes sense to limit that person's role to one that performs project management instead of any technical work.

A. Shareholders

The lawyers are the shareholders. Since the shareholders are both the boss and the customer of the department, it is important to distinguish between the two roles. Where the customer wants to know how their individual client-matter projects are going, the shareholders want to know the overall state of the department from a financial and utilization perspective.

The shareholders need to know about how the customers view the department, potential work "coming down the pipe," operations and finally, accounting. The Litigation Support Department "COO" role can provide this information, thanks to the individual(s) filling the role of the department VP of Marketing, Operations and Finance.

Operating the department as a company will provide the structure and rules required for successful long-term operations. Without them, projects may suffer and the department becomes a financial drain on the firm. When the Department asks for additional resources, it is the shareholders who allocate the budget. Trending and financial reports provide validity to the argument for allocation.

If one's department is small enough that all of these roles are played by one or two people, the firm should consider out-sourcing technical work by using a "hosted" or ASP solution. This book attempts to provide guidance in implementing this process on an individual case basis and across the firm. The strategies in the book try to account for both small and large cases and firms.

Regarding work loads, the Accounting Department tracks and prints the financial reports for the Litigation Support Department. Therefore your Litigation Support Department COO only needs to concentrate on cost code use, marketing and operations.

B. Chief Operating Officer

The COO role is responsible for the overall achievement of the Litigation Support Department's Strategic Objectives. The Chief Operating Officer, or "COO," traditionally reports on the overall character, health and direction of the company to the shareholders. In a law firm where the partners are shareholders this analogy is quite apt. Instead of reporting about the state of a company, the COO reports on the state of the department as it relates to the firm as a whole.

The operations roles are responsible for supporting individual cases. The COO uses information from operations, finance and marketing to present the partners with a complete analysis of the Litigation Support Department. The COO uses these reports to achieve various goals such as establishment of standards and investment in additional Department resources.

If the department requires an additional technician, the COO makes the argument to the partners. Reports showing historical resource utilization, profit (or potential profit for firms not billing time) and anticipated future utilization provide the foundation for action by the firm. These reports come from the following Litigation Support Department roles: VP of Marketing, VP of Operations and the VP of Finance.

COO responsibilities include, but are not limited to:

- Provide overall operational leadership for the entire Litigation Support team, including project managers, production staff, sales and marketing, and administrative personnel.
- Communicate the department's plans for departmental and firm projects and goals to legal teams and firm management.
- Oversee plan implementation from conception to completion.
- Oversee interdepartmental projects.
- Manage a production manager and multiple project managers working at multiple locations.
- Work with partners and associates to accept and take advantage of the benefits the Litigation Support Department offers.

The COO should have a successful record of overseeing the completion of multiple large scale projects concurrently, in a high volume legal production environment with tight deadlines.

The COO also must have the ability to merge strategic and tactical vision into a real world production plan, and then communicate it to staff members to produce the required results.

C. VP of Marketing

"England and America are two countries separated by a common language."
-George Bernard Shaw

Litigation Support sees the world through technical eyes, while attorneys see the world as deadlines and obstacles. To solve this conflict, it is useful for Litigation Support to adopt an attorney. If your firm is lucky enough to have an attorney with the time and interest, get them involved in Litigation Support. The VP of Marketing's role is not to learn how to perform the technical duties, but to make certain that litigators and paralegals understand technical requirements, limitations and constraints.

This role is accountable for finding "customers" among the firm's attorneys (both those initiating new cases and those with case loads that would benefit from Litigation Support's help). The role also seeks new ways to provide greater satisfaction at lower cost and with greater ease. This position reports to the COO, and is best filled by an attorney.

There are many roles for the attorney to play. Some of these are daily or ongoing tasks, while others are incidental.

The "Litigation Support Attorney" is a member of the Litigation Support team, and works in both an active and an advisory role. This attorney provides guidance to the Litigation Support team, as well as to other attorneys in the firm. Ideally, this attorney should be senior in position, such as a partner, so that their guidance also carries authority within the firm. While each firm has a slightly different culture, Litigation Support still should have this role filled, in order to make the interface between Litigation Support and the rest of the firm as smooth as possible for both teams.

Because Litigation Support work is becoming increasingly technical, the background of the Litigation Support team members will shift from a strictly legal background to a database and IT background. In this changing situation, the Litigation Support Attorney's role is to help the Litigation Support team understand the goals of the review team, next steps in the case and case lifecycle.

The Litigation Support Attorney also helps guide the development and direction of Litigation Support for the entire firm; they help assess when work must go to an outside vendor, and helps the Litigation Support Department provide timely advice that compliments current electronic discovery laws. In certain firms, against advice, a partner may not wish to send work to a vendor. In cases like these, the Litigation Support Attorney may help the partner chose an appropriate course of action.

Most important, the attorney's role is to keep on top of projects and help mediate the inevitable conflicts between Litigation Support and the attorneys that they serve. For example, when three partners are all pressuring the department to get their work done first, the Litigation Support Attorney can help defuse the situation.

The Litigation Support Attorney's role is also to scout for incoming discovery, and make sure that Litigation Support has a chance to guide the project management and technical considerations of discovery.

Finally, the Litigation Support Attorney can push for the adoption of the Litigation Support Technical Standards on a given case and firm-wide. Because of the hierarchical structure of a law firm, it is nearly mandatory that the managing partners instruct everyone to use the Standard and follow documented operating procedures. Until this is done, expect to lose a lot of time to avoidable technological tangles.

The Standards document is a good marketing piece for the department. Lawyers and paralegals never want to admit that they do not know the answer to a given question. This relates directly to how attorneys cross examine a witness. When a vendor poses technical questions, the firm can provide this document.

Litigation Support can help the attorney understand that there are many technical decisions which affect the success of their project. For the new attorney or paralegal, it introduces them to the department. The document instructs legal team member, vendor sales person and technician to involve the Litigation Support professional for litigation technology issues.

VP of Marketing responsibilities include, but are not limited to:

- Scouting for new work;
- Gaining inclusion of Litigation Support into litigation not yet involving the department, if only in an advisory and project management role;
- Estimating upcoming work, including when and how much;
- Promoting Litigation Support inclusion in all litigation;
- Promoting Litigation Support Department firm level initiatives;
- Facilitating communications between the department and firm;
- Helping institute Accounting Department cost codes for litigation technology goods and services;
- Establishing "timekeeper" numbers to track department time;
- Explaining recent case law to Litigation Support about preservation, chain of custody, spoliation and so forth;

The VP of Marketing must ultimately educate the firm and partners that the Litigation Support Department has a technology plan applicable to each matter that will also benefit how the firm operates. As such, the successful execution of this plan and these efforts requires acceptance by the firm. Litigators will only delegate authority when they are confident the recipient will successfully perform the associated responsibilities. The VP of Marketing must also educate the Litigation Support Department about case law and sanctions and other legal factors that will affect both how the attorney litigates and Litigation Support operates.

The following are short, mid and long term goals for the department. The VP of Marketing plays a key role in the department achieving goals that involve persons outside of the Litigation Support Department.

Short Term Goals

Litigation Support should start using the standards and ideas as soon as possible. In this fashion all data becomes organized going forward. For example, start storing files according to the file folder conventions described in the book. Even if old folders and files do not conform to the standard, start using these standards for all new data (folders and files).

It does not matter whether or not the Firm has adopted the standard and requires vendors to match the outlined specifications. Litigation Support should go ahead and start using the system for folders that the legal team uses. After a while, enough folders should be out there to cause teams to adopt it themselves. Litigation Support should also provide a copy of the technical standard to every vendor. This idea and strategy is discussed throughout the book.

Get all of firm vendors qualified against the new firm Litigation Support Technical Standards. The Needs Assessment section will give the Department COO a good idea as to what issues the Department and firm need to address. Litigation Support should have a good comfort level with the standards and have a game plan for handling discovery before pushing them onto the rest of the firm.

Mid-Term Goals

Firmwide adoption of the technical standards and inclusion of Litigation Support in the pre-discovery phase of the case are the major mid-term goals of instituting the new processes. The managing partners will have to mandate that all attorneys and paralegals use the standards for all discovery projects. Litigation Support needs to educate the legal team about Litigation Support, services and consistency. Unless each project uses the technical standards document, Litigation Support will forever receive data from third parties that requires technical clean-up.

Even when a member of the legal team contracts with a discovery vendor directly, the resulting product should conform to firm standards. In the long term goals, only the Litigation Support Department vends discovery. Through use of the firm technical standard, 80% of materials coming to Litigation Support should pose technical challenge. The other 20% will still require some sort of attention to make it match firm technical requirements. Once the 80% is taken care of, one can address how to produce and receive discovery from sources other than the vendor, such as clients, friendly firms, and opposing counsel.

Long Term Goals

If the firm owns and operates a file server that did not historically use standards for folder naming and organization, it is likely that people have "squirreled-away" lots of work product in odd locations. Files may reside in any number of places that only certain people know about. It is not unusual to find a folder or file named "Smith-Wish" and have no clients named Smith or Wish. Organizing this information can be impossible, or at least so difficult that the time might not seem warranted. Nonetheless it ultimately is the firm's best interest to organize historical folders. At the least, the department should move all litigation folders to a standard repository location. Only in this manner can everyone be certain the disaster recovery plan and backup strategies outlined in the book are applied religiously.

D. VP of Finance

In a traditional business hierarchy, the VP of Finance is accountable for supporting both Marketing and Operations in the fulfillment of their financial goals—achieving the company's profitability and securing capital whenever it is needed at the best rates. This role answers to the COO role.

Fortunately for the Litigation Support Department, the law firm takes care of the actual collections and payments for services from outside vendors. The department will stay in business so long as the firm exists. This is not to say that this role is perfunctory; rather, this position leverages the revenue which past, current and future work represents to achieve better rates.

Note: While the role and department stay, employees will change. Because all responsibilities are assigned to roles, the persons fulfilling a role may change over the course of time with a minimal impact to the associated work.

The COO uses financial reports, in conjunction with reports from marketing and operations, to argue for firm investment in various resources. For example, the amount of money billed to clients for project management time as compared to the current and future needs, as reported by the VP of Operations, may allow the COO to create the business argument for the addition of another project manager or buying a robotic CD/DVD maker with optional label printer.

As the Accounting Department administrates all financial information, the Litigation Support Department VP of Finance role gets his reports from them. He, or she, therefore needs the Accounting Department to track separately litigation marketplace goods and services. Although Litigation Support time may be billable to the client, it may require another tracking system.

Persons, unlike goods and services, may require manual entry into the same system paralegals and attorneys use to bill their time. This may mean creation of billing numbers for each member of the Litigation Support Department. This is another task for the VP of Finance. One may question why it is important for the department to bill their time. In a firm where a Litigation Support Department technician or project manager expects to bill 1,000 hours a year, the question of additional resource is not of budget but bandwidth.

Note: When Litigation Support bills time, it becomes a more significant part of the legal team and litigation process. Billable time has side benefits covered in this book, including cost recovery as it applies to litigation case lifecycle and firm operations.

In firms where Litigation Support time is not billable, the goal is to have the potential billable revenue entered into the accounting books. The argument for doing so is that the resulting reports will build the foundation for all business decisions, including investment in the appropriate hardware, software and staff.

When in doubt, the Litigation Support Department should bill for the same goods and services as a vendor. Collection of these monies is not important to the department. Using the reports provides the foundation for all other efforts.

Through tracking of billable time, the department can also assess bandwidth. This information also helps the Operations Manager balance workload across staff.

The person in this role should understand how the department can use financial reports to justify actions which benefit the firm. These reports also provide a valuable index as to growth rates for various services. This role may need support from the Litigation Support Attorney in order to create cost codes and billing numbers. As Litigation Support relies upon established tracking mechanisms, beyond printing a monthly report, there is minimal impact upon normal firm operations.

VP of Finance responsibilities include, but are not limited to:

1. Establishment and use of cost codes by the Accounting Department;
2. Inclusion of cost codes on invoices by all litigation vendors; and
3. Creation of reports from the Accounting Department, for use by COO and other VPs.

As the Accounting Department handles the actual finances for the firm, this role's responsibilities center mostly on the generation of reports and the ongoing efforts to make certain all internal and external goods and services are tracked accordingly.

Depending upon the firm, the Litigation Support Attorney role can provide the clout to institute cost codes and billing numbers so department staff can enter time into the time and billing software.

E. VP of Operations

Where the VP of Marketing presents the legal team with a vision of strategic case lifecycle support, the VP of Operations is accountable for the successful execution of that vision. This role also tries to identify and incorporate new ways of serving customers at lower costs and with improved efficiency. This role reports to the COO.

The VP of Operations endeavors to develop the technical standards that all work created internally or outsourced through a vendor will match. Only through consistent approaches and technical standards can the Litigation Support Department hope to produce a consistent product and experience for the customer.

This role creates strategic alliances with prequalified vendors whose goods, services and resources comply with the firm's best practices and established standards. This role relies upon the VP of Marketing and COO roles to bring work through the Litigation Support Department, thereby restricting work to selected vendors.

As the software marketplace matures and new litigation software and service vendors attempt to establish themselves within the market, the VP determines whether they complement the firm and case technology plan. If a product alters this plan in some fashion, will the benefits outweigh the larger costs in terms of case lifecycle and technology issues?

VP of Operations' responsibilities include, but are not limited to:

1. Ensuring the Litigation Support Department successfully meets all project management and technical deadlines;
2. Monitoring the quality level of litigation goods and services, regardless of source;
3. Representing the interests of the Litigation Support Department to the IT Department;
4. Monitoring operational resources, including assessing bandwidth;
5. Ensuring technology is a benefit and not a burden to the legal team;
6. Overseeing the qualification process for outside vendors;
7. Maintaining a list of preferred litigation marketplace vendors;
8. Ensuring a consistent experience for all matters;
9. Updating the firm technology plan to accommodate market and legal changes;
10. Helping the team to budget for litigation goods and services;
11. Aiding the team to understand the real and intrinsic value of various goods and services;
12. Providing project management for both internal and outsourced litigation goods and services;
13. Identifying potential sources of electronic discovery to the legal team.

Note: Some responsibilities require the involvement of Litigation Support before as well as during the collection process. The VP of Marketing can help educate the team to involve Litigation Support sooner rather than later in the case lifecycle.

The VP of Operations should work closely with the Litigation Support Attorney to make certain current firm operations meet the requirements required by the judicial system.

This role makes certain all litigation goods and services the legal team, friendly firms, clients and experts will use for the collection, review and production process make sense from a technical and operational perspective. A good example of this is storage.

Understanding storage and backup technology is essential to proper collection of paper documents and electronic materials. An attorney and client may not fully appreciate the difference between copying files from a hard drive versus creating a forensic copy. Each type of copy serves a distinct purpose. Failure to appreciate this distinction can result in severe sanctions. The VP of Operations works with the legal team to help them understand how the distinction affects their case.

Most recently, litigation involving a large investment banking organization resulted in a major firm losing their client, employees and, more than likely, partners with major clients seeking "safer" firms in which to practice.

Technology and operational advice is invaluable to the legal team. Regardless of whether goods and services are out-sourced, the legal team should make certain that technology decisions support case strategy for the entire case lifecycle and potential legal contingencies.

F. Production Manager

In a very large firm the Litigation Support Production Manager's responsibilities can include overseeing technicians as they create goods and provide services to the legal team. In smaller departments, the VP of Operations, Production Manager and Technician may be the same person.

In cases where the production manager and technician is the same person, the balance between product management and technical work is critical to department health. For firms outsourcing all technical work, the Production Manager role is to ensure that vendors properly fulfill their responsibilities.

This role constantly researches ways to improve goods and services with minimal to no negative impact on current operations and costs. The Production Manager also works with the IT Department to identify any issues that could affect the legal team and Litigation Support Department's ability to work. As example, ensuring proper backup and restore abilities for all litigation folders on all servers.

Note: When firms outsource, they may abdicate authority to a third party. The Production Manager must evaluate the vendors to make certain they meet firm requirements. This is the difference between abdicating and delegating authority.

The Production Manager coordinates and oversees the workloads for both departmental and case specific projects. Firm projects, such as organizing historical server folders, may rank lower in importance than a case specific project, but deserve attention, and eventually, completion.

A technical person is best suited to evaluate how and whether technology goods and services actually provide what the provider promises. This task has the added benefit to the person in the Production Manager role. The Production Manager will learn how vendors use technology to provide goods and services. The Production Manager will become better equipped to evaluate and actually manage these same goods and services internally.

The legal team should route all electronic discovery materials through the Production Manager. This role can act as librarian for all digital media for all cases. As original media, especially if it is the only copy, should never leave the firm, the Production Manager must catalog all original media, vendor generated media and firm generated media for every litigation. The legal team should always store these types of materials in a central location. As every case needs to store the same types of materials, all storage should be centralized and cataloged in the same fashion.

The same approach holds true for legal video. Video may exist on analog media, such as VHS tape, or digital media, such as CDs and DVDs. In keeping with the aforementioned concept of a media library, the legal team and vendors should route materials through the department or, minimally, provide the Litigation Support Department with a copy of these materials.

The Project Manager is responsible for managing and coordinating all Litigation Support aspects of individually assigned cases. The Project Manager is the first and single point of contact for the case team (i.e., attorneys, paralegals, document clerks, imaging specialist, coding clerks, clients, and vendors).

Production Manager's responsibilities may include, but are not limited to:

- Preparing a case technology plan for legal team;
- Managing vendors to assure that high-quality data deliverables and services are provided within the negotiated schedules and budgets;
- Troubleshooting Litigation Support applications, databases;
- Consulting with the legal team and vendors to resolve technical issues relating to new case issues;
- Updating the legal team as to actual costs and budget;
- Updating the team as to dates and deadlines for work;
- Analyzing resulting vendor proposals and making processing recommendations to case team;
- Assisting with analysis and testing of new or updated versions of Litigation Support software;
- Ensuring client satisfaction through proactive communication;
- Monitoring resources and current level of utilization;
- Balancing workload and caseload among internal staff and outsourced vendors;
- Providing project management and prioritizing projects;
- Maintaining a media inventory of original and generated digital and analog media;
- Ensuring network infrastructure meets litigation data needs; and
- Understanding how to create and provide litigation goods and services.

Requirements for this position should include the following:

- Extensive Litigation Support experience (emphasis on technical work);
- Understanding of case lifecycle;
- Understanding of the case technology plan;
- Experience building and training a technical team;
- Comfort with multiple Litigation Support software applications;
- Experience training and mentoring legal team members; and
- Strong English-language communications skills.

The Production Manager is also responsible for the Litigation Support Department toolbox. Outlined under the hardware and software sections of this book is a list of the various types of utilities and hardware every firm should consider owning.

G. Clerk

The Clerk's primary responsibility is to organize the Litigation Support Department's data and records. The Litigation Support Department can generate a lot of CDs and DVDs, and receive even more from clients and outside sources. The Clerk organizes and archives these materials.

The clerk's main responsibility is allowing the project managers and technicians to concentrate on higher level duties, such as meetings with the legal team or updating a database for review by the same legal team.

The Clerk can act as the primary contact for support requests, obtaining status updates for the firm's attorneys, and, potentially, entering billable time for the Litigation Support Department staff.

The clerk is an entry level position. The person in this role may eventually become a technician or project manager.

1. Clerical Tasks

Clerical work is best done by the clerk role. The Clerk's primary responsibility is to organize the Litigation Support Department's data and records. The Litigation Support Department can generate a lot of CDs and DVDs, and receive even more from clients and outside sources. The Clerk can duplicate, organize and archives these materials.

The Clerk's duties can include technical and non-technical responsibilities:

Technical Duties

- Performing quality control ("QC") tests of inbound and outbound media, such as adding missing information to a media labels;
- Creating duplicates of media;
- Installing minor hardware and software upgrades; and
- Providing level 1 technical support.

Non-Technical Duties

- Maintaining a database of the media library;
- Shipping;
- Ordering supplies, such as blank media;
- Routing incoming calls and emails;
- Adding missing information, such as cost codes, to invoices;

- Contacting vendors to identify any issues such as missing information; and
- Project managing the routine creation of department status reports.

Reporting

The clerk works with the department COO, VP of Marketing, VP of Operations and VP of Finance. The clerk's duties call for this role to interact with the legal team, accounting department, vendors and other third parties when shipping materials. The clerk is in a prime position to maintain indexes on each area: marketing, operations and finance. The COO requires these indexes, presented as reports, to properly run the Litigation Support Department, argue for additional resources, and so forth.

The following are the reports the clerk should help to assemble and generate on a monthly basis.

1. Marketing

The clerk is the primary filter for calls and emails. As such this person has a good understanding of the department's reputation. The clerk can work with the VP of Marketing to identify potential projects which will impact workload and server capacity.

2. Operations

The firm assigns a "time keeper" number to all persons who bill their hours. The Litigation Support Department clerk reports total billable hours for each person in the Department. These numbers, compared with numbers from the last several months, provide the COO with critical bandwidth and operational capacity. The clerk can also present storage indexes and software license use statistics.

3. Financial

Although the time keeper number is also a financial indicator, the Operations report uses it to indicate capacity and use. The financial report outlines litigation technology goods and services spending, including internally generated billable hours.

The clerk uses the time keeper reports to indicate (potential) earnings for project management and technical work. Accounting Department reports, indicating litigation technology goods and services spending by cost code, provide the remainder of the fiscal picture. The department COO can use these reports to justify reinvestment in the firm, additional employees and political changes, such as routing all electronic discovery through the Litigation Support Department for processing.

II. Services

From a risk management perspective, all law firms must be very careful when considering what goods and services to render. The question is not always one of ability and capacity: one must also consider which responsibilities and liabilities accompany those services.

As example, the client of one of the attorneys supported by your Litigation Support Department brings in a former employee's laptop. The client believes the former employee deleted key files. Bob, from the law firm's IT department, retrieves deleted files. The technician's credentials should meet or exceed those required to meet the legal scrutiny by opposing counsel. Bob may have to take the stand and testify. Will he provide the other side with the opportunity they need to cast doubt over all resulting exhibits? Attorneys hesitate to buy goods and services on behalf of their clients unless they can justify the expense. There have already been cases, and I predict there will be more, where issues of this sort can result in rulings and sanctions against a firm and its client.

This is not to say that one should outsource all litigation industry goods and services. In reality, your Litigation Support Department should be able to perform basic technical duties—even if they refrain from doing so at particular points.

The need to perform basic technical work in-house is absolutely critical, because 30-minutes of in-house work is better than suffering through a 2 hour turnaround time from a vendor. Practically every time a CD arrives from a third party, there is some amount of technical work to perform. The CD may be missing a load file, or some Access database work may be required. Again, it is better to have that 30 minute in-house option when deadlines are tight and you don't have time to send the product back to be re-done by the vendor.

The basic reality of this situation is that firms with Litigation Support people who can perform sophisticated technical duties in-house will be much better off strategically than firms whose Litigation Support people cannot perform average to intermediate technical duties. This disadvantage can—and sometimes does--lose cases. Again, the ability to perform a service internally does not mean the department should do so for all cases.

Assessing Your Department's Abilities

If your Litigation Support Department cannot perform a service to the same standard as a vendor, it is wise to outsource it. Many technical people think, "If I can visualize the solution, I can undertake the task". This mindset disregards the fact that the need to complete the task successfully in a timely manner is the most important goal, and should support the good of the case.

Cases may last for years, moving from periods of high activity to long periods of dormancy. Litigation Support (or a vendor) can expect sudden technical requests with short turn-around times following these months of inactivity. For example, an attorney might call needing new CDs containing the results of various searches. If the database is complete with all appropriate images, fields, data and tags then such a request is simple to fulfill. If, however, the database is flawed or incomplete, Litigation Support may be unable to fulfill a request in a timely fashion. Bear this caution in mind as you decide what responsibilities Litigation Support should shoulder and providing it with the appropriate internal resources.

When the firm decides to offer a service, it must invest in the necessary resources to ensure successful support. As the Litigation Support Department can pay for itself and save clients money through the addition of a service, this opportunity has great appeal. A firm may be tempted to believe a minor investment will result in significant cost recovery for the firm and client. As the decision to bring a service in-house must be a business and legal decision, one must first address the state of the department.

One baseline for any Litigation Support Department is the division between project management and technical work. In both small firms with one Litigation Support professional and large firms with multiple professionals, a single person will fulfill both the project management role and technical role. The larger departments may divide the work for every case by the role, and subsequently responsibilities.

When a department decides to provide a new good or service to the firm, the initial consideration is who will actually perform these new duties and whether they have the time to do so without detriment to their other responsibilities.

Assessing Your Bandwidth

Your firm needs to decide how much time to spend on project management versus technical work, both with regards to the department as a whole and each person individually.

Depending upon your firm, the Litigation Support project manager will also spend a certain amount of time performing technical duties. For a firm where all electronic discovery is processed by an external vendor, the amount of technical time the project manager must spend to load new materials into a database should be low. If your firm has not yet instituted Litigation Support Technical Standards, the amount of technical time may represent a significant portion of the project manager's time.

For firms that perform electronic discovery in-house, the required amount of technical time is likely significant enough to warrant a full-time technician. The addition of this person will allow your project manager to concentrate on communications and other internal goals.

When the Litigation Support Department is a single person, the management of the balance between project management and technical work is vital to the success of each case, the department and, finally, the firm as a whole. When the project manager must spend an increasing amount of time performing technical work, their primary responsibilities may suffer. This can cause the department to enter a potentially damaging spiral of missed deadlines and bad communications; the results can be the attorney or paralegal bypassing the Litigation Support Department and contracting directly with outside vendors.

If the firm has no Litigation Support Technical Standards, it is likely that the vendor will return product which requires additional technical work to use within the firm. The Litigation Support Department must now perform additional technical work that could have been avoided. Due to expediency, the Litigation Support Department traditionally performs this work itself. In many firms the person performing the technical work will be the project manager. Depending upon the urgency of the work, all other scheduled meetings and efforts may be delayed. This scenario explains one way in which a project management oriented department can become swamped with technical work. This can be detrimental to the project management responsibilities and can harm internal efforts and deadlines for other cases.

If the department cannot mandate outsourcing, using technical standards or increasing department resources, both departmental reputation and cases can suffer. If the firm cannot or will not mandate standards, the department will always spend time correcting what the vendors deliver. Establishment of standards decreases the amount of unnecessary internal technical work and allows for prequalification and exclusion of vendors.

In deciding which services to perform in-house and which to out-source, remember that project management is a critical service. If project management is the sole departmental service, the firm must ensure the Litigation Support person performs mostly project management duties instead of technical duties. Whatever goods and services may be involved, project management is the first and most important duty of every Litigation Support Department. It would be wise to attend to the successful execution of this role and associated responsibilities before attempting to bring further goods and services in-house.

Many firms, especially small and mid-sized, should become familiar with at least two "hosted" solutions for purposes of discovery review and production. A hosted solution means that case data sits on a vendor's servers. Because the database and associated electronic files reside with a vendor, any technical administration happens by their own technicians. This means that the Litigation Support Department can concentrate on project management. This may also mean the vendor bills hourly for their work. When a technical issue, such as a corrupt or missing file, causes a problem for the team, the vendor can allocate additional resources to resolve the issue. In contrast, the law firm must take resources away from one case to provide resources for another.

The firm should consider outsourcing services until the department has the necessary people, hardware, software and training to provide them in-house. It is more important that the department has a chance to organize itself than to load additional work onto an overburdened and under-equipped department.

When the firm decides what roles and, consequently, what responsibilities, it wishes the Litigation Support Department to undertake, it must support adherence by the attorneys, paralegals and vendors to new documented protocols. One major benefit to the team is a technology plan which follows a consistent pattern from matter to matter. This does not limit litigation strategies which may change radically from matter to matter. It does provide for minimal effort by Litigation Support Department to reuse all associated discovery databases and materials.

Before any law firm begins to perform a litigation technology service internally, it needs to see if doing so makes business sense. Just because one "can" does not mean that one "should." Through the use of cost codes, the firm can determine which types of services to address regarding cost recovery. The project manager can research and determine the resources necessary to provide first. Before adding any new services, make certain the existing services are successful from both case and firm perspectives.

When considering whether to have separate project managers and technicians, it is important to maintain outside vendors who can provide support for both "overflow" work and work deemed too risky to perform internally. Risk in this context is one of "risk management" for the firm, irrespective of the department's abilities. For departments that plan on performing technical work in-house, the need for separate project managers and technicians will increase. However, this does not negate the need for the project manager to be able to perform basic technical skills. The firm wants to make certain the department is organized in such a fashion that it can pay for itself, manage bandwidth (outsourcing when necessary) and make certain that one role does not impede the ability to fulfill the responsibilities of another.

Vendors

The firm may be tempted to outsource work to a single vendor, but this is not wise. Not all vendors are good at all tasks, and their technicians can and do switch jobs. If the key technicians move to other service bureaus, the firm should consider following them.

One problem a firm may face is when the sales person switches companies. The paralegals and attorneys may still provide work to this person. However, the work product may not meet firm requirements. The result may mean bad product and revisions which delay the legal team.

The legal team may not have the time to research vendors nor the skills to properly assess their technical work. The Litigation Support Department can not only create a list of preferred vendors but also keep the list current. While the case requirements may limit which vendor does the work, the Litigation Support Department does not need to limit vendor choice to geography. In today's world, one can overnight digital media containing millions of pages of discovery to any vendor in any state in the union. So, why limit the firm to local vendors? Due to restrictions such as weight, paper discovery will probably stay local for scanning, but the resulting product can go anywhere, again, overnight.

While the scanning vendor may offer OCR and bibliographic coding options, it may be outsourcing this work, too. As every vendor has a limit to their own capacity, the department may wish to limit how much work and what types of work to send to any given vendor. Again, this is the type of consideration that a dedicated department may have time to research while the legal team may not.

Through the use of a technical standard, the department can prequalify service bureaus in any part of the work. Once qualified, the project manager may retain their services and involve the vendors as necessary. The toughest part of employing the multiple vendor strategy is keeping track of all your projects, vendors, and inventory. If the firm needs to use multiple vendors within a single case, this can get tricky. This is a situation where it is critical for the person filling the Litigation Support Department project manager role to concentrate upon their responsibilities. Because technical work frequently deals with more immediate deadlines, one can see how it would take precedent over project management work.

In a firm with a small department, the decision to limit internal work to project management can be advantageous to both case and firm. As project management time can be billable time, any firm without a department should consider addition of this critical staff position. While vendors do provide a project manager, this person must attend to multiple projects for multiple firms. The Litigation Support Department project manager, even if only one person, can attend strictly to firm projects and represent firm interests when working with vendors and the team.

Departmental Project Management

The following is an overview of ongoing departmental and case related concerns as they relate to case project management and firm planning. These topics are addressed in more depth throughout the book.

Storage

How much server storage is available to the Litigation Department and when will storage reach capacity? How long will it take to expand capacity? Even firms that outsource their discovery review will probably require some internal storage for certain types of files related to each case.

Every IT Department has contingency plans for potential problems such as server crashes and losses of power. How do these plans accommodate the needs of litigation?

Litigation requires contingency plans that minimize potential and unavoidable interruptions to the team. This includes the potential for interruptions due to storage issues. If the firm provides storage to cases, the Litigation Support Department can work with the IT Department to represent litigation team needs.

The concerns are more complex when dealing with multiple offices and locations for storage. This line of thought brings us to network administration issues which will be addressed below.

Note: The same type of contingency planning anticipates potential storage issues, such as when Litigation Support must move case data to a third party (hosting company, other firm) due to legal or resource issues.

Gauging Total Storage

How much storage will a given case require? This is not a simple question. How much combined storage do all cases use? This can also be a difficult question to answer. When can Litigation Support move data to "near-line" storage, such as hard drives and thereby increase the available storage? For firms that host their document review systems and data in-house, these questions are significant. What is the firm storage consumption rate?

The Litigation Support Department should work with both the litigators and the IT Department in order to gain a full picture of storage. For the sake of the case and everyone's time, it is far better to use a hosting company in anticipation of storage issues.

Estimating Budgets

The legal team needs not only to generate a technology budget for their case, but be able to justify and explain it to the client. The Litigation Support Department can help the team do this. This book includes a budget spreadsheet to use on every client-matter. Because the budget is a spreadsheet file, it is simple for everyone to see how adjusting price and quantities effects overall cost.

Estimating litigation goods and services costs is very difficult. When estimating electronic discovery, one cannot know how many pages and documents a hard drive may contain. File sizes, types and quantity can help one to create an estimate, but it is only a scientific guess. What the litigator and client need to understand is how costs can and do increase as the scale of discovery increases. Litigation Support can work with the legal team and any vendors to cull the total number of documents and pages. The litigator and client need to also understand how a $30,000 estimate became a $10,000 invoice. In such a light, the client may appreciate that they are not simply spending ten thousand dollars, but saving twenty thousand dollars.

As the Litigation Support Department may estimate budgets for more litigation technology projects than any single litigator or paralegal, it can provide great value in understanding, budgeting and justifying associated costs. This book also attempts to provide the insight and strategies so that any person may better perform these tasks.

On Firmwide Standards

Both the Department and the firm must address capacity, resource and risk management concerns before offering any services to the client and legal teams. Standards will effect not only firm and client cost but may require delegation of some authority to Litigation Support and away from attorneys and paralegals. This can prove problematic when perceived as counter-intuitive to current firm culture and historic partner rights. The key is education. The legal team needs to understand how the changes affect their ability to litigate.

Many law firms operate like a small business incubator. They provide the partners with most or all of the resources necessary to operate: accounting, facilities, staff, and business technology such as phones and computers. How partners run cases is essentially up to their discretion. The Accounting Department can mandate or win financial arguments thanks to the backing of State and Federal laws and organizations such as the IRS. The Human Resources Department also relies upon backing from similar authorities. The firm must provide the Litigation Support Department with the appropriate authority. The Litigation Support Attorney role should represent the interests of the Litigation Support Department in this effort. Unlike a small business incubator, however, the success or failure of one partner affects the finances of the others. Therefore, it is in the best interest of the firm to act accordingly.

Technical versus Project Management Work

Because both services are critical to the successful litigation of every case, every law firm must provide appropriate resources for both. This may mean use of a consultant, outside vendor or investment in additional internal firm resources. One should avoid any compromise between time allocated for one type of work versus the other, lest the net result be detrimental to both efforts and therefore the associated matters and firm.

Department Administrative / Clerical Work

No service bureau or law firm can operate successfully without basic administrative and clerical work. As the Litigation Support Department can require as much general administration as any service bureau, responsibility for the maintenance of the overall organization of the department is a major consideration, a consideration addressed throughout this book. One may assign the responsibility for this type of work to the project management role but, again, if the amount of work warrants the investment, a low-level (low-cost) clerk may be the answer to this ongoing need. No case can afford sloppy organization. This is also true for the department, as it will inevitably affect the support for each matter.

1. Management

A. Implementing Best Practices

The following text outlines initiatives the Department should undertake in an effort to bring order to the Department and case support. Initiatives that do not require involvement of other departments are easier to implement. These include one-time initiatives such as customizing a technical standard. Other initiatives, such as the establishment of "cost codes", may require the addition of new accounting codes, but will not affect how the accountants perform their work. These are firm oriented initiatives.

Potentially the most difficult initiatives are those which affect the legal team or client. In firms where paralegals have "vended" paper discovery for years, it is natural that they would assume the responsibility of vending electronic discovery, too. Shifting the responsibility to the Litigation Support Department may require a mandate from managing partners and a change to firm culture. The success of any high level initiative has a greater chance of success when those involved understand how it benefits them. This is true for clients, vendors, attorneys, paralegals, technicians and so forth.

The easiest initiatives present the easiest concepts for the legal team, vendor and Accounting Department to understand, and adopt. For example, once the VP of Operations starts using the folder organization scheme, per the Network Folders section, he can address the Disaster Recovery and Security initiatives.

The following sections concentrate on firm level and case level initiatives. The text contains a list of roles and responsibilities for each initiative.

1. Department and Firm Level Initiatives

The goal of these tasks is to organize and manage internal firm operations. The Department COO undertakes these initiatives in an effort to bring order and consistency to litigation technology in the firm. One example of such an initiative is the organization of folders on file servers. This goal does not directly further any case goals. It does, however, benefit all litigation. Other initiatives require the support of the managing partners, such as instituting a firm technical standard or moving the responsibility for contracting electronic discovery goods and services to the Litigation Support Department.

Firm Level Initiatives
1. Assign Roles to Persons Roles (then assign responsibilities to roles)
2. Personalize the Technical Standards (publish a firm standard)
3. Assess the Firm (and determine course of action)
4. Initiate a "boot camp" where all Litigation Support persons learn the best practices template)
5. Begin Tracking Billables (to pay for resources)
6. Organize the Network (to begin applying security and disaster recovery)

7. Qualify Vendors (and exclude bad vendors)
8. Resource Initiatives (hardware, software and people)
9. Determine Services (what to perform internally and what to outsource)
10. Update the firm's "Client-Matter Intake" (at what stage legal should involve Litigation Support)
11. Initiate a "Network Clean-Up" (the search for errant historical folders)
12. Create an maintain a "Media Inventory" (the ability to locate any media for any case in moments)

Assign Persons to Roles

Print the department hierarchy, included on the attached CD, and assign people to roles. There is a good chance in most departments that the same person will wear several hats. All responsibilities relate to a specific role. When a new person assumes a role that had been previously staffed by another person, the responsibilities stay with the role. The book associates firm and case level initiatives with roles.

If there is no obvious partner for the VP of Marketing role, the COO should address the Litigation Department head. This role is critical to the success of the department, partially due to the authority a partner may wield. An associate is helpful in this role, but may not carry the weight necessary to bring about institutional change.

Please refer to the Hierarchy section of the book to learn more about the various roles and their associated responsibilities beyond these best practices initiatives. Roles, such as the VP of Marketing, are critical to the success of the department. The book outlines responsibilities and strategies for this and other roles. This concept applies to case work, too. For an example, please refer to the "Roles & Responsibilities" worksheet of the Litigation Budget Spreadsheet, also included on the CD.

Personalize the Technical Standards

The VP of Operations should edit the Litigation Support Technical Standards document and make the changes necessary for use by an individual firm. When the VP of Operations edits the document, they must be careful not to change naming conventions, path structures or things of a similar nature. Adherence to technical specifications and organization rules affect the ability to achieve key initiatives, such as backup and security. Finally, please do not remove the Ad Litem Consulting, Inc. copyright.

The Department must provide this document to every vendor for use with every litigation technology goods and services project. The standards document provides technicians with the structure and rules for a standardized discovery process—although it gives the technician enough flexibility to determine how exactly to achieve the explicit end-results.

Eventually, all legacy folders, files and databases will match the firm standard. The sooner the department begins to use the standard itself, the fewer materials it must "correct," as part of a later initiative.

The latest version of the Litigation Support Technical Standards document is available at the http://www.eDiscovery.org website and included on the accompanying CD.

Needs Assessment

The Department COO should perform the Needs Assessment for the firm. If the reader is an attorney or paralegal or otherwise not a member of a Litigation Support Department, the assessment provides insight into the level of support possible, from Disaster Recovery to workstation monitor configurations and training. Document reviewers know the positive and negative aspects of the current system. The attorneys know if Litigation Support provides good value for their goods and services.

Litigators may not know how to use the Litigation Support Department to advantage for every stage of the case lifecycle. No matter one's background, the Needs Assessment provides the reader with a list of key considerations and an explanation of the ideal manners in which to address them. The book explains how to use billable hours and hosting to pay for additional resources, resources required to provide an appropriate level of service.

Electronic discovery has changed both litigation and technology. Everyone from a legal student to a grey-haired partner should understand the business and financial implications to both the practice and the cases. It is in the client's best interest that their attorneys employ a technology plan. The attorney should read the support sections, relative to each assessment, until they understand how it benefits the firm and the case.

Status Reports

Where the included Needs Assessment provides the reader with more of a "qualified" idea as to the current state of the department, the status reports provide actual quantified answers. Further, the Department COO can use these reports to show actual trends such as server and worker capacity versus use.

Each report is concise. As such, the book does not include actual sample status reports. It does, however, provide a list of demographics one should strongly consider including in a report. These reports cover the three areas after which they are named: Marketing, Operations, and Financial.

The clerk role is responsible for generating these reports. In a department with no clerk, it is the responsibility of the department COO.

Boot Camp

The Operations Manual describes the operation of the Litigation Support Department, as well as how to support individual cases through technology. A successful Litigation Support professional has to be attentive to firm, legal team, client, vendors, experts, and both opposing and friendly firms. Each of these parties has a particular interest in the case, and Litigation Support is often in a position of mediating these interests. Yes, the Litigation Support professional must be something of a diplomat.

In order to be a diplomat for technology, one must understand:

1. The case lifecycle;
2. The firm technical standards;
3. How software helps discovery journey from pleading to trial;
4. How the legal team will use the software during case lifecycle to achieve goals;
5. Nuances of the legal mindset (or, passive aggressive persons unite!);
6. Firm culture and perception of the Litigation Support Department ;
7. How to handle all of the above.

The primary goal of this book is to provide any reader, regardless of background, with a strong understanding of how to use litigation technology to win cases while saving the client and firm money by providing the right tools, training and information in a timely, consistent and professional manner. It is, therefore, in the best interest for everyone to understand the associated responsibilities and how the results of their efforts directly benefit both case and firm.

Please see other sections of this book for strategies and overviews of the discovery lifecycle, storage concerns and other associated Litigation Support issues. In the end, the Department should work well within the firm as a whole as well as providing top level support to everyone involved in each case.

Begin Tracking Billables

The Department COO or VP of Operations will require all litigation technology goods and services vendors to use the appropriate cost codes on their invoices. The requirement appears in the technical standards document. Any vendor will include the code if the firm requires it. This helps the Accounting Department begin to use the new codes. These codes allow the Department VP of Finance to run critical reports. They also form the basis for the business arguments outlined throughout the book.

Note: The inclusion of the cost code, along with client-matter number and attorney name, helps to expedite payment to the vendor.

For those Departments that do not bill their time, establishment of a "time entry ID" is the second part to this initiative. These reports allow the Department VP of Operations to monitor work load. The money earned, or written off, through billable time provides the basis for hiring more staff.

The Accounting section of the book speaks to both cost codes and billing time.

Organize the Network

There are two types of folders, those the end users access and those they never see. The VP of Operations should follow the instructions in the Network Folders, and Needs Assessment network configuration sections to create the folder structure and backup requirements for the locations. Inside of each root folder, the VP of Operations should create client number folders and matter number subfolders to help subsequent visitors, technicians and end users to follow the organizational pattern.

The VP of Operations or COO should perform the Disaster Recovery section instructions to make certain all data on the network meets expectations of the legal team and Litigation Support Department.

The VP of Operations can also create a test environment where technicians can work without risk to the production environment, where the legal team operates. To learn more about this environment, please reference the "Administrative Hardware" and "Production v. Staging" sections.

Organizing all legacy folders, which are not subfolders of a recognized root folder, is an important initiative. These files can be lost and, depending on the type of data, may not receive the appropriate backup or security treatments. The Litigation Support Department and legal team members should move errant folders in an ad hoc manner, but the actual clean-up is a separate initiative. The clerk's role is responsible for this long term clean-up project.

Inform Legal of Change

Litigation Support and the legal team need to eventually move all legacy folders to an appropriate client-matter number sub-folder. The sooner the department establishes these locations for use by the Litigation Department, the fewer legacy folders it will need to identify and migrate.

The VP of Operations identifies all litigation data repositories as part of the Disaster Recovery Plan section. If the Department does not yet promote the use of official repositories, the COO should send an email to the Litigation Department identifying them and explaining the benefits to the team for their use of them. The book, or CD, contains sample text to use. This email should contain:

1. A copy of the firm's Litigation Support Technical Standards document;
2. An explanation about the plans for network cleanup;
3. Identification of all directly accessible storage repositories;
4. An explanation of the client-matter foldering organization strategy;
5. A request for people to begin storing and moving data to the appropriate client-matter sub-folders.

Qualify Vendors

The VP of Operations should begin to introduce both the Litigation Department and all vendors with the new firm standard, official or not. Use of the standard by vendors can eliminate the majority of associated technical problems. While the Litigation Support Department qualifies vendors, as is illustrated in the "Vendors" section, the Department should also educate the legal team as to the value of the standard and using qualified vendors.

The Litigation Support Department faces similar issues with every case and legal team. The process of qualifying vendors for consideration is also a way to exclude bad vendors. If the law firm does not yet mandate use of qualified vendors, it is possible for bad ones to get future work. This, in turn, will require work on the part of the Litigation Support Technician to correct. Depending upon the culture of the firm, excluding bad vendors can be a long term project.

Resource Initiatives

Litigation Support Department resources include: hardware, software and people. Now that the Department has control of current and future litigation data and does not spend hours correcting deliveries, it is time to address the resources the firm provides to people to perform their work.

The Department COO should move the firm toward a homogenous software environment, per the User Tools section of this book. It is not advised to move any active or recently active cases from one software title to another. All new cases must use the sanctioned titles.

The Department COO should then acquire all the necessary software and hardware tools, as outlined in the Needs Assessment. This includes both the inexpensive software utilities as well as an administrative server on a separate network, as outlined in the Administrative Hardware section and "Production v. Staging" sections.

There is also hardware to benefit the legal team. As explained in the Monitor section, addition of a second monitor can speed review time by 10 seconds per record. On a large document review, a time savings of seconds grows into days. The Department COO should now work to provide this hardware to the legal team and Litigation Support Department.

If the Litigation Support Department is billing, then it is generating revenue for the firm. The revenue funds the purchase of desired hardware and software. The Department COO can use the Accounting, Hardware and Software sections of the book to provide the firm with the strategies and arguments for provisioning of resources.

When the Department COO is able to show how much time the Department spends on technical and project management, he, or she, is able to argue for addition of staff. If the new staff will perform new services, the COO should reference the Services initiative.

The COO should also update the hierarchy to reflect any change in the Department. The COO should then make the chart available to the rest of the department.

Determine Services

The Department must have the necessary hardware, software and people to perform any service. All services require project management at a minimum. Technical services also require a professional with the appropriate training to perform the services, as well as the time to do so.

The COO should reference the Services section of the book when considering how to handle various litigation technology goods and services.

Certain types of technical work carry short term or long term responsibilities. An example of a one time service is creating CDs. The party that creates the database from "native" files, such as a spreadsheet, is ultimately responsible for any issues thereof. The department must have a contingency plan in the form of a prequalified vendor for any technical service.

The Litigation Support Department should provide a minimum, if any, technical services until it has achieved all initiatives under the "Marketing," "Operations" and "Finance" categories. The Department does not need to generate and collect revenues. Ultimately, the law firm pays for the entire Department, including hardware, software and personnel. Therefore, the COO should consider a moratorium on some or all technical services until the Department is ready. If the law firm's network operations center is not as good as that of an outside provider, the Department may wish to outsource storage. Once an appropriate level of service is available internally, the need to outsource is eliminated.

At this point, the Litigation Support Department should not be putting out many new fires. It should be able to concentrate on historical or "legacy" issues.

Client-Matter Intake

Every law firm has a matter intake system. Whether the system consists of a person or an intranet application, part of this system should include alerting the Litigation Support Department about new matters.

Not all new matters are new cases. Litigation Support can provide the best level of support the earlier in the case their involvement begins. This is true whether the case is in the pleading or production phase.

The Department COO and the VP of Marketing, also a partner, should research the firm's current system to determine how to alert Litigation Support of new matters.

Network Clean-Up

Depending upon your firm, there may be client matter data squirreled away all over your network. The "Pareto Principle", also known as the 80-20 Rule, states that a small number of causes (20%) are responsible for a large percentage (80%) of an effect. This rule, initially created for the retail industry, applies to network organization as well. If the firm gives everyone a "home" directory on a server, the chances are excellent these folders contain files that should reside in a more appropriate location.

The firm's new directory standards provide your legal team with an appropriate place to store data. This small provision results in a much larger impact, as everyone can now find all case materials with minimal effort. After moving data to their new client-matter folder, one should not delete the original folder. Instead, place a "shortcut" directing people to the new folder location. The "clean-up" person, preferably the Clerk, should also leave a copy of the "Letter to Legal", as a text file, to explain what happened to the information and why.

Retire Folders

Accounting can use the client-matter numbers to determine if anyone recently billed time to a given matter. If there has not been any activity for a long period of time, the materials are candidates for emigration to less expensive storage, such as a backup tape. However, attorneys may not want their data moved off of a server.

The Department should not completely remove the client-matter folders, when able to retire materials from the server. The Department *must* leave a text file explaining what materials were removed and where they currently reside.

To identify folders and files for retirement, the Clerk or VP of Finance can compare the list from accounting of active matters against the list of client-matter folders on the servers, as provided by the VP of Operations.

Media Inventory

The VP of Operations should be able to locate any media relating to a case. The Department COO needs to work with the Litigation Department to collect all media currently residing with attorneys, paralegals and non-Litigation Support Department staff. The Litigation Support Department should return a copy of the media, if the person desires it.

The Clerk's role should create an inventory of all media in the Department, per the Media Inventory section. The Clerk will need to organize all media into binders. During this process the Clerk must apply labels to both media and binder, per the firm's technical standards. Acting as the Department librarian is an ongoing responsibility for this role.

Routing all media through the Department is the first step in moving the responsibility for vending discovery to the Department as well. The legal team gains office space and relinquishes any librarian duties to the Litigation Support Department.

2. Case Level Initiatives

The Department COO undertakes "case level initiatives" in an effort to bring order and management to the litigation technology goods and services that cases employ. The Litigation Support Department needs to provide a consistent experience for all cases. The case lifecycle is always the same. Therefore, the Litigation Support Department will undertake the same initiatives as each case reaches a given stage. The same culling strategies always apply for each case, regardless of scale or content. When the legal team and Litigation Support Department understand how litigation technology can aid the team in every stage of the lifecycle, and follow a proven technology plan, the case enjoys the highest quality experience. The Litigation Support Department provides this experience in a consistent fashion from any case to any other case and any case lifecycle stage to any subsequent lifecycle stage.

Case Level Initiatives include education and implementation initiatives.

Education

The Litigation Support Department has a technology plan. It also has the materials necessary to explain that plan to all parties involved, most especially the legal team and the vendors.

The VP of Marketing along with the COO should educate the Litigation Department about the availability of litigation technology goods and services. Ideally, by this point, the Department should be well organized and have a list of qualified vendors.

To aid in the education process, the Litigation Support Department can use the flowchart, budget spreadsheet and concepts from within the book. Education also includes the goal oriented training detailed in the Training section.

Implementation

No system is a complete success unless people accept and use it. A partial success is not entirely a failure, either. While best practices outline how to handle situations under ideal circumstances, real life is rarely ideal. Regardless of what the legal team does, the Litigation Support Department should endeavor to follow the technology plan and ideals as closely as possible.

This adherence means that the Litigation Support Department follows all steps outlined in the Case Lifecycle Task List. It also means adherence to the organization rules found in the book. The Litigation Department should view the Litigation Support Department as a resource beneficial to the case. Now that the legal team understands how the department helps them accomplish their goals, cooperation and implementation should be possible.

It is time to turn principle into practice.

B. Supporting Files

The book references a number of emails and other supporting documents the Litigation Support Department should use. One example is the vendor email, explaining about the qualification process. Another is the email to the Litigation Department outlining the clean-up initiative. The book also references items such as a lifecycle flowchart. All of these documents, detailed below, are available in the appendix and / or on the CD.

To help organize the supporting documents, they appear under two categories: for use in Department and Firm Level initiatives, and for use on a Case Level. The Litigation Support Department may use the same case level documents for every matter.

1. Department and Firm Level

The Litigation Support Department can use these documents to achieve major initiatives.

Vendor Compliance Email

The email encourages the vendor to begin the qualification process. Once qualified, the firm may consider this vendor for projects. The VP of Operations should send this document, along with a copy of the firm technical standards to every current, historical and prospective vendor.

Server Organization Email

This email explains to the Litigation Department about the organization initiative. It outlines what will happen, how it affects the legal team and the benefits to all. The VP of Operations should customize this document in preparation for this long term initiative.

Department Status Reports

A major responsibility of the Department COO is tracking the financial and operational aspects of the department. The COO should have a good idea when the Department will require additional capacity, licenses or people. The COO should also know of potential projects and their impact upon the Department. The included "Status Reports" are good templates for the Department COO to use in constructing their own department status reports. The COO can also use these reports when arguing for additional resources.

Litigation Support Technical Standards

By requiring all litigation technology goods and services match these specifications, the firm can be confident it will not require subsequent technical work prior to use by the legal team. Consistent use also means that the Litigation Support Department can institute appropriate security, backup and disaster recovery plans.

2. Case Level

The Litigation Support Department uses these texts to provide a consistent experience for the legal team. The COO will need to personalize the texts to match firm characteristics, such as names and dates.

New Matter Assessment Email

The "new matter assessment" email introduces the legal team to the Litigation Support Department. The email is a request for a meeting, so that the VP of Operations will get a technical assessment of the potential work. The email explains some of the benefits to the team and expectations in terms of the litigation technology goods and services.

Case Lifecycle Flowchart

The Case Lifecycle Flowchart is a visual tool that walks the reader through the entire discovery lifecycle: from Phase 1, collection, to Phase 5, production per the Case Lifecycle Task List. The legal team can use the flowchart for cases in any stage of review. Project management is a major key to the successful Litigation Support experience.

Deposition and Trial Resource Sheet

Through the use of the Internet and external hard drives, the legal team should have uninterrupted access to all litigation materials. Neither the total amount of storage, nor location of the attorney should prevent access to their files. For example, the team needs access to all pre-production and production documents in the document review system.

The team can use this opportunity to identify any hardware or media they require, such as copies of each production CD, or a projector. Deposition and trial support are services your Litigation Support Department may or may not provide. As such, the Department outlines for the legal team who to contact for support.

Litigation Support Technical Standards

By requiring that all litigation technology goods and services match these specifications, the Litigation Support Department will not need to perform subsequent work. For example, the VP of Operations will be able to load all new materials directly into the law firm document review software.

Discovery Budget Spreadsheet

During the lifecycle of the case, there are various details that need to be organized and tracked—and any method that is used to organize and track case information has to work for attorneys and techies alike. The book includes a spreadsheet that does just this. The attorney can use it to budget for the case and then track all projects and people relating to processing or handling discovery, while technicians can use it to learn the case history of each collection. This is important when a technician needs to obtain materials from the original vendor. The spreadsheet also includes a worksheet to help identify and limit discovery through the use of dates, names and terms.

2. *Marketing*

A. Legal Team Relations

Everyone who works in the Litigation Support Department needs to understand how to speak with the legal team in terms they understand. Everyone in the department should also endeavor to understand what the team is trying to accomplish at all times. Litigation Support professionals can act as liaison between technology and the accomplishment of case goals.

Communications

Litigation is date driven. Everyone on the legal team schedules their efforts around meeting, beating and accommodating deadlines. Therefore, the department should speak in terms of deadlines and maximum turnaround times whenever discussing tasks. Litigation Support should know how long it will take to generate and ship a production. It is critical that the legal team know this as well.

There are established points in the case lifecycle, such as during production, which require accommodation by the legal team. One of the best ways for Litigation Support to maintain good relations with the legal team is to help them understand and incorporate technical turnaround times as they schedule their efforts. If the Litigation Support Department requires two business days to generate a production set of CDs, the legal team needs to know this before they begin the review process.

Note: When the attorney directly contracts any technical service, without input from Litigation Support, the turnaround times can change. The review team may not know how this with affect their efforts.

The legal team needs to know how technical issues will affect their budget and ability to meet a deadline. This is especially true for surprise problems, such as a password protected email file. Whether a technical issue is anticipated or a surprise, the Litigation Support Department needs to provide the team with time and cost estimates, as soon as possible. There is a clear delineation between the technical work and legal work done for the case. In an ideal environment, the paralegals and attorneys are able to concentrate completely upon legal instead of technical considerations.

Litigation Support's job is to make sure the attorney realizes how technical decisions affect the legal team in terms of dates and cost. When scanning discovery, the vendor may offer "logical unitization" as an extra service. If the attorney understands that the additional four cents per page can buy the team extra review time, the cost may appear incidental.

The service, "logical unitization," ensures a ratio of one document per database record. During review, the attorney will designate the entire record as "privileged" or "productive." If the record contains both a privileged and productive document, the database must be corrected. Failure to make proper selection of technical attributes such as image file type and format can exacerbate unitization problems.

Litigation Support should speak with the legal team in terms of time, cost and lifecycle. This allows the attorney to make decisions which the department can support. As a technical liaison, the Litigation Support Department always acts in the best interest of the legal team and firm. To perform this service successfully, the department must present technical issues and options within a context the legal team can use.

Technology Liaison

The VP of Marketing facilitates internal communications between the department and the legal team. The Litigation Support Department VP of Operations acts as liaison between the legal team when there are technical issues. When the attorney creates a production agreement with opposing counsel, Litigation Support should first make certain that the firm can actually meet the technological requirements. At this point Litigation Support can provide an estimate of time and cost to the legal team.

Other situations which contain technological elements and therefore require input from the Litigation Support Department include:

1. Identifying potential storage sources of ediscovery for collection;
2. Communicating technology requirements to client and firm technicians;
3. Creating production format agreements with opposing counsel;
4. Creating agreements that involve electronic discovery; and
5. Contracting litigation technology goods and services providers.

Any conversation about the aforementioned points should be documented in email. In this manner the department keeps a history, available for when agreements conclude. Attorneys are very controlling by nature. They have to be if they want to succeed in litigation. The attorneys will delegate authority, but only when they believe they are handing authority to a competent person, or department.

The Litigation Support Department gains respect through the successful completion of tasks before deadline and within budget. When the attorneys trust the department, they delegate greater responsibility, and everyone wins. The firm can help the department develop both. First, through the adoption of the technical standard, and second, by ensuring Litigation Support has a voice as early in the case lifecycle as possible. The standard is the first step in controlling the format and quality of the work vendors create for the firm. As a published document, all parties can reference specific requirements when product does not match expectation. Litigation Support can show the team where a vendor did not meet the standard. Because technical jargon and finger-pointing only helps to frustrate the team, Litigation Support needs something tangible for "making their case." If the vendor got a copy of the standard at the start of a project, Litigation Support can point to section X on page Y when explaining the problem to legal and vendor. This process should help the attorneys and paralegals understand why only qualified vendors are worth the time and effort.

3. Financial

A. Accounting

The Litigation Support Department can be an entrepreneurial dream.

Litigation Support doesn't worry about collecting payments. It doesn't need to make sales calls to drum up more work (although it should). It is similar to a preferred vendor—one that will exist as long as the firm exists, except that the people may change at any moment. This is the mindset the team should adopt.

Litigation Support's single greatest attribute is that the workers and storage capacity can generate revenue for the firm; not only can it generate billable hours, it can (if warranted) take revenue from other vendors by bringing the work in-house. This is not to say that a firm should do so. This environment can be exciting for the entrepreneurially-minded Litigation Support staff—and for a firm's Accounting Department.

Of course, not all attorneys want to pass Litigation Support billables through to their clients, but instead will tend to "write off the time." Luckily, Litigation Support doesn't actually need that revenue to stay in business. It just needs the financials tracked by the Accounting Department.

Later in this text, we will discuss approaches to take toward billing, cover strategy, and describe how Accounting fits into the Litigation Support game plan. Initially, the following three steps are important to get Litigation Support services on the books:

Step 1: Create vendor cost codes.

If the Litigation Support Department does not yet bill for various services, it can use a selection of actual vendor bills to help the Accounting Department understand which services to track.

Litigation Support needs Accounting to understand how these new codes will help the law firm as a business. If a service such as the processing of electronic discovery uses the same cost code as legal research, the firm is getting a skewed financial picture.

Step 2: Provide codes to all vendors.

Make certain all of your vendors include the required code information on their invoices. If the vendor knows to include the cost code along with other key information, the Accounting Department persons will have an easier time performing their tasks.

Include the cost codes in your firm's *Litigation Support Technical Standards* document. In this fashion every vendor will always have access to the code and know to include it in all invoices.

Step 3: Use codes on all invoices.

The best vendors will match the law firm's standard. As this includes what information to include on an every invoice, this can naturally lead into steps four and five, accordingly.

Step 4: Start tracking potential revenues.

The 6-month and 12-month accounting reports on these cost codes will help the firm intelligently decide how much funding to allocate for the growth of the Litigation Support Department and the need for services. At the same time, the department will provide storage trend reports. As electronic discovery is data intensive, one must plan for the cost to store this information, whether internally or with a hosting company.

Whether your firm bills for Litigation Support time or not, tracking potential revenue is important. At a certain point, the department may need additional staff. If each person bills 1,000 hours a year, the question centers more upon the ability to meet said hours than increasing firm budgets.

Step 5: Identify lost versus captured revenue.

Now that your firm or practice can identify potential and lost Litigation Support Department revenue, the appropriate firm committee can address the question of whether to bill. They can understand how much the firm spends for any given type of service. It is not uncommon to have a discovery project cost $20,000. This cost may not be sufficient to warrant firmwide change. However, when the firm considers the aggregate cost for ten projects each year, the totals may warrant firmwide change.

Now that your department is able to justify income, it is time to justify expenses. There are certain hardware and software tools every law firm should have. These tools extend from the Litigation Support Department to the legal team. For the team, a second monitor will improve everyone's document review speed. This small cost will greatly improve moral and reduce eye strain. The firm can use the second monitor for all cases. The author's research determined that a second monitor, not simply a bigger monitor, provides a better result.

At the same time, the firm should consider risks and responsibilities before attempting to bring any new services in-house. One cannot deny that the single service of project management on the part of Litigation Support is a vital service and will ultimately impact the case as a boon or a burden.

1. What to Bill

Once upon a time, the amount of data stored for document review was relatively small. Even as recently at 2003, a Litigation Support Department might only have needed 500GB of storage. Today a single case can use a combined 500GB of "off-line," "near-line," and "on-line" storage. Server storage for these amounts of storage is not cheap; just look at the rates your vendors charge for hosting. Server hard drives are more expensive than regular hard drives. The difference is essentially industrial versus commercial strength.

If the Litigation Support Department performs any services for which a vendor would charge, it should consider charging accordingly. If the firm outsources a service, it should consider whether to bring it in-house. In order to make this an informed decision, the Accounting Department must track these services with cost codes.

One can think of the Litigation Support Department as the preferred vendor. Any profits derived from the department belong to the firm, and that is part of the point. The technical costs to litigate a case are significant. Storage is one of the greatest costs as the attorney may need to pay for years of this service.

If the firm already stores information in-house, Litigation Support should know both when it will need more storage space and the cost to increase it. It is possible that electronic discovery may represent half of your firm's overall storage.

One should bill for those services and resources that are limited in some fashion. Storage, technical time and project management are good examples. The firm has a limited amount of each of these. Should the firm reach 100% utilization, it will need to either outsource or pay to increase capacity. Recovering the cost to increase capacity is a smart business decision. The most logical way is to charge for limited services and resources. How much one charges clients for these "line items" is a question of cost recovery versus a profit center.

By tracking these items with cost codes, the Accounting Department will generate the reports to make the business case for investment in hardware, software or people. At the same time, the firm which outsources any of these services can use these reports to negotiate a better price from a favored vendor.

One question to consider is the value of all discovery data stored on the server. If the law firm knows that billing clients for storage can pay for the cost for a $50,000 storage solution, a purchase should be easier to implement.

If your Litigation Support work represents 1,000 hours of billable time per person, hiring a low level clerk may be in the budget after all. If employees can pay for themselves through billable hours then the firm can afford to expand the staff.

Make certain that each case has the appropriate litigation technology support. Through institution of firm standards, you ensure each case is handled appropriately. This means consistent project management, potential technical work and potential storage.

Provision of these services for free increases the speed of consumption. There are no incentives on the part of the attorney to conserve resources. One potential result is a department that continually needs a greater budget to produce a lower quality product.

Many attorneys will choose to "write off" as many expenses to the clients as possible. This is not possible when the cost appears as a line item on a vendor invoice. The attorney and firm may have different opinions about what to write off. Litigation Support needs to bill for goods and services: but which goods and services should it bill for? The model for Litigation Support should be that of a vendor: bill as a vendor would bill. Look at some line items from a vendor invoice; if they bill for time, Litigation should as well. If they charge for OCR and CD-burning, so should Litigation Support.

Litigation Support Expenses

It is important for Litigation Support to be able to track its expenses; even if they are written off, it will raise visibility to the amount of money hidden in the department, and Accounting will be able to bring that visibility to the attention of the firm's partners. It is an index that every partner understands.

It is Litigation Support's responsibility to track billable work and the real or potential revenue. At the same time, Litigation Support should require outside vendors to use the firm cost codes when invoicing.

Whereas one firm may use these numbers to justify taking one course of action, another may take another route. For firms that perform any services in-house, these revenues will ultimately justify new hires and added resources. For firms that out-source all services, the requirement for an internal project manager role is absolute.

Mitigating Risk

Litigators and paralegals, perform their "due diligence" by consulting with a Litigation Support professional regarding how technology choices will affect any given part of the case. A technical decision may result in a 12-hour versus 36-hour production window. Twenty-four additional hours for review is valuable.

Lawyers and paralegals are smart people. A top litigator must know the nuances of the law and apply them with the guile of a poker player. This same litigator may not know the difference between a flat-file and relational database. Treatment of this difference will significantly influence the team's ability to comprehend what they read and any subsequent use. How the team collects, reviews and, potentially, produces discovery will directly affect cost, the ability to create productions expediently, and potentially the ability to win the case. As most litigators use a variety of software throughout the case lifecycle, the ability to transition key types of data between stages and software titles is critical. It is unfortunate that non-technical persons may make decisions without the input of Litigation Support or any firm-wide standards.

Note: While this book addresses many such issues, the ability to work directly with an informed Litigation Support technician may be worth the expense. Even a solo practitioner may wish to pay the hourly fees, ad hoc. This is true "due diligence."

As certain technical decisions and lifecycle strategies are universal to all cases, the firm may wish to institute them for all cases. This "cookie cutter" approach allows the attorney to concentrate on the law instead of picking the new vendor. While this book attempts to provide as clear a picture as possible of a proven, successful, model, there is no substitute for dialogue with an expert.

Litigation Support should be able to provide a technology plan and identify the strategic devices available to your team. If your practice does not have an internal expert, one not paid by the vendor may be worth the expense.

One goal of this book is to help all involved parties recognize not just the need to use standards for their own cases, but to institutionalize these standards for all firm litigation. The book contains a template for a Litigation Support Department and case technology plan. When organizing how the firm handles case technology, one also has the opportunity to organize such information so as to accommodate the law firm as a business.

Note: A potentially dangerous scenario exists in many firms where (a) Litigation Support project management and technical time is not billable, (b) cannot mandate outsourcing and (c) is beholden to litigation deadlines. Litigators and paralegals can turn the department into a free services free-for-all. The end result will harm cases and increase turn-over.

If the firm hosts all data in-house, the vendor product may not work with existing systems. If the firm outsources the case to a hosting provider, the Litigation Support Department must consider how vendor technology and standards will affect future litigation or providers. Any such vendor would also need to match the reporting and invoicing requirements outlined in the firm standard, such as inclusion of appropriate accounting cost codes.

When the law firm provides a service, it takes on all of the vendor responsibilities. I would never recommend having the "guy from IT" get deleted files from a client laptop unless he will perform well on the stand and his work acceptable to legal and technical scrutiny.

Remember, although your law firm may not be an electronic discovery vendor, providing services means responsibility for the results and any long-term support. When the attorney requires Litigation Support to perform such services, the department must then be ready for the future support for previous work.

Note: It is a common practice for vendors to outsource work when they reach internal capacity. Do they know something your firm doesn't know about resource management?

2. Billable Hours

Each Litigation Support person might be seen as representing 1,000 billable hours per year in potential revenue. From this perspective, Litigation Support professionals become income-generators for the firm, rather than expenses. Their project management time and the technical time take on an additional value in the eyes of the firm. This shift in perspective can be an important step in changing firm culture. This is a step forward and will help with the effort to institutionalize litigation technology standards.

In a law firm, there is a clear delineation between those who bill clients and those who do not. The ability and requirement to bill brings a level of respect to the work, product and person. The litigation team views Litigation Support as a member of the team.

The department is not a resource free-for-all. These are professionals who can only perform a certain amount of work in a certain amount of time and at a certain amount of expense to the client. As the firm slowly brings all Litigation Support responsibilities into the project management hands of the department, the need for additional resources will increase. At the same time, the overall quality of each case technology experience should improve, resulting in lower bills and quicker turnaround times. Finally, using accounting reports or billable hours, the department can show the historical trend in billables and plan for the hiring of any additional resources.

Note: As each project manager and technician handles each case in a consistent fashion, work load balancing becomes much simpler.

Treating Litigation Support staff as income-generators instead of expenses has an impact on various decisions—such as what sort of salary package to pay Litigation Support employees. Should they be hourly or salaried? How would one make this decision? After talking with over a dozen law firms, it is my conclusion that an annual base with the ability to earn overtime pay is the best solution. Because the Litigation Support person must rely on the attorneys for work, a base salary removes the stress and anxiety of periods where work is not as available. At the same time, when the worker is working 60 or 80 hour weeks, overtime hours makes the additional work palatable. The firm can recoup the extra costs of overtime; after all, the hours are billable to the clients for whom Litigation Support is ultimately working. One way to determine your hourly rate is to divide your salary by 2,000. A person who earns $80,000/yr is a $40/hr worker. This is a good ballpark estimate. Of course, the real well from which to draw this water is, again, the vendor bill. See what your vendors charge for the project management, technical and consultative hours.

Vendors charge for technical and project management work. When properly staffed and supported, the Litigation Support Department may be able to perform the same work for a rate lower than that of a vendor. A senior project manager may bill $200/hour or more. A Litigation Support professional from the firm may only bill $150/hour. On a two-year case, this could easily represent significant savings to each client. Further, the Litigation Support professional has a larger interest in seeing the firm win the case.

Litigation Support's time is largely a factor of the attorneys' activities; however, there may be administrative, non-billable work that requires time each day. Depending upon how the department operates, it may be worth the cost to hire an assistant to do inventory and other administrative tasks that cannot be billed to clients. If your billable rate is $200/hr and you perform 20 non-billable hours of administrative work per month, it would be financially viable to hire administrative help.

The VP of Marketing can act as a mediator between legal teams and the Litigation Support Department. Optimally an attorney, this role helps the Litigation Support professional understand what is behind various requests and posturing by the legal team. As stated, law firms are hierarchical and position or status can trump any argument. A senior attorney can advise and help a less experienced attorney expand their efforts to include litigation technology expert advice.

This "adoptive attorney" can give your Litigation Support team a very clear understanding of what types of work represent billable hours. Depending upon the firm, this attorney can then help argue for inclusion of these hours when billing the client. In certain firms a litigator may decide to remove or "write off" Litigation Support time from a client bill.

Irrespective of whether time is "written off," Litigation Support should always concentrate on getting these billables into the accounting system. These accounting numbers provide the basis for business arguments the Litigation Support Department can use to help the firm institutionalize best practices changes. If the Management Committee decides that the accounting and budget issues warrant some type of business change, then that is their province.

3. Media

Law firms that use litigation technology vendors will eventually pay that vendor to create a CD, DVD, video tape or other such storage media. While a DVD can cost ten cents when bought in bulk, the time to organize the content for storage requires manual effort. This is also true when Litigation Support performs the same work for the firm.

If the law firm pays an average of $25 per CD (DVD, tape, etc.) and buys 1,000 CDs a year, the law firm may recover some of that cost by performing certain work internally. The firm must, however, provide the necessary hardware, software and training to support this new responsibility. Recovering costs while saving the client money is a dual benefit.

Note: Frequently, Litigation Support creates a set of CDs or DVDs when giving work to the vendor. The idea of cost recovery speaks clearly when the firm pays the vendor to create an additional set of discs.

Bringing media creation duties into the Litigation Support Department and charging for media can quickly pay for a robotic CD/DVD burner and loader with label printer—and this will ultimately be a cost-savings for the firm. When a vendor charges $300 per set of ten CDs and the firm needs four sets for a production, the department's ability to perform the duplication job expediently represents significant savings to the firm and client.

Another cost savings comes from the time the department saves by removing the vendor from this particular business process. If the vendor's data requires modification, the department may perform this work in order to save time. The institution of standards helps to minimize the amount of time spent on this type of unnecessary work.

As always, remember that the law firm is a business. As such the "powers that be" will take seriously any staff member or department presenting their business case with supporting arguments that speak to business interests.

When the Litigation Support Department can produce the same quality product CD for $20 instead of the vendor $25 rate, the client saves. This type of cost recovery enables the client to save money while the law firm pays for appropriate resources. Similarly, Litigation Support uses the appropriate cost codes to get these charges and any appropriate billable time on the books. When Litigation Support performs any services or produces any goods for which a vendor would charge, the quality must be equivalent or better while charging a rate that undercuts the market.

If the attorney forgives the fee to their client, that decision does not affect Litigation Support's ultimate goal: tracking all potential and real costs and revenues. One guiding principle is to charge like a vendor, but undercut their rates.

The Litigation Support Department, if only one person, is in a unique position to undercut the marketplace for several reasons: the department will not go bankrupt unless the law firm goes bankrupt; the law firm can provide significant amounts of various types of work; because cost recovery is important to the firm and client, achieving these goals through the department is important. Media duplication is a basic service that all client matters require. It is also very simple to produce this product in bulk by buying the right hardware. The same philosophy applies to network file server capacity. This topic appears later in the book as it deserves and requires a proper section unto itself.

A goal here is to get the firm to identify potential income that is currently "left on the table" and determine whether to capture it. Another is to show how cost recovery can save the firm current expenses while saving the client money by beating market prices.

Should the firm decide to provide media creation and duplication services, it must then consider how long it will take to perform these tasks. If the current hardware only supports the creation of 3 CDs or DVDs per hour, the technician will never have time to perform any other types of work. Let's consider the "services" aspect of Litigation Support as it relates to media. An investment of $2,000 or less for additional hardware will provide your firm and department with the ability to produce a lot of media while requiring very little technician time. The amount of time saved represents significant value. The appropriate use of time should result in an engaged worker instead of a bored worker. The same technician can now produce a great volume of media in a short period of time, just as the vendor does. Remember, the department will use a lot of technician time performing clerical tasks when the appropriate hardware and software resources are deficient. Unfortunately, this type of prolonged operation will result in employee burnout, lower quality product and missed deadlines. The technician will use the newfound time to administrate databases and perform other work. Managing all resources appropriately can save the firm and client. Tasks for any given client matter are completed more quickly. The legal team benefits directly.

Note: The "appropriate resources" approach pays big dividends when the document reviewer uses a second monitor that pivots. This point appears in more detail under the hardware section.

Robotic Burners and Cost Recovery

The up-front costs represented by a robotic CD loader and burner can be recouped quickly as the technician is freed from a long manual process and may perform billable work. Without a robotic CD-burner, copying media to the network and creating media is a slow, boring process. If a CD has a read error or burn error, Litigation Support can return to find they just wasted 30 minutes—and possibly missed a deadline. The attorneys may not realize it, but almost every Litigation Support person has, at some point, logged into as many machines at the same time as possible in order to copy a stack of CDs to the server all at once instead of one at a time.

Conversely, I have also logged into multiple machines in order to burn multiple CDs simultaneously. The robotic CD burner does not require attention every time it requires the next disc. This allows the Litigation Support to perform higher level functions such as updating a database or meeting with the team. This is not a hard concept, yet many firms are hesitant to spend the money until they understand the larger gain.

Finally, understand that expensive equipment becomes less expense when it recovers that cost through production in bulk those goods for which the firm already buys.

Compare the cost for media from vendors versus the cost to perform these tasks in-house using a robotic CD-burner. This type of comparison can provide the business argument to justify purchasing a robotic, networked burner with the thermal label printer option.

In this situation, the Accounting Department is Litigation Support's ally; because Accounting tracks all costs and income, they can help Litigation Support build the business case for charging based upon other firm's "line items."

4. Cost Codes

Work with the Accounting Department to establish vendor cost codes for all Litigation Support type services. This includes everything from scanning and bibliographic coding to remote hosting, electronic discovery and court reporting. Assign cost codes to specific services you wish to address later, such as media creation, trial support, scanning and printing.

Whenever an invoice comes into the firm, Accounting categorizes the service with a cost code. In this fashion, the firm can track how much it spends per year, collectively, for office supplies, photocopying, phone services, and so forth. Accounting will use whatever vendor cost code seems the most appropriate. Right now, there is a chance your electronic discovery bills are being grouped with invoices from on-line research services such as LexisNexis or WestLaw.

This is important when the partners decide to create budgets for legal research based upon the litigation department electronic discovery cost growth rate. Accounting reports may state the firm spends $1,000,000/yr on legal research when in fact it spends $200,000 on legal research, $500,000 on turning emails into databases and $300,000 on converting paper discovery into more databases.

Through the establishment of Litigation Support cost codes, the firm can identify and chart two main indexes:

1. Overall growth and trends in litigation technology spending; and
2. Your biggest litigation technology spenders and cases.

These tools will allow your department to achieve larger goals, including improving the level of support to the legal team, decreasing turnaround time and decreasing costs to firm and client. As a department one should set goals and formulate strategies to achieve these goals. This is true for the technician supporting a team on a case or the head of Litigation Support positioning their department to support every litigation case in some capacity.

1. Chart overall growth and trends in litigation technology spending.

If your firm sees that it spent $500,000 on electronic discovery last year, perhaps the partners would be willing to hire someone full-time to process it in-house, given the addition of any required storage, software titles and training. Your law firm may not realize how much money the processing of discovery represents. It may not fully appreciate the money and time wasted due to a lack of proper business processes. By spending $200,000 this year on the appropriate resources, the firm may recover $500,000 in pass-through expenses in subsequent years. Research suggests that the need for more server space and media creation will not diminish in the near or long term.

Note: The attorney may be concerned that these types of efforts may restrict how they litigate a case. To the contrary, these requirements ensure vendor products and services match the firm base line. Non-technical people can provide the vendors with a copy of the firm technical standards.

The other half of the argument comes from showing how the time factor comes into play. Supporting a case when the vendor uses firm standards can take dramatically less time than when a vendor simply delivers according to their own standards. This is because the firm may use its own technical standard to pre-qualify vendors beforehand. As the vendor is required to match these specifications for every project, on every case, it receives from the firm. This lowers cost, turnaround time and technical glitches. The vendor's technician knows exactly how to configure the software to match the firm standard. The standard also requires the vendors to include the appropriate cost codes, and other information, on every invoice. This is to make the accounting process easier and, subsequently, faster.

Make sure your vendors and your Accounting Department know to use these codes. In the Litigation Support Technical Standards document, there is a section on cost codes.

Work with accounting to create the code numbers in your firm. Then update them in your copy of the standard. Finally, provide a copy of the full document, including cost codes, to every prequalified and not-yet-qualified vendor.

Examples:

Cost Code	Description
001	Litigation Video and Graphics: Video and graphics used at depositions, arbitration and trial.
002	Litigation Support Data Services: This covers the range of work such as: database creation, hosting, administration and such. Value added services such as OCR, programming, forensics, conversions, and media creation are all "Litigation Support Data Services".
003	Scanning and Printing: Photocopying paper, scanning paper or printing a paper set from electronic source (a/k/a "blow backs").
004	Court Reporting Services – Non-Video

The Accounting role (covered later under Hierarchy) is to make sure both the vendors and Accounting Department use the codes. For the first several months, it is worthwhile for Accounting to make sure people use the codes. Most vendors will use the same codes for every invoice. Litigation Support should work with the vendors to make sure they understand how important the inclusion of cost codes, and other information, on invoices is to the firm. Other sections discuss this principle.

2.   Identify your biggest litigation technology spenders and cases.

If Litigation Support wants to centralize all vending and processing of discovery, there will always be those attorneys who take whatever actions they feel are appropriate for the client without input from Litigation Support. This is a control issue. Remember, if the attorney has a vendor preference, work with that vendor to match the firm standard. What should not be an attorney choice is deciding whether or not to involve Litigation Support before any not-yet-qualified vendor starts to process discovery. The work these vendors generate may be technologically unusable for the firm. The firm may then look to Litigation Support to "fix it." Interestingly, it is often these attorneys who also want to write-off Litigation Support's hours spent fixing the problem.

The Accounting Department can run cost code reports that the Litigation Support Department can use to identify "rogue" projects. Once identified, the department can work with the attorney and team. Remember to impress upon the attorney that the department is strictly looking out for the case and these technical requirements (firm endorsed or not) are necessary for avoiding time and cost pitfalls.

5. Revenue Sources

Think of Litigation Support as a preferred vendor that works on-site for their only "client," the firm. It is in the department's best interest to show a profit and bill in the same way as does any marketplace vendor. When the accounting department can provide the appropriate reports, the areas to target for cost recovery become visible.

Cost recovery of this nature not only saves the firm's clients money; it means the firm is reinvesting in itself by funding these initiatives. The situation is a win for everyone: firm, legal team and attorney's client. Litigation Support Department bills to pay for resources it needs by providing top level support to the legal team while the attorney's client money. This provides the Litigation Support Department with the clout to institute change. It can make the argument that the proper business processes, instituted across the firm, will benefit everyone.

Ultimately, Litigation Support wants to firm to look upon it as a model of cost recovery by providing great service, competitive rates and paying for its own resource needs.

I am not advocating bringing every possible good or service in-house; I am simply advocating this idea for those services which make business and case sense.

There are four basic potential revenue sources. The accounting department can provide these codes.

1. Media Creation [_____] cost code

CDs, DVDs, HDs – Vendors charge big dollars for media. Make sure that you track potential revenues in order to help justify capital expenses by the firm for the appropriate hardware and software.

2. Storage - Access [____] cost code

Per GB, Per MB, Per Image, Per User and Per GB transmitted to the computer screen – Vendors charge for storage, access to the storage and sometimes both.

Compare the cost for all outsourced storage against the cost for providing an equivalent system within the firm. The expensive word is "equivalent." As with all products, there is industrial and commercial grade data storage. The price for industrial storage is significantly more expensive. The firm will eventually need to replace these systems with larger and updated systems. There is also the need for supporting infrastructure and system administration by the IT Department. The question is which party will pay.

The clients will pay for these services for the life of the litigation. There are many times the attorneys will keep the information on-line as a reference for additional cases. With the introduction of electronic discovery, the amount of information gathered and stored for each case has increased dramatically.

Together, these factors show us a future of big storage requirements. The law firm needs to set aside a budget to buy the hardware and software to support that storage. Does litigation bill enough to cover these inevitable costs or will non-litigation partners need to pay for things they will never use? Litigation Support can compare potential storage revenues against the cost for future storage expansion. Interestingly, these numbers can also help show a firm when having a vendor host their discovery is a prudent move.

3. Administration [____] cost code

Litigation Support may decide that administrative work, such as the initial setup of a new database for a new case and adding users, falls under the normal hourly billing rate for Litigation Support. I see no problem with that, as long as the department bills for the service.

4. Technical / Strategic Support [____] cost code

Again, this is an hourly service and a cost that every litigator should anticipate. Whether it is helping the attorney to estimate discovery costs or strategizing on collection and production efforts, Litigation Support provides a valuable service and these billable hours may represent the largest revenue source for the department. Remember that the advice Litigation Support provides today can save the client tens of thousands of dollars tomorrow.

5. Paper [____] cost code

Both the scanning and printing processes are labor intensive and the profit margins may not justify the risks of doing such work in-house. However, once paper discovery is scanned, all value-added services, such as OCR, can occur in-house, once you have the .TIF files. Some firms prefer to scan everything in-house. If your firm takes this approach, make sure that the Accounting Department tracks this cost separately. The head of Litigation Support may wish to use these numbers to justify further firm investment in people and hardware or transitioning the firm's work to a vendor.

Firms that do outsource should still qualify several different vendors to provide this service as a precautionary move. Adherence to the firm standard ensures vendor product will match internal product and software requirements.

4. Operations

A. Budget Estimation

Creating a budget for litigation technology goods and services is not an easy chore. Before electronic discovery, one could multiply the number of boxes by 2,500 and estimate the page count. An industry average of 3 pages per document was generally sufficient for estimating the costs for any special treatments, such as bibliographic coding. Electronic discovery changed this.

While a "pages per box" ratio is simple, it is more difficult to estimate the total number of pages by the total GBs. This is because the format and content of electronic discovery can be as varied as the number of software titles which run on anyone's computer. A GB of one type of file may yield thousands of pages, while another file type would only yield hundreds or dozens of pages. This makes any generalized pages per GB ratio almost useless. Fortunately, the bulk of ediscovery is of a single file type, email, and this can be estimated, after all. Therefore, one can create a fair estimate based upon the pages per email ratio. Use the included budget spreadsheet to perform this task.

Note: For large ediscovery projects where the vendor delivers the discovery database incrementally, the Litigation Support Department can update the spreadsheet to reflect real versus estimated costs.

Before ediscovery, the number of treatment options, such as bibliographic coding, was limited. One could scan, OCR, code and annotate images. This all changed with introduction of ediscovery. Not only may ediscovery require treatments and services, unknown to paper, but it may afford the legal team new options. Almost every option, such as hosting and native file review, present new potential costs. Some one these costs occur only once. Some costs are recurring. To estimate hosting, one should know the total storage size in GBs, number of months required and number of people who will need to access the system. Fortunately, the budget spreadsheet accommodates this option, amongst others.

Litigation Support should use the budget spreadsheet to explain potential technology costs to the attorney. The spreadsheet is a very straightforward way for anyone to understand the relationship between price and quantity. The attorney can then use the spreadsheet to explain costs to the client.

The budget spreadsheet includes multiple worksheets. The first worksheet is for the budget. Subsequent sheets are for tracking projects, keywords and names, and finally a place to store everyone's contact information. This information is especially useful for cases that were dormant for a long time, or if one person must track multiple matters.

Note: This spreadsheet used in conjunction with the case lifecycle project plan can prove invaluable to resuming work or learning the case's ediscovery history.

The spreadsheet allows the user to enter certain broad assumptions and fill in the numbers according. It also contains multiple worksheets that the team and Litigation Support Department can use to track discovery projects. It also assumes certain percentages of paper will be light, medium and heavy. This can help give a better estimate.

The spreadsheet contains several worksheets:

• Budget Estimator Worksheet

This worksheet is the summation of the discovery collection and processing effort. The attorney can use this worksheet to explain costs to the client. As the case progresses, one can track the total cost here.

• Discovery Matrix Worksheet

The Litigation Support Department VP of Operations, or project manager, can use this worksheet to track project information as it relates to each collection. This worksheet shows the actual page and document counts, so the reader may compare them against the estimate totals.

• Limiting Discovery Worksheet

The team and Litigation Support use this worksheet to limit and cull discovery by key words and terms. It also accommodates date range limits, culling duplicate records and key words for extracting the most important documents first. To help the persons who view these options, it explains the difference between deduplication by custodian versus across custodians and lets the reader type an "X" in the desired box.

The information contained on this worksheet can save the client significant amounts of money. It can also save the team hours, days or weeks worth of review time. As example, at the attorney's direction, the vendor can limit extraction to only those documents that contain key words. In such a fashion, the team can focus on the 10 - 20% of the ediscovery collection which is most likely to be significant. This strategy will also decrease costs significantly.

Note: Fact management software, such as CaseSoft's CaseMap, is the proper final central location for these important names, dates and keywords.

• Roles & Responsibilities Worksheet

Only update as necessary. This worksheet lets the reader know who filled a given role: Lead Attorney, Lead Paralegal, Client Technical Contact, and so forth. If you need to know who the Lead Attorney was on a given case, then consult the worksheet. The worksheet also includes space to store all contact information from each role.

Budget estimation is a critical service for the Litigation Support Department to provide to the attorney. Not only will the department help estimate cost, but also help reduce the potential exposure to large bills.

B. Computer Forensics

Computer forensics work is one of the most expensive services to contract and is therefore one of the most potentially lucrative litigation services available to the Litigation Support Department. Each litigator and paralegal should understand which case circumstances require forensic work and which do not. From the Litigation Support perspective the question is whether the team will want to search inside of deleted files for information. The legal team must also understand the exposure to the firm and risk to the case as determining factors when deciding who should perform computer forensic work.

Certification

An attorney would not use a non-CPA from the accounting department to audit accounting records for a case. The person should at least be a CPA. The attorney should also want the expert to be third party to the firm, unless they are qualified and ready to testify. There are no sanctioning bodies for many kinds of litigation technology services. There is certification for computer forensics. The Litigation Support Department should make certain the service and product meet litigation requirements. This includes the computer forensics certification.

One requirement for the Litigation Support Department to provide computer forensics work is that the technician has the appropriate certification and credentials.

Matching firm technical standards

No matter which vendor provides a good or service, the resulting product must meet the firm's technical standards document. Regardless of how many providers a case requires, the end technical result must match the firm standard.

A forensic copy of a hard drive can appear as one giant file. Through various searches, a technician will extract all files that meet key values, such as a date range or appearance of a word. The electronic discovery service bureau converts, or processes, the files to generate a database load file and all associated .TIF files. Because the final database matches the firm technical standard, the Litigation Support Department can make the discovery immediately available to the review team. This is true for all the products outlined in the technical standard.

If the Litigation Support Department must spend two hours manipulating a load file, the client is double billed and the review team is denied access. Litigation Support should strive to minimize or eliminate any wait time for the review team. Use of prequalified providers ensures the most qualified, and appropriate, persons perform case critical tasks.

It also ensures that the final product requires minimal department technical time. The legal team may access the data with a minimum of internal technical effort.

C. Document Review Systems

These days there are many discovery review systems. Along with the established titles like Summation and Concordance, it seems every vendor in the marketplace is developing or currently offering its own custom document review system. A lot of these systems have special abilities, such as native file review, concept searching, automatic foldering, and so forth. However, if the manner in which these systems handle discovery does not match existing firm technical requirements and lifecycle planning, the effect on the case can be increased costs and time.

The Litigation Support Department should promote not only the services but the software available to the firm. It is also the responsibility of the legal team to involve Litigation Support before making any purchasing decisions. Even if this approval is perfunctory, at least the legal team can feel comfortable they are not making any bad technological and strategic decisions. There are real world examples of attorneys who purchase an entire document review system which does not allow for network printing or lack the ability to accommodate more than one reviewer concurrently. The answer is to make certain the litigators involve Litigation Support before making technical decisions.

Even if your firm hosts all data on firm servers, it is still worth knowing what new options exist in the marketplace. Trying a small case on a new type of system is the best way to see if the new technology warrants further exploration. Litigation Support needs to ensure the new system will not present any major logistical or case lifecycle problems. One key to running a successful department is using an established technology plan that provides a painless path from collection to trial.

D. Electronic Discovery

How the Litigation Support Department, litigators, paralegals and firm handle the issue of electronic discovery on a per-matter and firmwide level should be critical issues for the management committee. Before questioning whether your firm should do more than review a discovery database, a firm needs to make certain all teams and the Litigation Support Department handle electronic discovery according to the same standards.

Because a small electronic discovery collection can suddenly expand to include twenty unexpected DVDs containing native files, the Litigation Support Department must be allowed to mandate outsourcing to a vendor. Without this ability, any case may overwhelm in-house capacity to the detriment of all cases and firm. The conflict between the partner who does not want any pass-through costs and the department is really a matter between the partner and the firm. The included hierarchy recommends that the VP of Marketing be an attorney. A partner is best suited for this task.

Electronic discovery processing is a young science for litigation. What is clear is that to underestimate the potential size and technical complexity for a given case is to risk the outcome of the case. To bring any type of work in-house, the firm should first master the project management aspect of the service. Before any internalization should happen the firm needs to first organize the entire department and how it handles current goods and services.

There are a lot of considerations when dealing with software; covered later, throughout the book. For the moment, let us consider "native files" and electronic discovery. As a matter of course, native files, such as email, are converted into an image file (.TIF or .PDF) and text for use in the discovery review software by the legal team.

While I believe that native files will become more important in the future, today's industry software leaders work best with the .TIF and text approach. Currently, litigators produce in this format. The software accommodates the case lifecycle. Because the law will eventually change the collection, review and production requirements, software and business processes will adjust accordingly. The Litigation Support Department must be nimble enough to adjust to these changes.

As any electronic discovery vendor can attest, the process of handling electronic discovery would fill a book itself. This book concentrates on helping firms determine whether to provide services in-house, but not necessarily how to perform every possible service. Just be certain that your firm is ready for the responsibility.

E. Paper Discovery

Many law firms perform some or all scanning and printing ("blow-backs") inside the firm. First, never underestimate how long it can take to print 5 boxes of paper. This is especially true if your Litigation Support Department is not properly trained or equipped.

With so many scanning and printing companies around, the prices are fairly reasonable should a firm decide to outsource this task. If the source of a blow-back is a .TIF file instead of a paper page, the cost is lower, too. If you are blowing back paper for a production, it may even be cheaper to ship your CDs to the other firm's home town for blow-back and, finally, delivery.

The larger question, then, is what to scan and print internally. Internal and important documents, such as a pleading should be scanned. It is the start of the case and the source of issues, keywords and so forth. The scanned images should go, as identified elsewhere in the book, into the client-matter folder area. The scanning process reduces the amount of paper used in the case by keeping each page archived electronically, ready for review or printing whenever necessary.

At a minimum, firms should look at the cost to provide for this scanning ability, if only for smaller projects.

F. Project Management

A project manager uses a case lifecycle technology plan and task list to provide everyone and every case with a consistent Litigation Support experience. The manager uses the same tools, in the same sequence, to achieve successful and predictable results. The project manager knows which actions to take during every stage, in anticipation of needs in other stages of the case. Because every case follows the same lifecycle, the legal team and Litigation Support Department can follow a standard case technology plan.

Every role requires a task list. The tasks for non-Litigation Support Department persons are not difficult and usually amount to providing or receiving information. Due to the predictable case lifecycle, it is possible for each Litigation Support Department project manager to follow the same task list. As such anyone with the right skills can assume responsibility for a legacy case or new case with minimal problems. Through the use of the standard and task list, everyone knows both where to find the required files and where work stopped or encountered an issue.

It is important to note that the task list outlines the required results, but does not necessarily tell the person how to achieve them. This is because there are many legitimate ways for a technician to produce the required result. The list may, however, tell the person which tools to use in order to achieve the results. The tasks are not limited to the Litigation Support roles as all roles possess critical information necessary to the successful production of goods and provisioning of services. To properly execute the firm's technology plan, each person on the team must understand their role's responsibilities. The project manager can help educate each person accordingly.

With the consistent use of a case lifecycle task list for all matters, there is a minimal learning curve for any new department project manager or technician. This also means the department can look to IT professionals as a source of new Litigation Support Department technicians. While it is relatively simple to teach a technician to follow a technology plan, it can be more difficult to teach technical skills to a paralegal. Paralegals may perform better as project managers. The project manager is more interested in the results of current efforts and organizing resources for the next. Technicians are more interested in how to achieve the documented results. A task list ensures the results of both roles are harmonic.

Note: The age of paper discovery is over. The technical nature of electronic discovery and litigation technology goods and services requires a technical expertise in the Litigation Support technical roles.

The advantages of the project management standard workflow include:

1.   The ability for any technician to perform quality control tests on work performed by another other technician or vendor.
2.   The benefit that all roles can learn a system and associated responsibilities, which they use for each case.

3. A standard lifecycle makes training a simpler task.
4. The ability to shift work from one technician and project manager to another with minimal disruption.
5. The ability to resume support on long dormant cases with a minimal learning curve.

Work Case Lifecycle Task List

Use this task list, in Microsoft Project file format, to walk the legal team and Litigation Support Department through all the tasks and steps needed to successfully execute a successful technology plan which: provides appropriate support, matches the flowchart and matches all departmental and firm best practices. Please note that some task sequences repeat, such as with a "rolling production," where deliveries and productions may happen multiple times. The Discovery – Flowchart illustrates the process very well. One may think of it as a road map, where the task list outlines the actual directions.

Work Case Lifecycle Sample

To provide a better picture of what is involved, here are to excerpts from the task list. In the first excerpt from the task list, the Litigation Support Department helps the team plan for discovery, budget, vendor and software selection and so forth. The second excerpt walks the department and team through the final steps in closing the case.

The full Microsoft Project file is included on the CD. As with the Litigation Budget Spreadsheet, the project manager should create a copy of this file for use with each case. The project managers can then update the task list as the case progresses.

Sample Tasks -

Key: LS is short for Litigation Support. The bullet points may not appear in the project file.

Step	Description
15	Phase 2: Discovery Planning
	• In phase 1, Litigation Support learned about all the potential collections, names of deponents and other case demographics.
16	LS prepares a discovery flow-chart for case
	• Use the included lifecycle flow chart to illustrate for the legal team how the technology plan and case lifecycle work together.
17	LS checks availability and price of prequalified vendors
18	Paralegal schedules the Discovery Planning Meeting w/ Team & Client
19	30 minutes before Discovery Planning Meeting
20	Review and update budget spreadsheet discovery matrix worksheet
	• LS presents the legal team with a litigation technology budget; based upon vendor quotes and team estimates about quantities.
21	Review and update budget if necessary

22	LS finalizes collection names and internal doc control number prefixes
23	Review of discovery flow-chart
24	LS makes recommendation on database treatment options
25	LS makes recommendation on in-house work versus vendor involvement
26	LS recommends firm DRS or ASP solution
27	LS approves technical considerations in doc requests to client and opposing
28	Discovery Planning Meeting
29	LS & Team & Client formalize discovery matrix, ability to produce and schedule
30	Production method (by Client, by Vendor) to Firm by Client noted per collection
31	Identification of native review only collections such as a relational database
32	Client designates a point of contact for each collection and ongoing issues.
33	Attorney and Client agree on budget
34	LS enters client roles in the Roles & Responsibilities worksheet
35	If client has vendor choice unknown to the firm, LS must prequalify
36	Team member updates CaseMap with all case names, terms, dates, etc.
37	Attorney formalizes the request for production by opposing counsel
38	Attorney uses kit strategies to limit discovery
39	Attorney gets formal agreement about production technical specifications
40	Attorney gets formal agreement about end-of-case destruct orders
41	Results: budget, discovery matrix/request, production format, CaseMap

As one can see, the tasks are very simple and walk each person through the Litigation Support and litigation goods and services needs for the case. The next excerpt shows how each case lifecycle ends, from the litigation technology goods and services perspective.

Step	Description
193	Phase 8: Case "Tear Down"
194	LS executes Destruction Orders (if any)
195	Alerts Team as to completion of Destruct Orders
196	Paralegal returns rented equipment
197	Paralegal returns firm equipment to IT
198	LS updates LS Inventory Spreadsheet
199	Case Summary
200	LS provides Estimated and Final Budget Spreadsheets
201	LS provides Discovery Summary Worksheet
202	Results: Case Over

Each phase, whether collection, production or tear down, appears in the project plan. As one can see, the tasks in no way limit how the attorney litigates a case. The tasks do, however, provide for best practices, consistent experience across matters and quality Litigation Support. It also provides vital information when a dormant case becomes active. This project plan allows a computer science college graduate, with the necessary instructions, to provide top level Litigation Support project management to the legal team. Of course, the individual would still need hardware, software and, perhaps, training before executing the plan without incident. If the Litigation Support Department has enough work to warrant the addition of another project manager, the project plan minimizes the learning curve. Additionally, any person who has worked on other firm matters is already familiar with the technology lifecycle and can aid the new worker as they learn.

Although the litigation case lifecycle is consistent, the Litigation Support professionals may only experience every phase themselves after working on many cases for many years. While some cases may not go to trial for years, other cases exist on a "rocket docket." A Litigation Support professional may only get to experience the discovery phase where team reviews for privilege.

Proper project management means the ability to know what work has been performed, is outstanding and is pending, once the case matures. A task list provides the project manager with this information, no matter how long the case has been dormant.

G. Storage

Thanks to the client-matter number directory structure, we know how to organize the data. Now we deal with where the data will be stored. Even firms that outsource the majority of their storage will still need to use the outlined structures for whatever data is actually stored on the firm network.

Storage is a big deal these days. With "ediscovery" upon us, there are fewer small cases and more GBs of email to handle. As I point out in my client production planning document, even medium sized firms should expect to be at multiple TBs of storage very quickly. Through culling, however, the data that actually makes it onto the server may be greatly reduced.

While an accurate page count to storage ratio estimate is impossible, some guideline numbers say there are 100,000 pages of email per GB (Applied Discovery, 2005). So how much electronic discovery is coming your way? I would estimate the average business person has between 1 and 2 GB of email.

If you think your firm may have email from 100 deponents, expect 100 -200 GB from email alone. This doesn't include all your other electronic discovery files, such as word processing, spreadsheets and more.

Questions one should be asking oneself include:

- How much storage is left?
- How soon will it be until you run out of space?
- Do you have a backup system able to accommodate this amount of storage?
- How expensive will it be to increase that capacity?

There are ways to reduce your current active storage size. Start by using external hard drives, as outlined in this book. This is regardless of whether you plan on hosting your own data and database or using an outside vendor. If the review team doesn't need to see the data, don't stick it on an expensive server. Just make sure everything is backed up on tape and either CDs, DVDs or external hard drives.

The final question, as alluded to above, is whether to house your discovery or arrange something with an ASP. On the plus side, the ASP will house your data, perform technical duties and provide full review capabilities. On the down side, the majority of ASPs charge you monthly for storage, access and other "line items." Do not be surprised if the ASP's rookie technician costs as much as an associate and their top person as much as some partners.

1. Small Firm

Small firms are not exempt from electronic discovery and the flood of native files that are part of every case and daily correspondence. These firms can buy exemption from the technical requirements if they pay a vendor.

Due to staff size, there may not be the time to provide the serious attention required by the technical aspects of running Litigation Support. Further, the funds to increase storage may be limited. In the Needs Assessment section of this book is a section on storage. Find out how much is left and the cost to increase it.

Another mistake a small firm can make is not handling electronic discovery like a big firm. The issue of how the firm handled electronic discovery collection, review and production is crucial enough to be the difference in winning or losing cases. Thanks to the Internet, even a solo practitioner can use the same document review software, via an ASP, as the attorneys from large firms.

Personally, I suggest that every small firm use the ASP route.

Using an ASP will remove all major issues such as storage, data analysis and technical support. The attorneys will get the same technology as a large firm for nominal cost. Litigation Support should evaluate the ASP from a technical perspective and then fulfill the role of project management.

The ASP will also provide service level guarantees the practice may not yet match. Use of an outside vendor also provides the firm time to plan and implement a long-term solution while getting the benefits and work done today. Every vendor can create CDs for internal firm inventory as well as productions to third parties.

The ASP route means the ability to use a different document review system for every case. This lets your firm sample different solutions until it finds a favorite. Watch out - If each case uses a different interface for review, reviewers may become confused.

As noted above, there are certain negatives when using an ASP. They cost more, and the firm can incur monthly bills for the life of the case—and after, if left on their servers. The costs will vary depending on the total file size, amount of their technical time, total quantity of blow-backs and optical media productions. The Firm may also need to pay some fee to get back its data at the end of the case. Be sure to read the agreement carefully.

If your firm still believes that paper is better than staying electronic, vendors can always turn electronic discovery into paper. Everyone is comfortable with paper. There are significant negatives with this route, however. Boxes of paper take up space. Small firms have less space than big firms. Also, if a page is lost, it is probably lost for good. Perhaps most importantly, all metadata stored by the electronic version of a record is lost when the record is printed. Metadata is stuff like the subject field in your email. In a database, you can search by author, date, document type or some combination. You can't do that with paper. Finally, paper is heavy and expensive to ship, especially when compared to CDs.

However, it should also be noted that creating paper from a .TIF file is cheaper than a photocopy, because there is less manual labor.

The small firm can choose to do in-house electronic review. Storage is relatively cheap, but not for the type of servers and backup systems you must require for this "mission critical" data. If you consider the price for possibly losing all work against the price of proper storage, you may decide that an ASP is the route to go.

Finally, firms frequently host documents in electronic or virtual repositories. Hosted repositories save firms the IT and financial resources by transferring the infrastructure investments to a vendor. A hosted environment also facilitates 24/7 access to documents from anywhere in the world at any time. If your firm does not have an actual server room, you should consider a repository.

2. Medium and Large Firms

If you work in a medium or large firms, chances are excellent your firm already has some amount of electronic discovery (native files or .TIF/.PDF files) stored on the network. Hopefully it is organized in such a way that anyone can easily determine the client-matter number for each item. Depending upon your firm, attorneys might even have client CDs sitting in their offices. This would be electronic discovery that Litigation Support might not even know about.

Your firm may also be supporting more than one in-house document review program, such as Concordance, Summation or iCONECT. Along with the need to consolidate data and educate legal teams about how to handle discovery there is the need to consolidate software titles.

A medium to large firm is in a better position than a small firm to invest in server and storage space for its clients. At the same time, this service can be charged to clients, just as if it were done by an outside vendor. If your firm plans to charge its clients for storage, as any vendor does, then you had better be able to identify everything for a given client matter. Use the directory structure mentioned elsewhere in this document. If your firm has GB and later TB worth of storage, you could be making tens of thousands per year in storage fees. This money will help you afford future investments in storage.

For the medium to large firm, there are several positives to storing data in-house. It allows total control of client data and team work product, the ability to perform technical administration internally by Litigation Support for billable hours, and the option to charging a monthly fee to the client for storage. Also, the reduction in vendor involvement means less pass-through of data, and quicker turnaround times.

At the same time, bringing storage in-house adds several burdens to Litigation Support. It compounds the burden of technical administration to that of project management - dealing with the team and the vendors. As many cases go through very active to dormant phases, Litigation Support never knows when some old case will suddenly consume an afternoon. Added costs for storage and backup also mean added administration time by other IT persons.

Like a smaller firm, a medium to large firm may also decide to go with an ASP. This option means that there is no impact on firm networks and IT departments, and allows Litigation Support to concentrate on non-technical issues, such as contracts, rates, training, etc. Using an ASP also allows the firm to point fingers at a third party instead of taking all the blame for an error. However, as with a small firm using an ASP, medium and large firms must be careful not to run up high bills for hourly service from the ASP.

3. Hosting and Storage Options

In the following paragraphs, I will describe in a general fashion the various options for hosting and storage available to law firms, as well as the pros and cons of each method. Most firms seem to employ somewhat of a hybrid approach where some information and software runs on different systems even within the same matter. For certain types of information and software, a hybrid approach may be the best approach. No matter how the firm decides to host its information, it should be consistent across all matters and litigators. A consistent approach employed across all cases helps to ensure a better experience for all involved.

Option #1 - Firms Houses Everything

This option requires that the firm store all information in-house and removes the need for outside storage. The firm may still require vendor assistance to process data, but the resulting databases and files exist on the law firm servers.

Scenario:

In the morning mail delivery, Litigation Support receives three FedEx envelopes and a smallish box. In each envelope is a CD with the latest batch of .TIF files, cross reference and database load files from the vendor. The technician evaluates the filenames and spot-checks some images to identify any obvious issues. If there is a problem, Litigation Support may have to ask the vendor to fix the problem or be able to perform the work internally.

Once the data is copied to the server and loaded into the database, Litigation Support runs various reports to make sure there are no technical errors, such as gaps or missing images.

Pros:

1. Firm has the greatest control of data, including: storage, access, database administration, technical work and productions;
2. Firm controls internal and external access to the data;
3. Potential cost recovery for both project management and technical time;
4. All data is centralized within the firm; and
5. Ability to create productions and multiple sets of media internally.

Cons:

Note: Most of these "cons" should be the responsibility of the IT Department and not the Litigation Support Department.

1. Firm has to administer the software (e.g., perform installs, tech support);
2. Firm has to administer network servers;
3. Firm is responsible for "up time," backup and restoring of data; and
4. Firm has to buy additional storage and software licenses.

This list should not give the impression that the "pros" outweigh the "cons". It is simply a reference the reader should use to determine the best approach for their firm.

Option #2 - Firm Houses Nothing

All native files and paper discovery go directly to the service bureau, which, in turn, provides access via the Internet. Via the browser, the legal team then "tags" or identifies documents for blow-back to paper, electronic productions, and online review by other team members. The Litigation Support Department can concentrate completely upon project management and internal department initiatives outlined in this text. As these initiatives help the department pay for itself and provide true cost recovery for the firm and the client, a temporary suspension of internal technical work can be very advantageous.

There are certain types of cases where the attorneys already know the discovery collection process alone will be extremely involved. The Litigation Support Department needs to be able to determine how much technical and project management effort the case will require. From the perspective of both roles, there is the need to identify high risk Litigation Support work. Due to the technical nature of electronic discovery, there are problems which may arise through no fault of anyone involved. In such cases, mitigating the risk to a vendor can save the firm a problem later.

There are other types of cases where the scale of discovery unexpectedly increases more quickly than resources and bandwidth can accommodate. Under this circumstance, any lapse in access by the legal team due to the migration of the case materials from the internal firm systems to a service bureau is worth the inconvenience. If the department and legal team coordinate efforts, there should be no interruption in service to the team. Other ongoing matters should experience minor disruptions, but this inconvenience eliminates the potential of greater problems ahead.

The following is an incomplete list of the benefits and potential costs for using a "hosted solution." As the reader progresses through this text, begin to visualize how the Litigation Support Department affects the firm as well as the individual cases. Further, one should look at how one can use this knowledge to the advantage of both firm and case.

Pros:

1. Minimal firm investment in hardware, software or technicians;
2. Project management is the main consideration for Litigation Support;
3. Department time available for internal projects such as clean-up and institution of cost codes;
4. Another company is responsible for all server administration, backup and "up time"; and
5. Ability to test alternative solutions with small cases.

Cons:

1. Monthly bill for the client from an outside vendor;
2. Must rely on vendor for technical work, thereby accruing billed time;
3. Most matters that use hosted solutions still require some internal storage;
4. Decentralized hosting of case files;
5. Vendor technical work billed to client on an hourly basis; and
6. Difficult to make certain the resulting work will meet firm standards.

Hosting Requirements

The following is a list of hosting requirements. Your firm should pay careful attention to these points when determining whether to store discovery internally or employ a vendor to host case data and work product. If your firm IT Department cannot meet the same service levels, you are a great candidate for an ASP solution. If you are a medium or large firm, the IT facilities requirement may be easier to meet. Once the accounting reports can show a large enough amount of money spent on hosted storage, the firm may realize the need to invest in resources and meet those needs internally.

Don't forget, these service levels represent a requirement. Don't back down if you believe the case is exposing itself to a potential problem. Make sure that you keep the email where the team was advised. It is the responsibility of Litigation Support to look out for the team. As such, it needs to advise the team as to the safest place for the database. This is also about mitigating risk. That's a fancy way of saying that you need to cover your rear. If there is a technical issue, all eyes will turn to the Litigation Support Department. Lit support is responsible for the technical side of the case. These considerations are aside from the functionality of the document review system. This will not guarantee that your team will like the document review software. It does guarantee that the chance of losing access or data is very low.

When using a vendor, does all firm data reside on a private or shared server? Find out if your vendor puts multiple law firms on the same server. How does the vendor keep everything separated? Logins are only one type of separation. The other type of separation centers around folder storage on the server. Again, if Litigation Support does not have the technical background, find a provider who does.

Your network/hardware administrator from IT should be able to identify any potential problems. For the server, desired/required hardware includes, but is not limited to, redundant power supply, RAID 5 array and a certain amount of memory. Again, your IT person will let you know if your data is both safe and sitting on a server powerful enough to handle firm needs.

Other hosting considerations include backups, restoring and guaranteeing access at all times.

Data Center

1. Connection to the Internet: The host should employ multiple dedicated connections to the Internet from different Tier-1 providers. In this context, "dedicated" means the connection is always on; much like the difference between dial-up modem and a cable modem. Find out the speeds of the ASP connections. Also find out the connection from the "pop" to the server. The pop is the "point of presence." It is where the Internet meets your vendor's network.

2. Internal Network: Your network operations center ("NOC") should have a fast gigabit Ethernet backbone. This means your data can go from your server to your PC screen in the fastest time possible. At the same time, the vendor's network should employ full network redundancy.

3. Physical Plant: The data center should employ fully redundant power and air conditioning supply, with state of the art fire protection. This provides the maximum possible protection against potential disasters that could affect access to your data. Computers don't like water. As such, there are special computer room fire suppression systems. What system protects your NOC?

4. Monitoring: The hosting company, or IT Department, should know there is a problem when it occurs. This means you require 24X7 monitoring of the building and data infrastructure by a local staff along with immediate access to those who can fix the problem. Your hosting provider should use software that will page people when it detects a problem.

5. Phone Houses: If your firm is on one coast and the ASP on the other coast, will this affect the firm's ability to access vendor staff?

24x7 Physical Security

The Internet is not the only way for bad people to reach your data. Who is to say how far people will go to win a case. Closed-circuit cameras, 24hour guards and physical location monitoring help make sure your servers are safe. Other security precautions include: Biometric scanners, secure card-key access, lock doors and locked cages enclosing all equipment.

Backup, Restore and Disaster Recovery

These three concepts are critical to the security picture. These are the same requirements the firm needs to meet if hosting data internally.

Your data requires enterprise-class backup and restore technology. This means weekly full backups of certain data (such as .TIF image files) and daily incremental backups of databases and other native files.

There needs to be off-site retention. There are companies that make a weekly visit to drop off backup tapes and take others off-site. After all, what good is a backup if it melts in the fire next to your crispy server?

Operating Systems

Whether your software sits on a Windows or Linux server, there are always "patches" or updates to install. There are also patches for network hardware, such as routers and even network cards. Whether it is the law firm's IT department or an ASP's technicians, someone needs to take responsibility for this.

OS administration may be best done by non-Litigation Support Department personnel. It doesn't matter whether the Litigation Support technicians are capable of performing the work. If the firm already has an IT person patching and administrating other servers, this server also should be his (or her) role's responsibility. Every person should understand their role and the associated responsibilities.

4. On Hosted Solutions ("ASPs")

Not all services are provided internally. This section discusses hosting companies and how they provide service to the law firm. The ASP lets a law firm try a new document review system without having to buy and install it at the firm. Hosted solutions allow the firm to estimate potential earnings to offset expenses incurred by moving work in-house.

All legal teams at a single firm should use the same document review system for all cases. The cost to install and then support each application is significant. If the firm wishes to test a new system on a single case, an ASP is the best approach. Litigation Support can perform a project management role and the vendor performs the technical role.

Here is how a traditional ASP works:

1. All electronic discovery is given to the ASP;
2. The ASP processes the discovery and turns it into a Brand Y database;
3. The ASP loads the database into its own servers and provides logins to the legal team;
4. The review team accesses its database over the Internet; searching, tagging and issue coding;
5. The ASP creates "production cds" based on tagging; and
6. At the end of the case, all data may be returned to the firm.

While using an ASP is cheaper than buying and testing a new document review system in-house, there are certain costs associated with the process. Here are a few:

1. Hosting

> ASPs charge for hosting the firm's files. It is a monthly recurring fee based on factors such as access, storage, hourly work, and media creation. Try and determine the grand total you will store and then figure out how many months you'll need.

2. Access

> ASPs usually charge for access either per login or amount of bandwidth per month. In other words, they either charge a lot of "up front" costs for access, or a smaller bill each month.

3. Front-Load Fees

> The Vendor may charge fees to get everything loaded and set up.

4. End-Load Fees

The vendor may charge you to get your data back.

5. Incidental Fees

You may use a certain amount of the vendor's time each month for various service-related issues. Is there an hourly fee for this time? Remember, this might be a recurring cost for the next 24 months.

6. Media

Every CD produced for the firm can be $25 - $35. If all data for a given client-matter takes up 1,000 CDs, that's $25,000. If the ASP produces 10 CDs, that's another $350 bill. The firm can use an external hard drive to bring the media cost down to $500--although the firm still needs to make a second backup. NOTE: Many vendors don't even fill an entire CD before moving to the next one.

The firm can also save money by using an ASP. Here are some of the ways in which using an ASP can save the firm money.

1. Storage

While a 300GB external hard drive is cheap, server hard drives can be quite expensive. There are very sophisticated storage technologies that are the best choice for critical data. These are also very expensive. Ask your network tech person to critique the vendor's hardware. If all firm electronic files reside on a remote ASP server, your firm may not need to increase capacity.

2. Backup

The more GBs of data on the server, the more tapes required for backups.

3. Technical Work

The Firm can pay an ASP technician on an hourly basis versus an in-house employee or on-site consultant.

Printing

Most firms have attorneys and paralegals who prefer to review using paper. If the ASP is going to have to provide paper, it may need a local vendor who can handle the printing for them. This is preferably a local shop, so as to minimize shipping costs. Watch for these incidental costs. In this case, the firm may end up paying for both CDs (from vendor to printer) and paper. Be sure to check this up front with your potential ASP.

An ASP allows the Firm to test-drive a review system before committing to it internally. ASPs are more than happy to drop by the firm, demonstrate their system, and provide answers to the Firm's questions about their wares and prices.

H. Technical Work

To litigate cases, every law firm uses a slightly different set of technical goods and services. Every firm provides some level and quantity of technical work for each case, if only modifying a load file. Each law firm faces the same operational issues related to using the right person for the right type of work and legal risks associated with internal performing of technical work. Some lawyers involve the firm IT Department in cases by asking them to perform technical tasks. These persons and their work must meet the scrutiny of the courts without risking the entire firm. If required to testify, the firm will lose their support and possibly have to hire a temporary replacement. To use the IT Department as a source of inexpensive labor may impact both the case and the firm.

The introduction of electronic discovery has added major costs to litigation. There are a myriad of new services and invoice "line items," all of which are very expensive. The need to review electronic discovery has many attorneys searching for inexpensive labor. The firm needs to contemplate the addition of various technical goods and services to the Litigation Support Department in an effort to save the client money. Those technical goods and services which the firm cannot or should not perform internally are mandated for outsourcing by the firm management.

Technical work in a Litigation Support Department can range from loading data, to performing computer forensics work. Later in this book, the reader will find technical checklists for performing routine tasks such as processing incoming media and creating a production set. This particular section raises points that address whether a firm should perform technical work internally and help the reader to assess their own firm's abilities. The firm's Litigation Support Department technicians should only provide a service when it:

1. Is ready for the associated legal and logistical risks, and;
2. Has already invested in the proper resources and training;
3. Has successfully performed the required work on several smaller projects; and
4. Has prequalified outside partners for large or risky projects.

Legal Risks

The law firm must always consider the exposure to law suits deriving from both outsourced and internally performed technical work. In firms where the attorney will ask the Litigation Support Department to convert native files into a discovery database with images, the exposure it is to both the case and the firm. The firm should decide which technical work the Litigation Support Department may and may not perform for cases. While the managing partners must decide how they wish to mitigate risk, the final decision about whether the department is capable of providing a technical good or service properly comes from the Litigation Support Department.

Resources and Training

Before the department performs a litigation technology good or service, it must have all the necessary resources: hardware, software and people. Litigation Support's VP of Operations should research vendors to learn which hardware and software tools they use to perform a given type of work. Vendors and trainers can provide all the necessary training.

Once the department performs technical work, it may be responsible for any subsequent technical support. The need to perform work on historical technical work often comes back at inopportune times. At this point the VP of Operations and Litigation Support Attorney can help prioritize work. As example, an old dormant case may suddenly become "hot," and the attorney may require an immediate production with little warning. If the Litigation Support Department performed the original technical work it may need to prioritize this case over other cases until the production is complete.

The best way to *mitigate* risk for internally performing technical work is for the firm to provide the Litigation Support Department with the necessary resources as well as the training to use the resources.

The best way to *avoid* risk is to pay someone else to perform a task. These people are known as "overflow" partners, and every firm should have them.

Overflow Partners

Through partnerships with prequalified vendors, the Litigation Support Department is able to limit its role to project management. This is critical when the department is already operating at capacity. Performing a technical good or service internally does not eliminate the strategic need for partnerships with outside providers who perform the same technical services. It is recommended that the firm send a certain amount of work each year to the overflow partners. Even small projects allow the department to make certain a partner can still match the firm technical standards.

By outsourcing high risk work to a third party, the firm limits exposure should something go wrong. In order to minimize the risk of receiving bad work product from the vendor, the Litigation Support Department must use prequalified service bureaus.

Any cases that involve old servers, not used for five years, stored in a damp basement, should be considered high risk work. It is in the best interest of the firm that the vendor performs every task, from collecting the hardware to turning it on for the first time. These types of risks fall under the category of "logistical" risks.

Logistical Risks

If a firm employee performs services which result in his, or her, absence later due to testifying, the firm must perform that person's work until they return. If the technician is also responsible for project management and clerical tasks, the firm must be prepared to support this work, too. Litigation Support's VP of Operations must balance project management work and technical work. First the department must be ready to balance work loads and nimble enough to lose one or all technicians to legal proceedings.

If the department is prepared for this "absence" contingency, it may be ready to perform the services. The IT Department may not be prepared for a key employee's absence. The employee may not have the proper background to perform well on the stand. A Litigation Support Department should be prepared for this type of absence. Further, the technician should be experienced at testifying and therefore be an asset to the team instead of a potential liability. The firm should make the determination.

Best Practices

The easiest way for the firm and the department to minimize risks is through standards and the use of a reusable technology plan. A standard is the best defense against technical issues. It is in the best interest of the case and firm that the right roles perform the right responsibilities. This may mean outsourcing of litigation technology goods and services, even if the attorney wants internal technical support staff to perform the work for "free."

1. Staging Areas

In the computer world there are the concepts of a "staging" or "test" environment versus the "production" environment. The idea is to prepare software or load data in a safe area that won't affect other business, such as document review. When the work is ready for the end-users, the data or program gets "released" to the production environment, where the legal team operates. Legal folks might also consider these as the technician's "preproduction" and "production" data.

However, this procedure is sometimes thwarted by human nature. Attorneys and paralegals, when they receive files from clients, may want to take a peek at the files before they are staged by Litigation Support. This is dangerous.

One of the biggest rules in the IT department is not to copy files containing viruses to the network. Viruses can delete all of your data or scramble it just enough to cause giant problems. Some types of virus arrive in email. If the attorney opens client emails, that virus may take down all firm email. Won't that attorney feel foolish when the virus gets tracked back to him or her? There are other unforeseen perils. One could result in emails getting sent from the firm to any email addresses in the world. One of those might even result in losing the case or creating a new one--against the firm.

It is for this reason that the data should first get loaded to the test environment. The destruction of the test environment will in no way impact the business of the firm. Virus and other malignant code will not affect the legal team or firm. Litigation Support should use this information to help persuade the managing partners to take an appropriate stand. It is their company, too, after all.

It is Litigation Support's ongoing task to educate the attorneys about how to handle native files. The legal staff needs to know how to handle electronic discovery when it arrives.

What is difficult here is that attorneys receive native files, such as Word and Excel, from clients on a daily basis. It is therefore important to differentiate between business communications and electronic files collected for the purpose of review and possible production. One way to achieve buy-in from your legal team is to get them into the following mindset: if it may be produced some day, it must go to Litigation Support Department.

There are several places to use as staging areas: local pc, external hard drives, and administrative server in a staging environment.

a. Local PC

While the local PC is the most accessible location to perform technical work, it is not the best environment. Local PCs are not subject to daily backups. They typically have only one hard drive, offering no disaster recovery ability. Further, these machines are also used for other types of work, such as business correspondence and time keeping. The machines may run antivirus or other types of software which may affect native files from clients. Worst of all, each person's work is not visible or accessible to other members of the Litigation Support Department.

b. External Hard Drives

External hard drives hold hundreds of GBs. They quickly transfer information to and from network file servers, are inexpensive to buy and ship. This makes them an ideal staging area for technical work. It is also easy to move a hard drive from one technician to another. On the down side, these drives offer no redundancy, so a hard drive crash can mean a total loss of data. The second concern is whether a file containing virus could access the production environment and the Internet via the technician's PC.

Hard drives are also the preferred method for sending and receiving large quantities of data. It is advantageous to have a fleet of external hard drives with both USB and Firewire ports. One can store a lot of emails and other native files on a drive. When a lot of data arrives, it is advantageous to have a test environment where the Litigation Support Department can evaluate the materials and determine the best course of action. Through the use of multiple external drives, it is even possible to have multiple test environments.

As a side benefit, when producing or supplying a large quantity of data to a vendor or third party, an external drive is always welcome because it is a real time saver for their technician. Just remember to put big FIRM stickers on each drive and keep track of who sent which drive is where and when for what client-matter. Also, a hard drive is not recommended as production media. CDs and DVDs are better because they are read-only.

No one will be able to delete or accidentally modify your production.

c. Administrative Server

The same work the Litigation Support Technicians would perform on their local PCs or on external hard drives is performed on this server. All technicians can access each other's work. The IT Department backs up the server on a regular basis, per the Disaster Recovery Plan. There is no need for the legal team to ever access this area.

Unfortunately, if this server is on the production network, it is possible for software and virus on the administrative server to infect other machines. The safest environment for the Litigation Support Department to perform their work is in a "test" or "staging" network. The staging network is not connected to the production network used by the legal team and rest of the firm.

i. Staging Network

All incoming data and all outgoing data need a staging area. The staging, or "test," area may be the Litigation Support Department workstations or a server, isolated from the production environment. The legal team can only access the production environment. After the Litigation Support Department technician creates a database in the test environment, he, or she, copies it to the production server for use by the legal team.

ii. Test Environment

The test environment provides a secure area in which the technician can work without risk to review team efforts. Whichever solution your firm chooses to employ (external hard drives or a test server); the Litigation Support Department should be able to pay for it by billing for the same resources it uses.

The test environment is also a safe environment where the Litigation Support Department can install and test new software before releasing it to the users. This is done to make certain the software will not create problems for other installed software due to technical reasons such as driver or ".dll" versions.

For those Litigation Support Departments performing technical services such as generating OCR or processing native discovery into a review database, the need for a test environment is of utmost concern. Native files are unpredictable. They may contain virus, malicious macros and other malevolent attributes which could harm the firm production environment. A single virus can delete terabytes of discovery files overnight with devastating effects to cases and the firm.

Note: Potentially infecting the network is one reason that the firm needs institutionalized policies which stop the users from indiscriminately opening files from clients and channels all materials through the Litigation Support Department.

The database that the legal team reviews may be the grandchild of several earlier versions. When the vendor delivers new data for the discovery review system, there is a chance that the structure and organization of the data may not match the firm technical standard. The use of prequalified vendors helps to alleviate this concern. Nevertheless, the Litigation Support Department should not perform database administration on the same database the legal team uses for review.

Litigation Support will make a backup copy of each database before working on it. There are occasions when the Litigation Support technician will need to spend hours correcting technical problems. Sometimes the database has to go through several steps before the finished product is ready for the firm. As a precaution, the Litigation Support Department technician should keep multiple versions, as a way to backtrack if new issues arise.

2. Network Folders

The client matter numbers are central to organizing every aspect of data and efforts by the Litigation Support Department, legal team and vendors. The client-matter number theme repeats in applications, such as email folders, financial trend reports from accounting and storage trend reports from the VP of Operations. The client folder, matter subfolder organization rule applies to all information repositories on both the test and production environments.

There are two main delineations regarding litigation data: discovery files and all other case files. Discovery and electronic discovery materials require more storage capacity than other litigation files such as legal video and transcripts. The following sections concentrate upon organization rules and examples. To learn more about security and backup routines, please reference the appropriate sections in the book.

Discovery Folders

The Litigation Support Department can use the client number folder, matter number subfolder as a way to organize all discovery data. Unlike other litigation files, however, these materials require special backup and security concerns. The administration of these files is not covered in this section. This text concentrates upon how to organize the data.

There are two main methods for organizing the folders. One can either group the attachments, database and image files under a single database folder, or in separate subfolders.

Single folder

        \\SERVER\DATABASE\010221\00001\DB1\

The advantage of this organization method is relatively obvious. It is easy to identify all materials for any client matter database. The disadvantage is the need for the backup administrator to create multiple backup routines for each new matter: daily or hourly for the database, weekly or biweekly for the images, and daily for the attachments and load files. The use of single folder organization can result in the need for users to access databases through multiple drive letters, as each repository fills.

The single folder method is difficult to maintain as each repository reaches capacity. The administrator must either move all client-matter information to a separate server or use multiple folders on multiple servers.

Separate folders

        \\SERVER\DATABASE\010221\00001\DB1\

\\SERVER\IMAGES\010221\00001\DB1\

\\SERVER\ATTACH\010221\00001\DB1\

\\SERVER\LOAD\010221\00001\DB1\

The advantage to this organizational method includes the ability to store database files on one server and the other files, such as images, on another machine. Because the image files and the attachment files constitute the bulk of discovery storage, placing them on a separate repository reserves capacity on the database server for databases.

Using separate folders helps the administrator group all databases on a single repository. This makes navigation easier for the end users and the administrators. A major advantage is that the IT department backup administrator need only establish three backup routines. Regardless of the additions and deletions below the database, images and attach folders, the backup routines never change. This eliminates the ongoing need to create new routines associated with "single" folder storage.

The following is a sample tree, using multiple folders, followed by an explanation of the purpose for each one.

Client Matter Foldering Tree Example

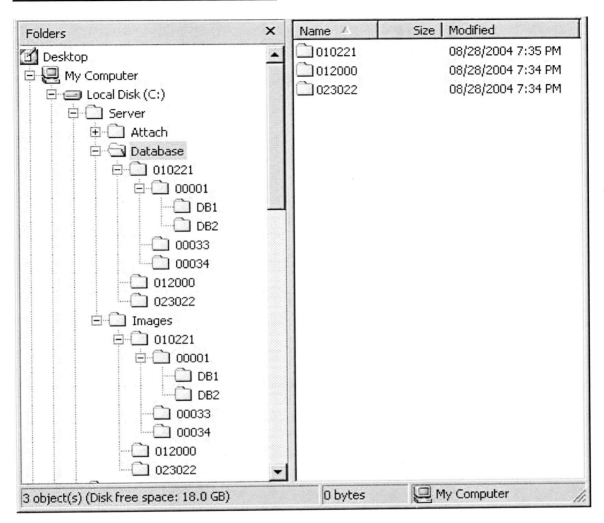

Root Folders:

1. X:\DATABASE\

This folder contains the actual database files, such as a Concordance .DCB or Summation .SWF files. These files require daily backups. These files contain the actual work product, or efforts of the review team. An hourly incremental backup of certain key files can ensure minimal review effort loss.

2. Y:\IMAGES\

This folder contains all image files for every database. The reason the text assigns the "Y" drive letter is to emphasize that these folders and these files may reside on any network repository. Restoring hundreds of GBs or TBs of files from CDs would take an unacceptable amount of time. Therefore the Litigation Support Department should consider maintaining the files on near line storage, such as external hard drives or another server.

3. X:\ATTACH\

Depending upon the discovery review software, the database records may link or otherwise reference the native files stored under this folder. The IT Department should schedule weekly backups for these files.

4. Y:\LOAD\

All the load files and working area of the server reside here. More advanced firms should employ an "administrative server" to house load files and act as a test environment. This directory represents your latest efforts to get work in front of reviewers or out the door. This material needs a daily backup.

About Subfolders

The client number, matter number, database name subfolders appear under all root folders. All data must reside under a client matter. This makes finding the data for any given client matter a simple task.

Example: X:\DATABASE\[client number]\[matter number]\[database name]\

Each matter may include multiple databases. Depending upon collections and productions, there could be a large number of databases. Each individual database must reside in a separate folder. This folder appears after the matter number folder. The administrator should name the folder for the database.

In this fashion, it is simple to identify all files relating to a given database for a given client-matter. If the files for multiple databases reside in the same folder, there can be confusion and restoring from backup tapes more involved.

* * *

The system outlined here is all about continuity throughout a single case and across all cases. What this means is that once one understands how to find and store data for one case, one can do so for all cases. It also means being able to find and retrieve data used in any stage of a case and associated applications.

As you can see from the tree, it is very easy to find each database for each client-matter, and it is equally easy to find the folder that contains the images for each database.

Shared Folders

All teams must collaborate. This means there is the need for the legal team to have access to one or more shared network folders. The shared folders may contain transcripts, work product, video and files for litigation programs ranging from titles such as "CaseMap" to "Sanction 2." These folders contain files the legal team and the Litigation Support Department generates.

Just as the administrator used database folders to separate content within each matter folder, the department should create folders for the software titles under each matter folder. Because litigating a case requires the use of multiple programs, there are also multiple data files for each application. The administration helps guide the team to organize these files by storing them in the associated application folders.

This organizational structure benefits the legal team as well as the Litigation Support and IT Department technicians. When it is time to add an associate or paralegal to the team, they instantly know where to look for everything. If the team goes off-site, gathering (or removing) all their data from the server is also simple and fast. The IT Department can establish a single backup routine for each repository that will not need updating. The network administrator will still need to update network permissions in order to both restrict and provide access to case materials and legal team work product.

The client folder, matter subfolder scheme also allows the department VP of Operations to calculate monthly storage for each client matter. As the firm does not have unlimited storage and adding capacity is expensive, a monthly hosting fee can encourage attorneys move older cases off the server and onto less expensive storage, such as "near line," a hard drive, or "off line," a backup tape or CD.

Note: When backing up folders for future internal use, the path should include the full path. This means including client matter number folders. When creating media, the client matter number folders are not included. This is true for all repositories.

File Server Paths

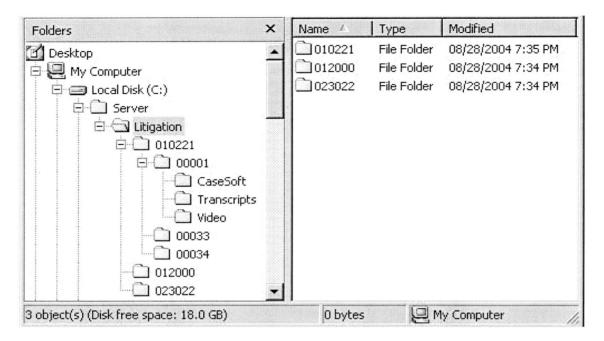

The server administrator should minimize the "path length" between the drive letter and client number folder. The path length is 21 characters in "C:\SERVER\LITIGATION\".

In the example, "C:\" is the root of the path. The path length includes the number of characters from the drive letter, "C" to the final "\". Some litigation programs can only read the first 255 characters. If the path length is 100 characters, before including the client number folder, subfolders, and filename length, the total path length may exceed the 255 character limit.

It is easier to perform administrative and technical duties with a short and simple path. These folders should appear on every repository that contains litigation files.

Network permissions should be set to make certain that only administrators can view and modify the contents of certain folders. As the review team does not need to delete images, network permissions can impose this restriction. Each of the database folders may require different permissions, depending on who needs access to them.

A Slightly Different Approach

There are two methods for organizing shared folders. As already detailed, the application folders can reside inside of the matter folders. The alternative is to create a single application folder which then contains client-matter subfolders. The server folders would look like the following picture.

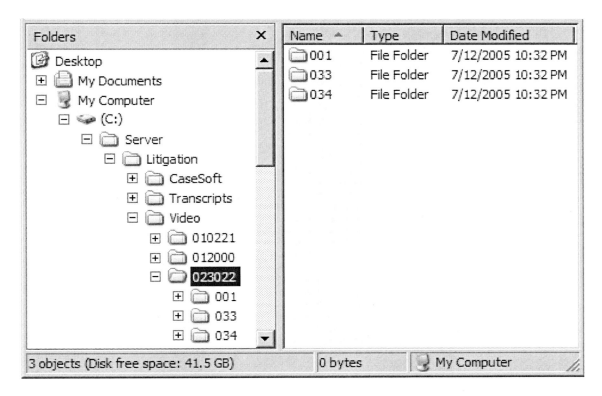

The problem with this approach is the way that this organization of client-matter materials affects the administration of backups and network permissions. It also adversely affects Litigation Support's ability to identify all client-matter materials in an expedient manner.

About Active Directory

The technology of Active Directories can present the Litigation Support Department administrators with new approaches to the use of shared folders.

Even though the folders exist on different machines, Active Directory removes the need for multiple network drive letters. A folder from one server can appear inside of the folder from a different server. In this fashion, the legal team could browse a single, Litigation Department, "L:\" drive for client matters that reside on multiple servers.

If Active Directories is of interest to the Litigation Support Department, the IT Department network administrators will know whether the technology is in place at the firm, or when it may be available for use for the department and firm.

Security

The following text illustrates how security relates to the suggested folder rules. There are three main ways to apply network security when the firm uses either the [client number]\[matter number]\[application name] foldering schema or the [application name]\[client number]\[matter number] organization. The security options are:

1. Provide equal access to every client matter folder to everyone in the Litigation network group. This choice means low administrative overhead, because each person can access all files in a folder, or none of them.

2. Create client network groups. For example, if you are a member of the ACME group, you can access and see all the ACME matter number folders. If you are not, you can not even see the ACME client number folder.

3. Create client matter network groups. As a member of the ACME-SMITH network group, one can see and access these subfolders. If you have many matters going on at the same time and need to keep matter 3 people away from matter 4 folders, this is your solution.

It is important to note that although some software titles offer an apparent level of security, limiting access based upon user name, this may not actually provide complete security. Unless the network administrator applies security, team members can use Windows Explorer to bypass software level security and browse the server folders directly.

I. Training

Training is an effort to give the student guidelines and strategies to use when achieving a legal goal. The student can be a member of the legal team or Litigation Support Department. Litigation follows a deliberate pattern; this pattern allows us to predict the topics and situations that might arise, and train our internal people how to both use tools and decide when to use them. As a firm, we also need to train our clients and vendors.

Software as Case Tool

Software exists to perform functions. But these functions by themselves are pointless without a larger context. A search function is worthless until it is tied to a goal in litigating the case. We must train our Litigation Support Department to understand the litigation lifecycle, strategies, and goals. We also must train them how to use the available software and hardware to execute strategies and achieve goals.

The following pages describe when to train each role to achieve goals. For example, the first review of discovery is for production. This means evaluating each document for privilege and production, not for issues. To achieve this goal it is more important for your document reviewers to understand how to create folders and tags than perform searches. Training on complex searches and report writing or "how to use every option in the total package" is of limited value. People who work primarily in the document review stage need to know how to use the available software to achieve the goals necessary for this stage, rather than how to use every available software option.

After the production period ends (see Discovery Lifecycle flowchart), the team only reviews documents for issues. To achieve this goal, the Litigation Support Department must train, or arrange to train, the legal team how to search for subjective issues and tag key documents.

The main point here is to train people to achieve the immediate goals of the case using the tools provided. Train them to understand how these goals fit into the overall case strategy. As the case moves forward, continue to train people how to achieve the new goals required by each stage, while reminding them how the new goals fit into the overall strategy.

This also means that one should not spend time studying or teaching anything that doesn't help achieve the immediate goals.

Cheat Sheets

Almost every application has some sort of cheat sheet available. A cheat sheet is a very simplified "how-to" guide for major software functions like searching or tagging. Litigation Support should make sure to provide a copy of these cheat sheets, either printed or via email, to all end-users. Make sure to provide them whenever users are starting to use a given application for the first time.

1. Litigation Support

Teach all Litigation Support Department project managers and technicians to achieve both department level and case level goals. Overall success depends upon the people understanding their roles and responsibilities to both the case and the department.

Immediate Needs

Within many firms, there are no best practices. Teach everyone in the department to follow the same case lifecycle and use the same strategies. Once the department understands the best practices, it is time to teach the Litigation Department, the firm and vendors.

The COO should execute an initiative called "Boot Camp." The goal of Boot Camp is to provide any Litigation Support student, regardless of background, with a strong understanding of how to use litigation technology to win cases while saving the client and firm money by providing the right tools, training and information in a timely, consistent and professional manner. It is, therefore, in the best interest for every litigation role to understand the associated responsibilities and how the results of their efforts directly benefit both the case and the firm.

Ongoing Needs

The litigation technology industry continues to evolve. Once the Litigation Support professional understands the case lifecycle, discovery lifecycle and software lifecycle, they are ready to look for ways to improve upon the tools. Vendor demonstrations, industry trade shows, "webinars," periodicals and the Internet all provide educational opportunities, many for free. If a new tool presents interesting benefits to the team, the Litigation Support professional should be able to advise them of the impact on the lifecycle.

Future Needs

Based upon the expansion of department, accounting reports and market maturation, the Litigation Support Department COO may wish to provide new services to the firm, such as computer forensics or electronic discovery processing. These are major initiatives that require training and, sometimes, certification.

2. Legal Team

Training usually concentrates on how to use a piece of software, not as a tool they use to achieve specific goals; instead of concentrating on key functions the people will use to achieve these goals, it tries to explain everything the software can do. If training does not tie the functions to specific goals and strategies, people may not remember what functions to use to achieve specific goals.

Ideally, training should involve the actual case data. While this limits the time to train the team, it can be a direct benefit to review speed and end user satisfaction. Most people forget the bulk of their training because they don't actually use the majority of the functions. In goal oriented training, the entire class might only take 30 to 40 minutes at the start of the day, with another 10 or 20 minutes of review while the trainer is present.

For example, if you are training people how to review for privilege, the goal is to see people successfully find their review batch, assign designations and navigate to the next document. Once people can successfully achieve this goal, the team is on course for a successful production. After production, the goal might be to identify key documents relating to various issues or characteristics, such as date and author; this new goal requires new training.

In all training, the team needs to understand what their results should look like, and how the team will use these results to further the case. The discovery lifecycle flowchart is a good tool to help the team understand how the tool helps them achieve goals. The Litigation Support Department should be able to answer questions about strategy and next steps. Litigation Support should explain to the legal team how it will use their tagging work to produce, and achieve other goals.

Lifecycle Training

An understanding of how to use a software tool to achieve an immediate goal provides a solid foundation for understanding the technology plan as it relates to the entire case lifecycle. The legal team should understand how to tag documents for production purposes. It should then understand what will become of their pre-production and production databases as the case matures.

Training is an ongoing process. Fortunately, through a standard approach to Litigation Support, the larger strategies remain consistent from matter to matter. The same is true for organization rules and the entire litigation technology experience. Through a formal classroom environment, emails or general discussion, training can be an ongoing process.

3. Vendors

A lot of vendors promote a "100% error free product." This sounds great. To be sure, we all want that—in everything that we do.

But there's a problem with this type of claim, one which lawyers, and those who deal with lawyers, may have when hearing it: what constitutes an error? Aside from obvious errors, such as omitted files, what else can one classify as an error? Does the vendor compare the final product against their own technical standard, to determine if work is "error-free?"

As your client pays for the product, then the technical character of the product must match your documented specifications. Any requirement not documented is not a requirement. The adoption of the Litigation Support Technical Standards means the firm can provide requirements to vendors as a measuring stick by which Litigation Support will test for errors. When a vendor does not meet the standard, Litigation Support may use the document to illustrate the particulars of the problem to any party. At the same time, Litigation Support can make a good case for using vendors who can already match the Firm's technical standard and do not require subsequent work.

The following subsections outline how to use the technical standard with existing and potential vendors. The document is available on the CD or through eDiscovery.org. When the firm uses an ASP solution, the technical standards means that any productions, including the final delivery upon cessation of the case, will be homogenous with all other work the firm contracts, regardless of the vendor(s) and solution(s) used.

Existing Vendors

The goal in instituting a standard is to qualify existing vendors to match their product to that standard. Vendors know that this qualification provides them with a greater chance to bid successfully on projects and perform work for the firm. Qualifying is a process of inclusion and exclusion. Once the department has both pre-qualified vendors for consideration and a way to qualify new vendors, the Department can require exclusive use of qualified vendors, per the business and technical reasons outlined in this book.

The Litigation Support Department's ability to perform technical work will literally save cases. However, the elimination of unnecessary technical work by outside vendors will also save time and cost. The pre-qualified vendors work product requires the least amount of subsequent technical work by the vendor or Litigation Support Department. This can significantly save turnaround time, thereby expediting review and lowering the number of billable hours the Litigation Support technician bills.

The Litigation Support Department must understand the standard and use it internally before gaining any real value from qualifying vendors. These concerns can happen independently of the firm as a whole. The firm does not need to have officially adopted the standards for Litigation Support to undertake the following steps. In truth, the sooner the department starts to use the technical standard internally the sooner unnecessary work is eliminated and the department can concentrate on bigger issues.

Provide a copy of the standard to each vendor, along with the *Vendor Compliance Email*, as included in the Supporting Documents section. It is very important to let the vendor know when they have done things correctly or incorrectly. Litigation Support wants a friendly relationship with qualified vendors. These vendors will always match the standard and also alert Litigation Support of "rogue" projects, begun by others in the firm, independent of department involvement.

Litigation Support should not rely on the legal team to provide the Standard to the vendors. The Litigation Support Department and the vendors want to provide the best goods and services possible. The only vendors worth contracting are those that meet both the legal team and department needs at the same time.

The qualifying process

Depending upon the vendor, the qualification process may take several tries by the technicians. Expect this to be an iterative process. It is better for the vendor to learn to match the firm standards on generic, rather than client materials. The Department may chose to disqualify and exclude a vendor due to the quality of the initial delivery or the number of iterations. Unlike the iterative process most departments experience with their vendors on all projects, this process only happens one time per vendor. As this process can take many hours or even days, it is important to qualify vendors as a separate Departmental task from supporting actual cases. The Department should not take that type of risk with the case. Once a vendor is qualified, the firm can consider them for work on projects for every case.

New Vendors

Prequalify new vendors, whether referred by the client, attorney or chance. Firms are more likely to contract with those vendors that are able to match the firm standard. It is important for the Litigation Support Department to have a standard qualification process that is open to everyone. This is not to say that everyone deserves unlimited chances. Provide the Standard and ask the vendor to provide a CD matching the requirements. Once they can match the Standard, they are a contender for future work.

If a vendor does not succeed at creating a CD matching the standard, let the vendor know what was wrong with the sample media and let the vendor try again. Pass or fail, Litigation Support should save the sample and results for future reference. Once the vendor passes the test, add them to the intranet list of qualified vendors. It is, after all, in Litigation Support's best interest to have multiple qualified vendors. One never knows when the technician behind the vendor's work will switch jobs.

If the vendor provides a hosted service, such as an ASP does, consider them for a lunch meeting. While the vendor may want to show all the bells and whistles of their software, it will be Litigation Support's job to see how the vendor's product fits into existing business processes. For example, no one wants to use a document review solution that cannot be used for blow-backs and exhibits.

Litigation Support should find out why the client prefers a vendor. Traditionally the reason is financial. Vendors will match rates. This is especially true for preferred vendors. If the client or attorney prefers a vendor, which is unable to meet the technical standard, Litigation Support must be certain that the client or attorney understands that the department gave the vendor every chance, and is ready to offer alternatives. The decision to exclude a vendor needs to be based upon documented technical issues. In the end, the client and attorney will not want to use a vendor who cannot produce a usable product. The client will choose the law firm over the vendor.

J. Vendor Relations

Every litigation practice should have a person who can fulfill the role of Vendor Relations. The legal team does not have the time and may not have the background to keep abreast of market pricing and technology development.

The cost to process and use electronic discovery in litigation has increased the market value of providing the associated services and subsequently, the number of vendors. Vendors include a range of software companies which specialize in conceptual searching or native file review to the ubiquitous service bureau offering to turn electronic discovery into the familiar .TIF and associate text files.

The Vendor Relations role will research this software and determine whether it will accommodate all the technology the firm employs throughout the case lifecycle. The person in this role also knows which service bureaus provide the best services for the best prices. It is very beneficial to the firm to have all vending go through the Litigation Support Department because this role eliminates the need for each legal team to perform the same research.

The person in this role should plan a meeting with a current or potential vendor—for lunch, perhaps—at least once a month. Everyone in Litigation Support should attend. Litigators and paralegals also may wish to attend and should, therefore, be given the option to attend. The choice of lunch-time vendor can be for any litigation technology good or service.

Pre-Qualify Vendors for Future Work

Provide a copy of your Firm Litigation Support Technical Standards to each vendor. Work with your vendors until their product matches your requirements. After this process is completed, the overhead of loading new discovery into the document review system will become much simpler and require less technical time. The vendors who are capable of matching the firm standards are now qualified for future work.

The Litigation Support Department should maintain and update this list of qualified vendors for future out-sourcing. All litigation firms should consider employing at least one full-time Litigation Support professional. All vending of discovery should go through the person acting in the Vendor Relations role. For firms with a Litigation Support Department, all vending of discovery should go through this department.

For firms where the department does not have the ability to centralize all out-sourcing, the Vendor Relations person can still evaluate and qualify vendors. This list, along with a copy of the firm Litigation Support Technical Standards, should provide essentially the same results. Because the same technical standards apply to all firm related work, the preferred vendor knows how to configure their product.

Remember, any time Litigation Support has to perform technical work on vendor product is unnecessary work. Through the employment of standards and qualified vendors, the amount of time decreases.

When an attorney or client has a vendor preference, provide the Standard to the associated parties. Make sure the parties understand the importance of the Standard and importance that all vendors are qualified against the firm standard. The new vendor must perform the qualification in order to provide appropriate services. The VP of Marketing, preferably an attorney, can provide significant assistance since legal and political considerations, in additional to the technical considerations, may determine the final course of action. The department attorney can represent the interests of the firm and department in addition to the client and case.

III. Needs Assessment

The goal of the following pages is to provide the reader with a complete assessment of Litigation Support technology and operations at their own firm. The purpose of this assessment is to help the firm identify areas which need may require attention. The book outlines many strategies and approaches toward resources and rights. The needs assessment section provides the reader with the ability to compare current practice to the template outlined in the book. The Litigation Support Department COO should perform the assessment.

Assessment Areas

- Financials
- User Tools
- Storage Assessment
- Firm Technical Standards
- Litigation Support Software
- Department Hardware Capabilities
- Video
- Media Inventory
- Project Management
- Network Configuration
- Backup Routines
- Disaster Recovery Plan
- Training
- Departmental Operations
- Political Abilities
- Ability to Bill
- Vendors

The book outlines a template for a Litigation Support Department. The department identifies areas that require consideration. As the reader assesses their own department and firm, they should use the book as a reference. The book will explain why considerations in a given area are important and identify interdependence with other areas, such as folder organization, backups and security.

The question of which area to concentrate upon first is difficult. From a Litigation Support Department VP of Operations standpoint, the first recommended area is the adoption of the technical standard. The results will eliminate a lot of unnecessary technical work and thereby allow the technician time to work on other areas, such as storage and backup. A VP of Finance would recommend addressing cost codes and billable time, as the financial reports provide the basis for all business arguments. Further, these changes are administrative and require the least work resulting in a large benefit for the department and firm.

Although this book also outlines an implementation strategy, the unique culture and tradition found at each firm may dictate a different route. Regardless of the firm, the department can still execute most of the strategies, including the use of the budget spreadsheet, case lifecycle task list and departmental organization of files, folders and data. Use of cost codes may be the most important victory for the department as the resulting reports provide the best arguments for firmwide institutionalization of technical standards, prequalified vendors and documented Litigation Support best practices. The final result of this phase is the collection of revenues for internal goods and services. The department invests this revenue in hardware, software and personnel.

1. Financials

Any financial analysis of the Litigation Support Department should evaluate the department as if it were an independent company -- as if it were a vendor to the law firm rather than an internal support group. This is because the department should operate exactly as a business. Only through this method can the department provide the highest level of service to each legal team and the lowest operational costs to the firm and client.

The Litigation Support Department should charge for time (technical and project management), firm storage and the products they manufacture. It is in the best interest of Litigation Support to track the accounting numbers associated with each good or service. This is because the Litigation Support COO will use accounting reports to argue for investment by the firm in additional hardware, software and people. The law firm is a business, after all; the people running the business use financial numbers to help make budget decisions. Other reports show whether there is enough work to allow the resource to pay for itself. The revenue reports illustrate the department's ability to actually buy these resources.

A lot of the considerations noted below provide the Litigation Support Department with ancillary benefits. For example, through the use of vendor cost codes, one can identify attorneys who are contracting services without the involvement of the Litigation Support Department. The VP of Finance can negotiate better rates with vendors based upon the total amount spent to date.

In firms where accounting does not specifically track litigation technology goods and services, partners may be surprised by how much money this expense actually represents. Through these reports and some research, the department can make the argument for investment by the firm. It is possible that a firm annually buys $500,000 of a litigation good which Litigation Support Department technicians could produce internally for a one-time investment of $300,000 and annual reinvestment of $100,000.

Timeline reports show trends, critical for proper management of the department. To properly manage the Litigation Support Department, the Accounting Department must track all actual expenses and potential revenues. It does not matter whether Litigation Support line items are removed from every client bill. What does matter is the proper tracking.

Using the following spreadsheets, fill out the categories below as accurately as possible. Doing so will allow you to estimate how much money the firm is leaving "on the table" today. It also provides targets for Litigation Support and the firm to try and achieve.

Tracking   **(Yes / No)**

1. Accounting and vendors use a firm vendor cost code   _____

2. Litigation Support bills for internal goods (i.e., hosting)   _____

3. Litigation Support can bill time   _____

a. <u>Potential Income – w/o Processing Discovery (Accounts Receivable)</u>
Internally Provided Goods and Services -

Vendors bill for these fundamental goods and services. Estimate the department's potential income based upon current figures. One should also think of the figures in terms of purchasing goals. Storage fees can generate sufficient income to pay for any additional capacity the department requires. If the department can generate enough billable hours, it may be able to afford additional staff. Media creation can pay for a high end machine

Fill out the following numbers for each line item as best as possible:

Server Storage   _____ GB|TB * $_____ /m (Market Rate) * 12 $_____

Billable Time   1,000 hrs per person, per yr * $_____ / hr $_____

Media Creation $___/CD * ____CDs/yr $_____

                                        Potential Total Income   **$_____**

b. <u>Current Estimated Liabilities - Besides Processing Discovery (Accounts Payable)</u>

Outsourced Goods and Services -

The Litigation Support Department can use these types of figures to argue for better rates with the vendor. The department can use these totals to identify goods and services which it could afford to provide. Remember, these are totals for all litigation cases at the firm, not a single matter.

Server Storage   _____ GB|TB * $_____ /m Market Rate * 12 $_____

Billable Time   _____ hrs/yr * $_____ /hr $_____

Media Creation $___/CD * ____CDs/yr $_____

                                   Potential Total Liability   **$_____**

Use the final category to estimate how much money the firm spends on key litigation technology goods and services. Once accounting begins to use litigation technology cost codes, it will be able to create reports to provide actual totals and illustrate trends.

Many firms are contemplating which services to provide internally. One factor is cost. The firm needs to recuperate the initial and ongoing investment, should it decide to provide a service.

c. Outsourced Litigation Goods and Services

Electronic discovery $_____

Paper discovery $_____

Bibliographic coding $_____

Video, court reporting, exhibits $_____

Potential Total in Discovery Goods and Services $_____

These figures provide the grand total spent on litigation technology goods and services. They also show how much of the revenue is captured versus contracted to a vendor.

Use the estimated totals to determine how much money the firm spends on Litigation Support goods and services.

By running the Litigation Support Department as a business, it is able to pay for itself. The department is also able to gauge whether the firm spends enough on a good or service to afford investment in the resources so as to provide it internally. The Litigation Support Department can pay for an appropriate storage solution, whether $5,000 or $50,000 dollars. This is important because in five years, the firm's current solution may not be appropriate.

2. User Tools

Hardware, software and the Internet are all tools the modern legal team uses to litigate a case. The following assessment of the firm evaluates what resources the firm provides to the department and legal team. The reader can also estimate the necessary investment to provide the most appropriate tools, such as the cost to upgrade all review workstation monitors. The benefits include increased review speed, increased morale, and higher quality work.

All law firms want to keep costs down for the partners and the clients. If the firm could increase review speed, it would also reduce the number of review hours billed. The law firm can show the client that they are doing all they can to expedite the review process and keep costs down. Providing technical goods and services internally is not the only method of cost recovery.

Review speed is a result of three factors: hardware, software and training. This section of the needs analysis will provide you with an understanding of your current situation with regards to document review hardware and software. Training is handled in a separate section.

a. Hardware

Please note that the book covers video monitors as a separate topic under the Tools section. This section will help the user estimate the cost for hardware. The other section provides the full explanation and justification. The following text succinctly explains how the Litigation Support Department can justify investment by the firm.

Even older laptops and PCs can display a database record and the associated images more quickly than a reviewer can read. The attorney clicks next and reads the bibliographic coding. They then turn their eyes and look at the image. Finally, they return to the database window and click on issue tags, thereby coding the record. The attorney repeats this process for hundreds of documents an hour and potentially for months on end. The question is how to expedite this process. In the law firm of 2005, most reviewers use a 17"-19" monitor. Therefore we should consider this is our "baseline" configuration for a review workstation. If a dual 17" monitor workstation makes the reviewer 10 seconds faster per record than with a single 17" monitor workstation, they save 1 hour of review time for every 360 documents.

Time Savings Explained:

Savings Per Record	# of Records	Time Saved	Total Seconds
10 seconds	6	1 minute	60
10 seconds	360	1 hour	360
10 seconds	36,000	~4 days	36,000

The extra time freed up to prepare the case has real value to the legal team. The one time investment in monitors results in the same benefit for all cases. Addition of a second monitor has a nominal learning curve, so the team realizes the benefit immediately.

Hardware may also hinder the review process. If the attorney uses a 15" laptop screen for document review, their inability to simultaneously interact with the database and view the document hinders speed. The trade-off is between speed and quality. The attorney should be able to view and use both, without eye strain or shuffling windows. If the right monitor can save 10 seconds per record, surely the wrong monitor can slow the process by 10 seconds per record. The hardware investment can result in a net 20 seconds per record gain in review speed.

Most law firms have a standard hardware setup for everyone. Law firms are very conscious of status and status symbols. While a second monitor on a desktop is certain to cause questions, the justification is one of functionality and cost recovery related to document review and not status.

Enter the following information to gauge the type of document review workstation the firm provides to the review teams. This worksheet will also help the reader estimate the cost to upgrade the firm and whether the current hardware is potentially hindering performance.

The IT Department should be able to provide precise answers to these questions. Please only account for document review workstations.

Workstation Hardware	Quantity
1st monitor size	
15" or less	_____(a)
17" or greater	_____(b)
Total (a + b)	_____(c)
2nd monitor size	
15" or less	_____(d)
17" or greater	_____(e)
Total (d + e)	_____(f)

Determine the cost to replace all 15", or smaller, monitors with a minimum of a 17" screen. For laptops, the external 17" screen can display the document image in full-screen mode, while the laptop screen displays the database and team work product.

_____(a + d) * $_____ = _____(g)

Explained: Total number of 15" monitors * cost = total cost to upgrade.

To upgrade each workstation to a dual monitor configuration, each machine may require a second graphics card. For the cost, include both the monitor and card price. It is critical that the second monitor be able to pivot between landscape and portrait modes.

_____(c - f) * $_____ = _____(h)

Explained: Total stations without a second monitor * cost = total cost to upgrade.

While it is possible to use a 15" monitor as the second monitor, a minimum of a 17" screen is more appropriate. The purpose of upgrading monitors is to provide the team with screens that make it easier to read the information. The other legibility factor for a monitor is the screen resolution.

Resolution is total area, in "pixels," on a screen. One multiplies length by width to calculate the area. The most common resolutions are 800x600 and 1024x768. Use of a higher resolution provides more area on the screen to show information. The limiting factor, of course, is the physical monitor size. A 1024x768 resolution for a 17" or greater monitor is a good configuration. Any person using a resolution less than 1024x768 will need to scroll windows, thereby slowing review speed.

The IT Department should be able to supply a list of all document review workstation screen resolutions. These attorneys and paralegals, and their cases, will benefit the most from new monitors, optimal for the work they perform.

The investment by the firm in hardware will yield results in terms of faster review speed and more time for the legal team to prepare. The Litigation Support Department also requires the same hardware configuration. Litigation Support Department professionals use the same document review software and can also benefit when performing administrative work. If the department can perform more work of higher quality in less time, it can begin additional projects.

Software

The following items are the most common categories for litigation software. The list will help Litigation Support determine where there is duplication in the user environment, such as the review teams using both Concordance and Summation. This list is only concerned with what the litigation team uses for work.

Do not include titles if they are used only by the Litigation Support Department for technical work. The reason for this is that while Litigation Support may need to run both Concordance and Summation for import/export reasons, the team should only use a single software title. In this fashion, the attorney uses the same tools for every matter, thereby decreasing the learning curve. The book covers the topic of software options and selection in greater depth in other sections.

Note that there is only room for one document review system, one image viewer and so forth. The reason for this is that all review teams should use the same software.

b. Software Category	**Title**	**Version**	**16 or 32-Bit**
1. Document Review Software	_____	_____	_____
A. Able to display images in 2nd monitor?	(Yes | No)		
B. Internet Enabled	(Yes | No)		
2. Image Viewer	_____	_____	_____
A. Redact / Annotate	(Yes | No)		
B. Create .TIFs	(Yes | No)		
3. Adobe .PDFs Software	_____	_____	_____
A. Read	(Yes | No)		
B. Create / Edit / Modify	(Yes | No)		
4. Case – Fact Organization	_____	_____	_____
5. Trial Presentation	_____	_____	_____
6. Transcript Software	_____	_____	_____

Note: 16 v. 32-bit software is an important consideration, as 16 bit software limits file and folder names whereas 32-bit software does not.

Once all litigators and paralegals use the same titles for every case, technical support requires less time. Users become familiar with the software, which they encounter on every case. Through the use of the technical standard, they automatically know where to find their case files. The folders match the client matter number.

Limiting the team to one transcript application does not limit its ability to litigate. The vendors also produce a better product as the firm standard provides them with examples for each title.

3. Storage Assessment

a. Identify Repositories

The first step for the Litigation Support Department VP of Operations is to build a storage matrix which identifies all litigation repositories and supporting infrastructure, such as servers. A simple spreadsheet is sufficient for this task, even for large decentralized firms.

Data repositories are defined as any locations where one might find files or data relating to litigation. Example locations include:

- Desktop personal computers hard drives
- Laptop computers
- Handheld devices (Blackberry, Trio)
- E-mail systems
- Network file servers
- Document Management System
- Database and SQL Servers
- Web / Intranet / Extranet servers
- Backup tapes

Considering all the locations where the litigation team and Litigation Support Department may store case information, the reader should appreciate the value in restricting storage to specific predefined areas. Only then can the Litigation Support Department be certain that all litigation data and infrastructure is protected by backup routines and the disaster recovery plan.

Note: The Litigation Support Department can use this same matrix when addressing network security.

b. Drive Letters

It is possible for everyone in the Litigation Department to lose access to their work if the IT Department changes a network drive letter. Therefore, along with knowing where all data resides, the VP of Operations must also know all the ways the users may access the information repositories.

The amount of information relating to every case has increased dramatically. This is due to electronic discovery. The file servers will run out of free space, or capacity, at a dramatically increased rate with electronic discovery. The IT Department will ask the Litigation Support Department to remove as many files as possible to make room. The attorneys will not want their materials removed. The IT Department will also need time and money to increase capacity. The question is when the server will be full, again. The longer the storage trend history, the better the storage estimates the VP of Operations may offer the firm. This estimate must also accommodate reports from the VP of Marketing, identifying trends for workload and future workload. It may be fruitless to spend ten hours creating 1GB of free space if a case with 100GB of data begins the following month.

To learn more about tracking current and potential work loads, please visit the sections referencing the VP of Marketing.

c. Capacity

Electronic discovery constitutes the majority of data for any case. The VP of Operations should still monitor the growth rate for the remaining litigation files, such as transcripts and video. While PowerPoint presentations can get rather large, the storage of video and 3D animations may soon constitute a capacity concern of their own, like ediscovery.

The reader should assess the firm's capacity picture. Rapid change is expensive; planned and slow change is less expensive. The VP of Operations should be able to estimate or chart capacity use and thereby estimate the date when there will be no more. The department COO should use information from the VP of Marketing, Operations and Finance to determine the most appropriate storage solution. The IT Department needs time to shop for and install the new capacity. It is important to realize that more capacity also means the need for more investment in infrastructure, backup hardware and software.

d. Estimate Current Capacity Picture

As every firm stores some information locally on its network, even those firms that employ a hosted solution will still have the same internal capacity issues, just on a smaller scale. Use the data repository spreadsheet to calculate the following values, or simply estimate.

Total aggregated capacity for litigation files   _____

Total capacity available (%)   _____

Estimated date when litigation runs out of storage space   _____

Cost to increase capacity   _____

Time for capacity project to complete (estimate by IT Department)   _____

4. Firm Technical Standards

The Department should create a document which specifies all technical preferences and requirements for every project for the Firm. The standards document is the firm's Litigation Support Technical Standard, or "technical standard". The firm's network structure and software does not change from case to case. The technical character, therefore, does not change. Only the technical aspect of vendor deliveries changes, sometimes from CD to CD within the same case, and also from case to case. It should never change. It only changes because the firm did not provide a technical standard.

Note: While the included CD contains a generic version of the "Litigation Support Technical Standards," the latest version is available at http://www.eDiscovery.org.

Through use of a firm standard:

- Vendors create a better product because they can match documented requirements;
- Vendors can consistently do a better job because they process everything the same way every time;
- The department can eliminate the need to redo or modify vendor product, resulting in the team gaining access to data with minimal delay; and
- The department does not waste time performing unnecessary work, which it may bill to the client.

In the absence of a documented firm preference, vendors will substitute their own. If the firm does not already enjoy a technical standard, distribute and make the new Standard available to all legal staff.

Training the attorneys and paralegals to use the Standard is not difficult. In the section, Implementing Best Practices, the book outlines how to introduce the Standard. Proper introduction may require endorsement by the appropriate partners and firm CIO.

Until such time as the firm mandates both the inclusion of the Standard for every litigation matter, and the use of vendors qualified against the document, the department COO should place the Standard in a logical location any user can find. The appropriate partners or firm CIO should send a copy of the document to all legal staff with an explanation of when to use it. This is also a good opportunity to reintroduce Litigation Support and the associated goods and services the department provides.

5. Litigation Support Software

Litigation Support technicians need an array of different software tools to overcome strange and obscure technical issues as well as to handle common problems such as comparing the contents of a 500GB external hard drive against the contents of a network folder, or simultaneously modifying text inside of multiple load files. Although the Tools section of this book contains recommended software titles, the best tools may be those your Litigation Support Department technician prefers.

Please note that the firm should limit the legal team to the use of one software title per category (e.g., transcript maintenance, document review, image viewer). This is not true for the Litigation Support Department. The technician may receive data in any software format, software version and operating system. The Litigation Support Department uses these tools to migrate data into either the tools the legal team uses for litigation, or the appropriate format for production to a third party.

Below is a table of software that performs a given function. Fill in the titles that the department currently uses, if any. It is possible and likely that the department already uses additional categories of software. It is also possible that the reader will discover a type of tool as yet untried.

Category	Titles
Folder-2-Folder Comparisons:	
Mass File Folder Renaming:	
Image Viewing & Production:	
PDF Editing & Creation:	
Text Editors:	
Databases:	
Password Cracking:	
Email Readers:	MS Outlook, Lotus GroupWise, Mac/Unix mbox
Flowcharting:	
Spreadsheet:	
Operating Systems & Emulators:	

The cost to purchase this functionality is relatively minor when compared to the hours or days that the legal team would have to wait if the Litigation Support Department technician did not have the appropriate tools. Further, the Litigation Support Department technician's billable hours will pay for these tools. The law firm should provide the department with the resources, hardware, software and persons, necessary to perform the work.

6. Department Hardware Capabilities

Storage media exists in many physical shapes: discs, tape, postage sized squares of plastic and so forth. The Litigation Support Department must be able to read and write to as many of these formats as possible. Fortunately, most of the hardware is inexpensive. Fortunately, the department will be able to pay for all of this equipment.

A. Read Media Formats

Except for the "DLT" backup tape drive, all the hardware necessary to read all the listed formats is relatively inexpensive. There are multi-bay memory stick readers that accept many formats. This book covers media readers in the Hardware section.

Electronic Media Formats (Incoming data)
 Note: Internal scanning of paper is handled elsewhere.

Accepted media types (e.g., versions, specifications or models)	Associated formats or versions
1. CDs	(e.g., CD-R, CD+R, CD-RW, Mac format)
2. DVDs	(e.g., DVD+R, DVD+RW, dual layer, Mac format)
3. Firewire	(e.g., FireWire1 - 400, FireWire2 - 800)
4. USB	(e.g., USB, USB2.0)
5. Zip Disks	(e.g., 100MB, 200MB, 750MB)
6. Memory Cards	(e.g., Compact Flash, Microdrives, Sony Memory Sticks, SD, MultiMedia, SmartMedia)
7. DLT Drive ("DAT" Tapes)	(e.g., Types III, IIIXT, IV, and SDLT)
8. Floppy Disk	(e.g., 3.5", 5.25")
9. Hard Drives	(e.g., 2.5", IDE, EIDE, SCSI, SCSI ultrawide, Mac format)

B. Read Operating Systems Formats

Before one can store information on any media, they must first "format" it. During this process, the operating system, or "OS," writes key information to the media. This information is written in a format, or syntax, which is specific to the original OS, or "native" environment. This is why a Windows machine can not read a Macintosh CD. There is emulation software which allows one OS to read and write media formatted for another OS. This topic also is covered in the Hardware section under Tools.

Platform	Operating systems versions
1. Windows	
(e.g., 95, CE, ME, NT, XP, natively or via emulator)	
2. Macintosh	
(e.g., OS9, OSX, natively or via emulator)	
3. UNIX	
(e.g., UNIX, Mandrake, Red Hat, FreeBSD, Solaris)	

C. Optical Media Creation

There are two basic types of optical media makers: robotic or manual. Unattended, a robotic burner can create multiple sets of copies from a stack of originals and blanks. For a full discussion of burners and options, please reference the Hardware section.

Robotic Duplicator / Burner (No attendance required)
This type of burner is ideal for a linear approach to duplication. One CD after another, the burner will create as many duplicates as required. This solution is only as slow as the hardware installed. If time is not a significant factor, this hardware frees the technician to concentrate on other work. This is definitely a tool the department should purchase with revenues it generates.

Hardware Abilities	Formats
1. Create CDs	
(e.g., CD-R, CD+R, CD-RW)	
2. Create DVDs	
(e.g., DVD+R, DVD+RW, dual layer)	
3. Label Printer	
(e.g., thermal, ink jet, color, B&W)	
4. Networked	
(e.g., Yes, No)	

Single Burner (Manual attendance required)

This includes internal and external burners which the department would access. More than one Litigation Support specialist has engaged as many burners at one time as possible to quickly generate a production set. This solution is still necessary, even if the department owns a robotic burner. Because the department can burn multiple copies at the same time, also known as "parallel processing," it can create a new set of media more quickly than a robotic burner, which creates one CD after the next, in a linear fashion. It also requires the complete attention of the technician, effectively barring any other work.

Note: As identified in the hierarchy, the correct person to perform this low level task is the Litigation Support Department clerk. It is also worth noting that the robotic burner is far less expensive a solution than the clerk, although not versatile beyond its own programming.

Media Creation	Quantity	Internal or External Burner
1. CD Burners	_____	_____
2. DVD Burners	_____	_____

Note: Internal scanning and printing of paper is handled elsewhere in the text.

Video

Not all law firms provide internal video capabilities beyond the ability to view them. For information about video goods and services, please see the next section on Video.

7. Video

Deposition video is important for each case as it allows the jury to see the physical reaction and not just the dry text. Animations can recreate a series of events in a manner any juror can comprehend. The observers use video to make judgment calls as to the honesty and general likeability of the deponent. As the team should video every deposition, this will generate a lot of video. From this large collection, the team may identify a series of short Q&A segments for use as exhibits.

Whether or not a firm should provide legal video services internally is a decision that can only be made after careful deliberation of collected facts. This assessment should help the reader determine whether it is a service worth investigating further. At the very least, the Litigation Support Department should have partnerships with vendors to provide services as necessary. The firm technical standard also specifies format and technical requirements for any vendors, familiar or new to the firm.

It is advisable that the Litigation Support Department have the resources to provide some level of support. That level of support can be any service from the duplication or conversion of media to printing images from video or synchronizing transcript text to the speaker. All of these services, while possible, require the appropriate resources and training.

The following chart helps the reader assess their firm's abilities regarding legal video.

Ability: Fill in the answer as best as one can. _____

Convert or Duplicate Formats: _____
  (e.g., Hi8, VHS, SVHS, Beta)

Convert Formats: _____
  (e.g., Hi8 tape to .MPG file)

Desktop Editing: _____
  (e.g., Create excerpts, print screens, create compilations)

Synchronize Text: _____
  (e.g., In deposition video, synchronize transcript text to speaker audio)

Film: _____
  (e.g., Create day-in-the-life, deposition video)

Even if performing all video work internally, one must still have outside video partners. This is a strategic move and allows the department to shift work away from the firm.

8. Media Inventory

There are two basic methods for storing all media relating to each case. The first method involves each legal team member keeping a percentage of the client originals and vendor generated media for each case. There is no central database or catalog. Therefore, to locate any given CD, one must ask each team member if they can search their cache for the media.

The second method involves a central library of all media for all litigation cases in the firm. When any media arrives, the legal team automatically forwards it to the library, a/k/a the Litigation Support Department. The library contains original media from clients, vendor media, internally generated production CDs, and so forth. Through the proper management of the library, the department may quickly locate any requested media. The library helps to reinforce the role of the Litigation Support Department as the central resource for litigation technology goods and services.

Note: For both speed and space considerations, all media can be kept in nylon binders, instead of jewel cases. A nylon binder costs about $20, holds 128 or more CDs and is available from web sites, as well as office supply, music and computer stores.

Matching Role to Resource

The Litigation Support Department technician role requires the CDs to perform their data administration and clerical duties. There are many unforeseen scenarios that require the use of the media. If an image file on the server is missing, or becomes corrupt, the Litigation Support technician will retrieve a fresh copy of the file from the CD. The technician should not need to interrupt the review team to find media. It is important for the Litigation Support technician to have direct access to the media, so the person fulfilling this role can complete their work without the need to interrupt or involve the legal team.

For those firms that already route all ediscovery materials and vending through the Litigation Support Department, the benefits and logic of the media library may be obvious. For those firms that are working toward standards, including routing of media, the library may offer benefits the firm had not considered. Consider the following question to assess internal operations.

1. Does the legal team forward all media to Litigation Support? (It should.)
2. Does the firm mandate this course of action? (It should.)
3. Are client *originals* ever sent outside of the firm? (Only send copies.)
4. Does Litigation Support maintain an inventory of media? (It should.)
5. Is the inventory coded for client, matter, volume name, binder number, sleeve number? (It should be.)

9. *Project Management*

This section allows the reader to assess certain project management skills. To learn more about project management as a service, please reference the Project Management section of the Services chapter.

Project management is not just about a diary of what was done, although the history is very important, and it is important to know where on the server and shelves to find all the related data.

Project management is also about the ability to shift people from role to role with minimal disruption to the case. A project manager should be able to move from matter to matter, balancing workloads with other staff and following standardized procedures for each case. The ability to shift cases from one technician to another may save the case from irreparable harm. If each technician operates by their own methods, a subsequent technician may not be able to move projects forward, in a timely manner, if at all, without significant case history research.

By working with qualified vendors, it is possible to transfer work to an outsourced consultant or vendor with nominal impact to legal team efforts. The subject of outsourcing is covered elsewhere in the text.

Depending upon how your firm currently operates, it may or may not be able to isolate and track all work by the following factors. Please note that all of these abilities can be achieved through the use of: cost codes, billable time, and a budget spreadsheet and case lifecycle task list. All of these are included with this book.

Identify / Track Types of Work	**Department Has Ability?**
Internal Projects	
7. Identify every active project for every client matter along with associated information such as date and cost information.	Yes / No
Outsourced Projects	
8. Identify all currently outsourced work along with associated information such as data and cost information.	Yes / No
Client-Matter Specific Projects	
9. Identify all projects, internal and outsourced, relating to a specific client-matter.	Yes / No

Individual Collection History

10. Technical work is iterative. As the case progresses, the database and the images change. Whether this work, or project, occurs internally or through a vendor, it is important to know data history, from collection to current iteration, including vendor information.

Yes / No

Individual Project History

11. Large discovery collections may result in weekly deliveries. The project manager should know of any issues, current costs and ability to meet target deadlines.

Yes / No

Case Lifecycle Technical History

Yes / No

12. Provide a detailed case lifecycle history of all internal work performed for the client matter to date.

Media Inventory

Yes / No

13. Identify and locate all media relating to any project or client matter, including originals and production volumes.

The ability to shift work from one project manager to another project manager with minimal disruption to the case depends upon the rapid availability of key information. It also depends upon having all information appear in the appropriate locations, in keeping with the firm technical standard.

Only when every case is handled in a consistent manner from both a project management and data management perspective can the Litigation Support Department provide the optimal Litigation Support services to the firm. This includes the use of prequalified vendors, litigation technology cost codes, and the other best practices as outlined in the book. The strategies in this book do not limit the attorney's ability to litigate the case. They enhance the technological goods and services required to support their efforts.

"Any plan is better than no plan at all."
- Author Unknown

10. Network Configuration

Network configuration refers to the administration of how, when, and from where any user can access data, e.g., network drive letter, software menu or web address. It is the responsibility of the VP of Operations to document and manage access and security needs.

The Litigation Support Department organizes folders and files to make them easy for anyone to locate. The department organizes repositories in order to address network access and security requirements. The continued success of security measures relies upon the firmwide adherence to folder organization rules.

Because network configuration issues and backup concerns are closely tied together, there is opportunity for a certain amount of overlap from section to section in this book. In order to help organize the text and limit redundancy, backups are covered under the Backup Routines and Disaster Recovery Plan sections. Folder organization appears under the Network Folders section. This section concentrates on drive letters, access, and security.

1. Drive Letters

All computer users are familiar with the A: and C: drives. Each drive letter references a piece of storage media. If a PC has a second hard drive, or external USB drive, it may appear as the D: drive. This media is local to the PC. When a PC connects to a network, it gains access to hard drives that reside on remote PCs and servers. The network administrator can assign, or "map," a drive letter to a network folder when a person logs on. In such a fashion, everyone in the Litigation Department has an "L:" drive which points to the same folders. Persons not in the department either do not receive an "L:" drive, or it may map to another folder on a different server. This brings us to the next point which is how the end user accesses data.

Note: Law firm employees will quickly understand and adopt a logical storage scheme and drive letters if it is offered by the department.

2. Direct vs. Indirect Access

All software provides the user with two basic methods for accessing their data: "direct access" and "indirect access." Direct access tools have some form of "File - Open" menu option. This format requires the user to navigate the network in search of client-matter folders and data. Indirect access tools provide the user with a list of available targets, be they transcripts or databases.

An administrator must both provide and limit access to folders and data. Firms that use "direct access" software can use network permissions to this effect. Changing permissions requires the assistance of either an IT Department network administrator or Litigation Support Department technician who has network administrative rights.

The "indirect access" software administrator can add and remove items from the menu through the application itself. This does not negate the need for network level administration entirely. Most applications that use the web browser provide indirect access. The software administrator must rely upon the software's ability to limit access. If the software does not provide this facility, the administrator must rely upon network security permissions.

An administrator can manage network security so the user can access folders on a server that contains case files such as transcripts and databases. As users change cases, access rights may also change. A network administrator must update security settings, thereby granting or denying access to case folders. Indirect access software packages may remove the need for users to access the network folders. The administration of access rights is done through the software and not the network. This may shift the burden from the IT Department to the Litigation Support Department.

Note: One advantage of indirect access systems is the ability to act as interface between the data and the users. If the users cannot see the folders on the network where the data is stored, there is less of a chance of an unfortunate deletion. It is also much simpler to determine "what happened" if only an administrator can access sensitive folders.

3. Access and Security

The ability to apply access rights relies upon the litigious use of folder organization rules. The network administrator should be able to find the folders through the client and matter number alone. If Litigation Support does not provide a folder naming scheme and default repositories, people will create case folders wherever is convenient for them. The lack of folder organization inevitably causes an access or security issue. It can also cause problems when searching for all case related materials. The following are sample considerations and recommendations:

Question 01: How do you organize your data on the servers?

Answer: All folders should be organized by client number, with matter number subfolders. The client number folders should reside in predefined locations. Litigation Support should administrate this process.

Why: All names and nicknames change. Only the accounting client-matter number endures. Everyone relates their work to the client-matter number for billing purposes. The department uses predefined locations for security and backup management.

Question 02: How long will it take to identify all data related to a given client-matter?

Answer: Through the use of predefined repositories, it should take almost no time to identify locations for all materials.

Why: Every day the Litigation Support team performs tasks that require the ability to find any materials very quickly. There may be an order to remove all materials, or the team may need a copy for the war room. The team may need to find a key transcript or put a copy of a native file onto a CD.

Question 03: Which roles does identification of all materials require at the firm?

Answer: It should not require the involvement of the entire team; only the searcher, such as the Litigation Support Department.

Why: It is possible to store the materials with organization so that this task does not cause interruptions for other people.

Question 04: How do you limit access to case materials on the network?

Answer: The Litigation Support Department and IT Department can limit access through a combination of network security and software functionality.

Why: In the legal environment it is critical to limit access to repositories. Access is limited to those persons who specifically require it for their jobs. There is a legal term, "Chinese wall," or ethical wall, whereby the firm attests to clients and judiciary system that it is doing all possible to apply appropriate access rights.

Question 05: Are internal repositories available from outside the firm?

Answer: A qualified "yes" should be the answer.

Why: The firm or attorney may wish to limit which internal repositories are externally available. If the firm does not allow external access, the department must consider a hosted solution, should the team foresee the need for secure external access. It is possible to provide access to certain repositories while obscuring others.

Question 06: Are external repositories available to the legal team from inside the firm?

Answer: Due to both of the following considerations, the answer should be "yes."

Why: Many firms, even large ones, use hosted solutions for certain cases. To use these providers, the legal team must access the Internet. To expedite data deliveries, the department may wish to use an Internet communications protocol known as "FTP."

4. About Hosted Solutions

When the legal team uses a remotely hosted solution, the network administrator must provide secure access to the external system. Providing internal access to external services still requires secure access both from within the law firm and without, such as when the attorney works from client offices or a "war room." Law firms will also need to provide external access to internal files.

11. Backup Routines

The following is a scenario every Litigation Support Department and hosted solution provider will encounter. The speaker is a worried attorney. "After working from 7am, three reviewers stopped work for dinner at 7pm. When they resumed work, all the tags and foldering information were gone. We started reviewing at 7am, so this represents 36 hours worth of review time. The team was identifying documents for tomorrow's production. Tell us how much work we lost."

No one can rely completely upon their servers 100% of the time—whether those servers reside with the vendor or the firm. One truly should not consider any file storage solution until they find out how backups and restorations occur. Under the Disaster Recovery Plan, the text discusses how to plan for this type of disaster. Sometimes the only answer is to restore the last good version of the files in question. Knowing ahead of time how many versions to keep will limit the damage. Proper backup routines could potentially limit the example 36 hour loss of work to only 3 hours total. Folder organization helps to make this level of service easier to provide.

The different types of data need multiple backup routines based upon how people use them. Not everything needs to be backed up on a daily basis, or to a backup tape. The backup administrator may need to back up other types of files with less frequency. For example, all databases should be backed up daily, while weekly or monthly intervals may suit image files. A good Litigation Support Department knows the location for all litigation data repositories. The Litigation Support Department, in conjunction with the Litigation Department and IT Department, can create an appropriate backup schedule for each repository. Once the network backup administrator programs a backup schedule, the litigators and the Litigation Support Department can concentrate on other issues.

In the table below, identify where types of data reside and the backup routines associated with these data. This may require input from the technician who runs all the backups for the firm. Bear in mind one should store data based upon how you'll need it later. At the same time, a daily backup does not mean last night's backup tapes contain all of client-matter folder data. Depending on the "backup strategy" (see below) and the type of data, the backup administrator may require multiple backup tapes to restore every required file.

Your firm may retire backup tapes after one year of rotation. Case data should be kept for years. If the only backup copy of data resides on a "DLT", or backup, tape from three years ago, that tape better be available within an acceptable number of hours. Most law firms have a destruction policy. **Make sure your firm has no automatic destruction schedule that the Litigation and Litigation Support Departments did not approve.**

1. Backup Strategies

There are three main backup strategies:

1. **Incremental Backup**: Only backs up files added or changed since the last backup. Quick to back up, but restore requires multiple tapes (last full backup tape plus all incremental tapes since the last full backup).

2. **Differential Backup**: A differential backup only backs up files since last full backup. Each backup takes a little longer, but restore requires only two tapes (most recent full backup and most recent differential backup).

3. **Full Backup**: Back up all data. Takes the longest time to backup, but easy to restore since all files are at one place and you don't need previous back-ups.

2. Backup & Restore Times

The IT Department does not back up all data a nightly basis. This is because not all data needs to be backed up every night. Additionally, the more information backed up on a frequent basis, the greater the cost. Therefore, there is a constant struggle between the desire to make backups of everything as frequently as possible and the cost to provide this level of service. As such, the majority of IT Departments in firms back up only those files that changed since the prior nightly backup. This schedule traditionally includes a full backup on a weekly basis.

The IT Department backup schedule may not account for how litigation uses any specific cache of data. How people use data should determine the appropriate backup increment: hourly, nightly, or weekly. To document the current schedule, the Litigation Support Department VP of Operations first needs to identify all data caches. The VP must then determine what backup policies are in place for all litigation data and cross-correlate this information against the desired preferences as determined by both the Litigation Department and Litigation Support. The reader should reference the Backup Routines section for the list of data caches and backup increments.

The IT Department should provide the Litigation Support Department with an estimated time to restore files from each resource. The turnaround time and ability to restore information depends upon the resource and scale of the request. Because different resources are backed up on different schedules, the IT Department may require backup tapes from off-site storage. Other requests may take as little as fifteen minutes. Litigation Support should always provide the team with time estimates and the level of certainty.

Select a backup frequency and backup strategy for each type of data.

Type of Data	Backup Frequency	Backup Strategy
End-user working folders, e.g. transcripts, video files	Daily Weekly Monthly	Incremental Differential Full
Database Files	Daily Weekly Monthly	Incremental Differential Full
Image, OCR & Load Files	Daily Weekly Monthly	Incremental Differential Full
Native Files	Daily Weekly Monthly	Incremental Differential Full

12. Disaster Recovery Plan

If a law firm has an IT Department, then the head of that department should have a Disaster Recovery Plan. This is a contingency plan for potential situations that would cause work to cease, such as when the power dies, hard drives crash or the Internet connection fails. The plan may then outline solutions, such as a diesel generator, backup tapes and a second Internet connection through a different ISP. The resources in the plan are not just work aids—they allow firm personnel, including Litigation Support, to perform even the most elemental types of work. As Litigation is always racing against the clock, the IT Department must have a plan which allows people to resume their work within an acceptable period of time. The firm, and outsourced vendors, must employ a recovery plan that meets Litigation Support Department and Litigation Department needs in terms of cessation period and limiting the amount of work lost. The Litigation Support Department will pay for the required resources through legitimate billing, just as any vendor would.

To assess the firm's disaster recovery plan, Litigation Support VP of Operations must first identify all information repositories. The IT Department can specify how the current plan supports each repository. The Litigation Department can specify how they wish each repository supported. Finally, the IT Department can estimate any costs to achieve the desired support level. As stated previously, the Litigation Support Department pays for any additional resources through billed goods and services.

1. Identify Repositories

The first step in disaster recovery is for the Litigation Support Department to build a storage matrix which identifies all litigation repositories and supporting infrastructure, such as servers. A spreadsheet is sufficient for this task, even for large decentralized firms.

The Litigation Support Department VP of Operations should create and maintain this repository spreadsheet. To learn more about the spreadsheet, please visit the section, Storage Assessment.

2. Determine Support Level

The Litigation Support Department should work with the IT Department, on the spreadsheet, to list the backup increments, e.g., hourly, daily, weekly, for each repository. This information tells the reader how much work could be lost due to a disaster. The next factor to determine and enter into the spreadsheet is "down time". Litigation Support will need to tell the Litigation Department how long the legal team may lose access to any or all repositories.

Note: Litigation Support should work with IT to schedule planned down times to times which least affect the Litigation Department.

The servers which house litigation data, databases, and software, and the infrastructure, which routes information from and to the users, are all critical support elements. As such, the disaster recovery plan would not be complete without their consideration and inclusion. The question is whether the level of support provided for these repositories and the infrastructure meets the levels required by a litigation environment. A server crash may result in "down time," which halts document review. During down time, the team will not be able to access any data or software that relies upon the server. Litigation Support should use the spreadsheet to illustrate for the Litigation Department how loss of a given server may harm case efforts in terms of both down time and loss of any work product generated after the prior backup.

Litigation must determine how many hours of lost work is acceptable. Acting as technology liaison, the Litigation Support Department VP of Operations should speak with the IT Department in technical terms regarding disaster recovery and the legal team regarding limiting "down time", lost work and the associated costs.

3. Determine Desired Support Levels

The Litigation Support Department should work with the Litigation Department to determine how long of a lack of access to each repository and piece of supporting infrastructure is acceptable. When disaster occurs, the IT Department may restore normal functioning. They may also restore data from the last backup. Depending upon the backup interval for each repository, the legal team can lose all work performed since the interval. The Litigation Department will specify how much work product loss is acceptable on a repository by repository basis. Litigation must also specify the level of support required for hardware such as the document review server, without which access to every litigation case may halt. After this step is complete, the IT Department can, in turn, estimate the cost to provide the desired level of support.

Here is an example of how to determine the actual loss for a hypothetical repository. Assume that IT backs up a particular database every day at 12:00 a.m. If it should become corrupt at 8:00 p.m., the team could lose 12 business hours worth of document review time. Although the IT Department can probably restore the last backup within 30 minutes, the total potential loss is at least 12-1/2 hours. This figure does not yet include the time for each person to find where they began work 12-1/2 hours earlier. This type of experience is demoralizing to the team. There is also the financial consideration: whether the firm should bill the client for reviewing the same documents a second time. At a billable rate of $250 per hour, each reviewer's time represents $3,125. For a large firm with a team of 10 attorneys, the potential loss would be $31,250. An appropriate disaster recovery plan could limit this type of loss to a one hour maximum exposure. The ability to provide this level of support may require technically savvy staff and, potentially, investment by the firm in expensive hardware and software. Fortunately, the Litigation Support Department will generate the revenues necessary to pay for these resources.

4. Determining Cost, Justifying Investment

Based upon the disaster recovery / repository matrix, including the maximum acceptable downtime, one should have a pretty good idea whether current abilities meet user expectations. If not, Litigation Support needs IT to quote a cost and estimated completion date to upgrade disaster recovery abilities. Much of Litigation Support's work is managing expectations. If the attorneys need the IT Department to provide a certain level of support, then the firm may need to invest accordingly. This investment can come from IT's existing budget or through the Litigation Support Department revenues for billable goods and services.

While any level of service is technologically possible, the expense must be a good business decision. There are always opportunities for reinvestment in the department. The Litigation Support Department COO must decide which resources to bolster and to what level. It is recommended to use revenues from any given service area to reinvest in the same area. Use hosting fees to purchase more storage. If the Litigation Support Department is billing hours at capacity, an extra person may be the wise investment.

The IT Department can compare existing support level against desired support level to determine the cost to provide the new level of service. The Litigation Department should compare this cost against the potential financial loss as estimated by the Litigation Department. As budgets are finite, all parties should use the spreadsheet to determine which investments make the most sense. Eventually, the Litigation Support Department VP of Finance will be able to use Accounting Department reports to budget for the required resources.

Turnaround time is critical to the litigation process. For the appropriate price, the firm can provide the Litigation Department and Litigation Support Department with the requested level of support. If the Litigation Support Department can bill client-matters for hosting, the IT Department can purchase the necessary resources, required to support the Disaster Recovery Plan. Please reference the section on hosting to learn more.

After institution, IT, Litigation and Litigation Support staff should be able to recover from any disaster within a time frame the attorneys can accept.

One point worth revisiting here is that reinvestment capital can come from the Litigation Support Department billing for goods and services, such as hosting. The vendors reinvest hosting revenues into storage and backup resources. The law firm can do the same.

13. Training

There are many people who need to get trained for various purposes. A lot of firms concentrate on training the legal team while ignoring the continuing education requirements for the Litigation Support persons. This book is one method; sending staff to legal technical shows, another. Vendors and seminars provide education. This part of the needs assessment asks the reader to consider what kinds of training the firm currently provides and any budget needed for more training.

1. Litigation Support

Litigation Support needs training is the use of software as both an end-user and an administrator. Litigation Support also needs to be trained on how to use the software to achieve key case goals. Software is a tool and therefore a means to an end. The firm needs to train Litigation Support to understand how software and case lifecycle mesh.

Traditionally, paralegals would transition into the Litigation Support role. Today, Litigation Support needs to find new hires from the technical world. The job is a technical one, and it is easier to explain the case lifecycle to a technician than teach high level technical skills to a non-technical person. A great Litigation Support technician is one who can hear a request from the legal team and recognize what is needed versus what is wanted. The standard case lifecycle must influence how the technician approaches a problem.

Conventions and lectures occur throughout the year, such as those held by LawNet and LegalTech. Vendors provide free product demonstrations to any firm willing to listen. Whether the firm is shopping for a new product or not, demonstrations provide insights as to how the technology market will change and mature. This results in better support for the law firm, the case, and the client.

The Litigation Support Department is a pressure cooker environment. These are people who put in lots of overtime even though they know they will never make partner. Any minor perks for the support staff, such as education, that also benefit the firm may be worth the investment. When sending people to a convention, the firm should pay the extra cost so they may attend any lectures. A convention is a chance to hear experts from many sources present lectures on key issues, such as document review software and the future of native file review. The vendor exhibit halls also provide the Litigation Support Department person with the opportunity to evaluate multiple document review systems and talk with representatives.

Meeting with representatives is an ideal way to identify candidates for a future demonstration at the firm. Vendors are a great way to keep updated on the developing marketplace. There is no cost and the meeting can happen at the firm's convenience. One to two hours a month, twelve meetings a year, is a very small sacrifice for the Litigation Support Department attendees.

As an exercise, Litigation Support should evaluate each product by comparing how it would complement the firm's current technology case lifecycle. Discovery review software that does not export documents to exhibit software will cause problems for the legal team later in the case. A software title that does not allow for dual monitors may not be the best choice for the discovery review team.

At the same time, Litigation Support should identify how the software removes the need for certain steps or considerations in the technology plan. As example, a team that uses native file review software may produce in native format.

Litigation technology changes over time. Some companies and applications merge with others. A company introduces a new product to the market which attorneys may desire. The case lifecycle remains a constant through all of this change. Replacing one software title with another may cause a problem with titles in other phases of the case. Litigation Support should try and understand how any technology may benefit a case, within the context of current firm technology.

2. Training

> "We must all hang together, or we shall surely hang separately."
> - Benjamin Franklin

Every role, whether attorney, paralegal, technical or project manager, requires some type of training in order to achieve an overall successful Litigation Support experience. The purpose of one type of training is to move the legal team and Litigation Support Department from ad hoc problem solving to the execution of real lifecycle strategies only available through the application of a proper case lifecycle technology plan and firmwide litigation technical standards.

The Litigation Support Department's VP of Marketing role, a/k/a the "Litigation Support Attorney", facilitates the education process. The legal team needs to understand how to solve problems through the application of litigation technology. The Litigation Support Department needs to understand how software, goods and services not only functionally support the case but what the legal team hopes to accomplish by using them.

All people will resist performing new tasks when they do not understand how their work will benefit themselves or the case. People label this type of work "busy work" or "grunt work". When people understand the value of their efforts and know how to gauge the quality of the results, they perform better work.

Roles should have less concern for the "why" of required technical considerations than "how" these considerations will impact or benefit the ability to litigate in all phases of the case lifecycle. The person(s) behind each role may and should be encouraged to understand the "why" behind each consideration.

Every role should understand both the assigned responsibilities and how to achieve them. Litigation Support should always approach situations as an opportunity to educate the other roles about the case lifecycle perspective. The legal team needs to understand how their efforts today will aid their efforts in later stages of the case, such as creating a list of key names and terms, which is used in bibliographic coding, with court reporters and even identifying potential exhibits.

3. Legal Team

The Litigation Support Department should work to educate the legal team on two levels: first, how the Litigation Support Department and litigation technology benefit the case, and, second, how Litigation Support Department benefits the firm. The following bullet points illustrate three major considerations each person on the legal team should understand:

- How the outlined principles and practices in this text will benefit the team,
- How to use software throughout the case lifecycle to achieve case goals, and
- How the firm and client, as businesses, benefit through the use of the Litigation Support Department and by executing the principles in this text.

Training of the legal team should address the following issues:

1. The end users should know whom to contact with questions about how to use the software tools in order to achieve current case goals;
2. The legal team should know how the software and the case lifecycle mesh;
3. The legal team should understand the technology plan and how the Litigation Support Department, vendors and litigation technology will aid their work on the case from pleading to trial;
4. Everyone should understand the various roles and their associated responsibilities;
5. The legal team needs to know when to involve Litigation Support, such as when requesting discovery and dealing with vendors;
6. The legal team should adjust their schedules to plan and schedule for technical task turnaround times, such as when Litigation Support or the vendor needs to generate a production set of stamped images; and
7. The legal team may require coaching on communicating with technical people. Technical work and legal work each has its very own vocabulary.

An Example of a Training Scenario

General training where the teacher presents every function in discovery review software has limited value to specific efforts such as reviewing for privilege. The longer the gap between training and actual case work using the software, the less value the generalized training offers.

The better training style involves students as they learn how to use specific functions to achieve specific goals. This can make for a relatively short class, and therefore may not provide enough materials for a half-day or three-day training seminar. It should provide enough materials for a short goal oriented class.

On the first day of review, Litigation Support should have the team attend a 30 minute class that shows (1) how to find their personal batch of documents to review, and (2) how to mark them as productive or privileged. This can be followed by ten minutes of actual document review with the trainer present. It is easier to schedule the legal team for a 30 minute meeting then a half or full day class. In turn, the legal team can use the meeting as an opportunity to address other client-matter specific issues, which may or may not involve Litigation Support.

Note: This book includes a *Case Lifecycle Task List* in Microsoft PowerPoint format. The project plan identifies additional issues and materials required for milestone events such as the first day of review launch meeting. It also identifies the responsibilities of the other roles, such as Vendor and Lead Attorney.

Litigation Support should encourage the review team members to request additional help as needed. The legal team should understand that help includes both software training as well as the case lifecycle technology strategy. In most law firms, no one wishes to advertise ignorance in front of the entire team. As such, many attorneys and paralegals will remain silent when they should ask for clarification on a point. Litigation Support should promote the different forms of assistance available to the team, be it email, phone support or five minutes in private. Five minutes on the phone can save the reviewer thirty minutes of frustration. The legal team needs to understand this point, most of all.

As the firm can employ the same technology plan for every client-matter, the legal team should have an increasingly easier time using litigation technology to achieve routine goals such as reviewing for both privilege and issue. Litigation Support Department needs to educate the legal team and firm that this consistent approach benefits each case and the firm, in terms of cost, quality of work and overall speed.

4. Vendors

Litigation Support must train the vendor so that the technical nature of their products matches the firm standards and requirements. This can take substantial time, and it will be necessary to repeat at the start of each new project, due to potential vendor employee turnover. As regards how the vendor works with the firm, Litigation Support should focus on the business and technical training of the vendor, so as to bring them into compliance with firm operations.

a. Business Training

Litigation Support should endeavor to train the vendors to include such information and in such fashion as makes life easier for the Litigation Support role, legal team, client and Accounting Department. A good provider informs the team as to progress, results, ability to meet target deadlines and cost to date. Regardless of what other project names or codes appear, all vendor generated correspondence must include the firm's client-matter number. Work, internal or vended, always relates to a specific client-matter number. Ultimately, accounting will use this code to process payments and Litigation Support will use it to identify media and organize files on the server. If this code is absent from vendor correspondence or product, it creates work for the firm.

As the vendor can neither match an undocumented requirement nor include a firm client-matter number which was never provided, it is the responsibility of the Litigation Support Department to provide the client-matter number for each project to each vendor. A well trained vendor knows to ask for this information. The same vendor will know whom to ask for this information. Again, that training and those requirements come from the Litigation Support Department.

Vendors need to understand that they can either work with or against the Litigation Support Department. Litigation Support will encourage the use of those companies which make life easiest for the firm. One way is to include the right information in business correspondence; the other way is to provide products that match the firm technical standard and therefore require the least effort and time to use.

b. Technical Training

When the firm institutes a technical standard, those technical elements and preferences remain constant from project to project, matter to matter and vendor to vendor. The case, Litigation Support Department and firm rely upon this consistency in both the technical and business character of the litigation technology goods and services provider.

This type of consistency means that the Litigation Support Department may use the vendor on new or ongoing projects with a minimum of disruption to the case. While the scale of electronic discovery can suddenly grow exponentially, court deadlines may not move. In the same fashion that litigators will move paralegals from one case to another to boost capacity, the Litigation Support Department needs the ability to transition work to one or more vendors who can already match the firm litigation technical standards. This type of relationship is very valuable to the firm.

In the spirit of collaboration, the vendor is encouraged to inform the Litigation Support Department's VP of Operations role of any work coming from the firm but not through Litigation Support. Any vendor, qualified in the manner outlined above, who works with the department instead of around the department is the definition of a preferred vendor.

Firms that perform all technical work internally should still maintain a working relationship with vendors for litigation technology goods and services. Having this relationship is a matter of risk management. To restrict Litigation Support Department's ability to outsource will directly, and negatively, impact all active cases. It is worth the expense to send work intermittently and make certain the vendor can still produce what is required.

Faced with a resource problem, the law firm can either purchase additional software licenses and hardware, outsource work to vendors or, in decentralized firms with multiple offices, allocate someone else's resources.

Investing in software is a great way to increase bandwidth, but only if the firm also invests in the necessary hardware and people to properly use the additional resources. The time to prepare a project on the electronic discovery processing server remains consistent. If one technician only has the time for five projects per day, adding servers and software is not investment enough.

Adding resources to the Litigation Support Department should be planned. While the receipt of more technical work than the department can handle is inevitable, it is more difficult to plan for when it will happen. Any course of action that potentially sacrifices project management time for technical time as a support strategy is destined to hurt other projects, cases, the client and firm. Therefore, the department needs a contingency plan in the form of a vendor.

5. Other External Parties

Training is not limited to internal roles. Whenever the attorney deals with external parties, such as the client, opposing counsel and vendors, he or she should include the Litigation Support Department. The department can provide input on anything with a technical aspect. The attorney and Litigation Support can discuss technical strategies and then represent the resulting requirements to other parties on issues such as delivery format for productions, or outlining all the potential storage locations the client should look for potential discovery. Litigation Support should also evaluate the technical nature of inbound materials to make certain their character does not pose any significant technical issues.

14. Departmental Operations

The department should be managed so that the departmental COO can receive monthly reports that chart hardware and software resources, and provide information such as the anticipated date when the servers will be full, and when the firm will need to buy licenses. The COO also needs reports on the financial and workload trends for the department.

The only way to create certain critical reports is to organize how people perform and track all goods and services. The only way to create other reports is to organize how the department handles and stores all data. Through this approach, the Litigation Support Department is able to provide better service to the individual case while also benefiting the firm as a whole. Best practices, firmwide standards and a case lifecycle plan provide a foundation upon which the department may organize, track and report upon technical goods and services.

For more COO role responsibilities and the purpose of the reports, please reference the Hierarchy section.

Due to the increasing amount of storage space that electronic discovery and digital video represent for each case, it is easy to see how firm servers will run out of space at a greater rate than during the pre-electronic discovery age. Litigation Support should use storage trending reports to better gauge growth rate and, thereby, a date. However, it must be pointed out that the lead attorney on a small and simple case will suddenly receive additional files and occupy 50% of the previously free space on the server, thereby making all prior date estimates grossly inaccurate.

Because servers have limited storage, adding capacity costs the firm money, and the IT Department time, growth and storage reports help everyone to plan for this inevitability. Ideally, the IT Department should have the time to research, meet with vendors and schedule the project. At least it should have the option to do so.

Note: In order to reclaim server space, the Department should attempt to remove all files relating to a given client-matter. As the folders on the server are organized by client-matter, it is simple to compare a list of the folders against an accounting report of closed client-matter numbers.

Whether the department may remove information, such as discovery databases and associated native files, from the server is not always a question of case status. The attorney may require ongoing access, to closed cases from years ago. So, while Litigation Support Department should endeavor to retire old client-matter files in order to make room for new materials, doing so is not always an option.

Higher level management planning and abilities are built upon how the department organizes technical and project management time, storage and services. Through the use of accounting reports, it is possible and advantageous to track these types of items whether vended or generated internally.

There are resources, representing significant time and cost, that your Litigation Support Department COO should be able to track. These are questions that address how the department is organized as a whole in addition to how the department handles every matter.

Because this transparent view of operations requires consistency of effort by the department, there may be concern that people will have to change how they traditionally operate. This may be true. The operational rules do not limit how a person uses their expertise to solve technical problems. It simply lets each technician know what the results should look like and where to store it.

Like the attorneys whose ability to litigate is not limited by firm technical standards, the technician's abilities are not limited either. Rules can also help the department decide which technical goods and services to offer within the department versus outsourcing. Due to a standardized approach for department operations, it is possible to transition projects from one person to another with a minimal learning curve.

In a Litigation Support Department with multiple technicians and project managers and no documented plans, their work will still have similarities due to working on the same environment using the same software. However, these similarities should occur by design and not by default. For decentralized firms, there is significant need for consistency, for no less than the reputation of the entire firm is at stake.

Gauge your own Litigation Support Department and how it benefits both the case and firm. The earlier in the case lifecycle the attorney involves the Litigation Support Department, the greater the control the team will exercise over the technical aspects of the case including cost.

Something as simple as standardized folder naming and organization rules allow vendors to create an appropriate load file as well as organize folders on product their technicians generate.

At this point one should have a good idea as to how departmental operations and organization work together to provide better service to both the client and the firm. So, let us now look to "political abilities." Political abilities equate to delegating the final say on various issues to one party or another. Within a law firm, Litigation Support Department's political abilities include may center on the ability to outsource work, and bill for goods and services which it performs internally.

15. Political Abilities

There are a number of case-level decisions that should be made by Litigation Support, such as mandating the outsourcing of work, establishing a firmwide technical standard, restricting work to specific vendors, routing specific litigation goods and services through Litigation Support, and restricting software use to specific titles. Obviously the department will require the authorization by managing partners and the marketing savvy of the Litigation Support VP of Marketing.

These decisions may also affect how the department works with other departments, such as accounting. Situations may arise where decisions may effect the actions of legal staff. Litigation Support can not tell the attorney how to litigate a case, but Litigation Support should be able to mandate that technical decisions meet firm standards. Here now is a short list of political abilities. Note the value of each, whether your department is able to wield such power and how it would affect every role.

1. Ability To Outsource New Or Legacy Work

The department needs to self-regulate its work level. The COO, relying upon the VP of Marketing and VP of Operations, should decide what and when to outsource due to the complexity or scale of discovery in a case, or due to scheduled upcoming projects.

Litigation Support needs to be able to shift projects to vendors for the sake of all existing projects. This is a matter of knowing what the department can do, what is best for the case and the impact on other matters. Vendors outsource work. They subcontract that work which they can not or should not perform internally. They still perform project management and check the results for quality. Litigation Support should do no less.

In such circumstances as when the Litigation Support Attorney cannot persuade a legal team toward an appropriate course of action, the clout to force these decisions should come from firm management.

2. Firmwide Litigation Technical Standard Embraced

The law firm contracts with litigation technology goods and services vendors to create products such as a database with images. The resulting product should take a minimum of time and technical prowess to load and use. The best way to do this is to establish and publish a firmwide litigation technical standard.

Note: Visit eDiscovery.org to download the latest version of a mature Litigation Support Technical Standards document.

A firmwide standard is especially helpful if your firm is large enough to have multiple offices and departments. If non-Litigation Support persons can contract any vendor without input from Litigation Support, then a firm mandated technical standard will save you hours of needless labor.

The mandatory inclusion of this document with every project ensures the product will match firm technical requirements. For law firms where the attorneys and paralegals may contract discovery services without the involvement of the Litigation Support Department, this is a critical step toward the elimination of unnecessary technical work. This is also the first step toward moving all electronic discovery through the Litigation Support Process.

The ability to mandate inclusion of the Litigation Support Department can begin with the technical standard. Once the standard is published, the Litigation Support Department can then begin a qualification process for potential firm vendors.

In some firms, the legal team may not automatically include the Litigation Support Department. The department should use the arguments within this book to win the support of the CIO, Head of Litigation and, ultimately, Managing Partners.

3. Ability to Select and Exclude Vendors

There are good and bad vendors in the marketplace. When a vendor repeatedly requires multiple attempts to get a project's technical attributes correct, it may be time to stop using them. Litigation Support needs to be able to exclude vendors from future consideration. In order to exclude vendors, the department must also provide a list of preferred vendors. If the legal team wishes to chose a vendor, let the Litigation Support Department provide the list from which they may chose.

As with the establishment of technical standards, again the department should use the arguments within this book to win the support of the CIO, Head of Litigation and, ultimately, Managing Partners. Only through the education of the legal team and authority of the firm can everyone work toward change which is in the best interest of firm, team and client.

4. Routing Discovery Vending Through Litigation Support

In firms with an accounting department, it would be hard to imagine that an attorney or paralegal would contract an outside accounting vendor, and then have the internal accounting department use the vendor's work product for all firm accounts receivable ("AR") and accounts payable ("AP") needs. Yet, this is the same situation most Litigation Support Departments face. Although the field of accounting has standards and certifications to ensure that work product one accountant creates, another can use. The field of electronic discovery has no such luxuries. At some firms, paralegals and attorneys select the last vendor to give them chocolate chip cookies. The right roles should be responsible for making their appropriate and crucial decisions. There is a solution: route all discovery vending through the Litigation Support Department. Instead of the attorney abdicating this type of authority to a paralegal, the firm should delegate this authority to the Litigation Support Department.

It should be noted that when a firm institutes and publishes a firm technical standard, it can then prequalify vendors against that document. So long as the choice of vendor is limited to qualified vendors, the attorneys and paralegals who wish to vend discovery directly should not pose any significant problem for the firm or department. Either way, all electronic discovery should still, physically, go to the department for duplication (never send the originals to the vendor) and inventory.

5. Restrict Software Use To Select Titles

It is hard to imagine a single case where the legal team would use two programs for storing transcripts, three for document review, two for word processing, two for email and another two for deposition and trial exhibits. This would create a lot of confusion for the legal team. It also creates a myriad of problems for the Litigation Support Department and vendors.

Even those law firms that use a single program for storing transcripts may employ a different application from one case to another. Although to a lesser degree, this creates many of the same problems as when using redundant software titles on the same matter. Independent of input from the Litigation Support Department and IT Department, some attorneys may even purchase solutions that duplicate existing software but are limited in some significant fashion, such as the ability to export data to other programs. In these unfortunate circumstances, Litigation Support's first project may be the migration of the new database into a software title which the firm supports.

The law firm, through firmwide standardization on software titles, as outlined by Litigation Support, removes a level of complexity for support, the vendors and the end users. The Litigation Support Department need only be expert in a single title, not several. The department may select from a wider variety of vendors as the technical requirements are simpler. Finally, the end users enjoy a consistent software experience from matter to matter and collection to collection. Any learning curve on the part of the Litigation Support Department, vendor or legal team member is an impediment to speed and a successful litigation.

It sounds good in theory until the rainmaker partner prefers some obscure title. That is when the Litigation Support Department requires the backing of firm management to win the case for standardizing on titles and eliminating duplicate products.

6. Accounting Uses Vendor Cost Codes For Litigation Goods and Services

Some changes are easier to institute than others. One is the establishment of cost codes for litigation goods and services, such as litigation video and graphics, data services, paper services and court reporting services. The vendors will print the appropriate code on invoices and other such business communications.

As the addition of new vendor cost codes requires work on the part of the Accounting Department, Litigation Support should keep the number of codes to a minimum. The following is a four code example of how to categorize litigation technical goods and services. Absent is the billable hour which goes into the time entry system, such as Carpe Diem.

Litigation Video and Graphics (Code: <u>see Accounting</u>)

> This code represents video and graphics used at depositions, arbitration and trial.

Litigation Support Data Services (Code: <u>see Accounting</u>)

> This covers the range of work such as: electronic discovery and database creation, hosting and administration. Value added services such as OCR, programming, forensics, conversions, and media creation are all "Litigation Support Data Services."

Paper Services (Code: <u>see Accounting</u>)

> This includes photocopying paper, scanning paper or printing a paper set from electronic source (a/k/a "blow backs").

Court Reporting Services – Non-Video (Code: <u>see Accounting</u>)

> This is court reporters and their non-video associated costs.

These categories and descriptions are taken from the Litigation Support Technical Standards document, available at eDiscovery.org.

Accounting reports provide the foundation for making business decisions. As such, the Litigation Support Department's COO, or the VP of Marketing, should approach the CFO about the change. To help identify additional reasons, identify which cost codes the Accounting Department currently enters for electronic discovery and the other mentioned services. If accounting includes the cost for electronic discovery with legal research, as example, the firm has a skewed vision of expenses in the practice.

16. Ability to Bill

If the Litigation Support Department performs any of the same services and generates the any of the same goods as an outside vendor, it should bill them to the matter. The decision to take work in-house is one that comes with important risks and responsibilities. If the firm hosts databases and images, then the infrastructure should be as good as that of any vendor's hosted solution.

Attorneys may push to have work done internally if they know it will save the client costs. Litigation Support Departments which do not bill for time and creation of goods may be inundated by discount hunters looking for discounted internal work. When this scenario is compounded by lacking the ability to mandate out-sourcing, work for all cases may suffer. The ability to bill establishes the worth of the work Litigation Support performs. The legal team should use Litigation Support because of the quality of the work, not the ability to "write off" said work.

Almost every practice can afford a Litigation Support Department, even if the department is only a single person performing project management 90% of the time and technical work 10% of the time. When a person performs 1,000 hours a year of project management and technical work bills at a rate of $150/hour, they pay for themselves; 1,000 hours a year equals about 20 hours a week. An additional bonus from this arrangement is that the addition of staff becomes a question of meeting quotas instead of reallocating existing budgets.

The ability to bill for goods and services results in the ability to track and make the financial argument for additional resources such as software, hardware and staff.

1. Charging for Hosting

For firms that host all case materials on internal servers, storage is a significant issue. Electronic discovery has drastically increased the amount of data Litigation Support needs to store on a network. Until now most firms may include this service within their hourly rates, along with pens and paper. Someone will have to pay for the additional capacity. There is also infrastructure to purchase and maintain.

Ongoing hosting fees can raise the funds necessary to buy the new storage and backup systems every six years. This fee may also help attorneys decide whether to retire their case data from the servers.

If the appropriate storage solution requires a $36,000 investment, the department will need to bill $6,000 each year to recoup the cost. For a firm hosting one terabyte of data, this should not be difficult to do. This represents a billing of $500 per month. The resulting dollars per GB storage rate is certainly going to be far below that which any vendor would charge.

2. About Vendor Hosting

When the firm employs a hosted solution, one should be confident in the vendor's ability to provide appropriate infrastructure, redundant power, hard drives, Internet connections, and more. It is important that an IT Department technician evaluate the vendor's "network operations center" technical specifications. The Litigation Support Department should also evaluate vendor agreements for potential cost and lifecycle issues. The department should make certain the attorney is satisfied with the contract as it relates to damages and "up-time." None of the internal hosting, security and backup considerations change when using a hosted solution.

17. Vendors

Litigation Support should maintain a list of preferred vendors for each category, as identified by the cost codes. If lawyers wish to contract with an electronic discovery vendor directly, then the Litigation Support Department should provide a list of preferred vendors from which the attorney may choose. The preferred vendors will abide by the firm's instructions to involve the department before beginning any projects.

Many vendors may be concerned that the Litigation Support Department may exclude them, should the department manage the vending process. This is only true if the vendor cannot create a product or provide a service which matches the published firm litigation technical standards. The department needs to make the vendors understand that it has no personal stake in which vendor receives work, only that such work should meet the firm's standard.

How many projects come across Litigation Support's desk that:

1. Require no modification to use;
2. Require nominal modification to use;
3. Require major modification to use; or
4. Are not compatible with established firm systems?

Litigation Support wants to control vendor selection so that all incoming work requires little to no modification to use. If the department has a technical standards document, a technical template, the vendor should be able to meet these specifications. When the product provided by a vendor requires no modification to work on the firm's network, then you reuse that vendor. When a specific vendor cannot match the firm standard and deliveries repeatedly require technical effort by Litigation Support, the firm should not send them any more work. The work should go to a vendor who can match that standard, resulting in no extra effort by the department.

The department also should maintain an intranet list of good and bad vendors. The only way to truly weed out the bad vendors is to steer the legal team toward the great vendors. Everyone will be happy when there are no big problems. The need and argument for the department to be able to include and exclude vendors applies here.

Qualifying Vendors

Through the firm litigation technical standards document, all vendors, past, present, and aspiring, may attempt to qualify to work with the firm. The department should encourage the vendors to create sample media which can be evaluated for issues. In this fashion the department can prequalify or exclude vendors. When a client has a preferred vendor, the department should qualify them in the same fashion.

Keep the client's best interest in mind when dealing with vendors. It is in the client's best interest to have their technology costs kept low while the firm maintains only the highest quality vendors. Your firm has to use the results to litigate the case. A badly made database can cause the team to lose the case by missing deadlines or inability to migrate data to exhibit software without significant time and cost.

18. Printing

If the Litigation Support Department does not routinely print mass quantities of documents for the firm, then it is important to set some sort of maximum size for internal printing and minimum size for involving a vendor. Remember, just because the department is technologically capable of performing a task does not mean it should. Make certain there are established guidelines for when to take one route or the other.

Litigation Support should look at the source materials and help determine if printing is the best option for the case. An attorney or paralegal may believe that printing electronic discovery is the best way to process it. Some attorneys prefer to review documents in paper format as opposed to online. If the source materials would yield metadata and full text, then the print, scan and OCR sequence produces a lower quality product for the review team.

The legal team should know how long it takes the Litigation Support Department to print a banker box worth of paper, based upon the original source, such as paper, email and relational databases. The first question is what the team plans to do with the printed pages. The Litigation Support Department may be able to organize a printing by chronology, author, exhibit number or other combined factors.

A good Litigation Support Department must consider what the legal team hopes to accomplish by printing the discovery. The department can then advise the attorney whether printing is the best route to accomplish the desired goal, in relation to the lifecycle of the case. As example, if the attorney wishes to print documents to review for privilege and produce, then Litigation Support should be able to mandate a treatment in keeping with the best practices of the firm.

Determine through the Accounting department how much the firm pays for printing discovery. By tracking this number the department can assess trends and plan accordingly.

Printing Electronic discovery

Some firms print all incoming discovery and then scan it for subsequent OCR treatment. The resulting database and OCR text will never be of the same quality as when that electronic discovery is turned directly into a database with full text and associated metadata. Litigators, paralegals, vendors and Litigation Support Department persons who are familiar with the pre-electronic, paper-centric way of processing discovery need to learn about the new technology lifecycle plan.

Most teams print when it is time to produce or create exhibits. Only the Bates stamp and any text stamp which is specific to this printing should appear. It is bad form if the internal control number appears on a production printing. It gives the other side an idea as to the size of the original collection and how much was produced.

If a printing is for a production, the database administrator should update the database to reflect any new Bates numbers. The preproduction database should contain all control numbers assigned to a given document. Without the collaboration of the Litigation Support Department, the legal team may take steps which produce unwanted effects, such as undesirable stamps and loss of metadata.

For more information, please reference the case lifecycle flowchart for how to process incoming formats and generate productions.

IV. Tools

There are tools that each Litigation Support Department employee should have in order to work efficiently. The same is true of the person performing document review. When we do not have the proper tools, it may take longer to perform some or all tasks. Remember, litigation is deadline driven, so anything that helps get the job done more quickly is valuable.

Consider the robotic CD/DVD duplicator and burner which can free up hundreds of billable hours. If Litigation Support must generate each CD manually, then the technician must attend a manual, and essentially non-technical, process. The Litigation Support technician can load a stack of blank media and return in the morning to collect three complete sets of duplicates, labels included. A minor investment by the firm frees the technician to perform other, higher level, tasks for the firm.

The following sections cover the types of hardware and software recommended for any attorney performing review and for Litigation Support professional dealing with data. One may have a preference for one brand of spreadsheet program over another, but the need for a spreadsheet program of some sort exists.

The goal of software and hardware is to aid the speed and quality of the real work. These tools make your firm more profitable by:

1. Increasing the number of documents reviewed per hour;
2. Increasing the amount of time available for review;
3. Decreasing the amount of time spent performing or overseeing non-technical clerical tasks;
4. Decreasing the time required to perform technical tasks; and
5. Decreasing the turnaround time to create and load productions.

1. Software

In order to overcome the various problems Litigation Support staff encounters, a good toolbox of utilities is recommended. As is noted in the Needs Assessment section, it is important for the Litigation Support Department to have many titles, specific to the work. This is in direct contrast to the software tools, as they apply to the legal teams. The Software lifecycle and Needs Assessment sections help to explain why this is the case.

The following two sections identify the types of software that each role can use to achieve their goals; specifically, the Litigation Support Department and the legal team.

A. Litigation Support

The Litigation Support Department encounters technical problems on a daily basis. Technical problems require insight and the ability to identify the source of a problem. Some problems require modification of thousands of file and folder names. Other problems may require just as many changes to the text inside of thousands of load files. Technicians can use the following types of tools to address the majority of problems they will encounter on an irregular basis.

1. Spreadsheet Program

Most load files are text delimited. Each line looks something like this when opened in a text editor:

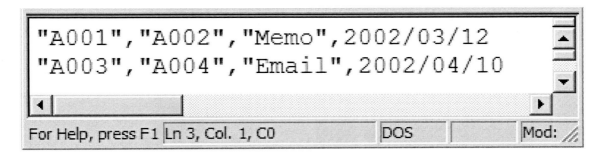

When loaded into the database, each line becomes a record and these values appear in the fields, such as "BegBates," "EndBates," document type and document date (or whichever fields happen to be first, second and so on). When we load this same load file into a spreadsheet program, the load file looks like this:

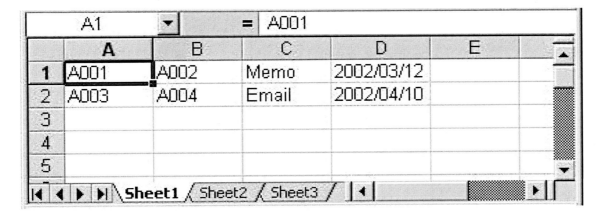

A spreadsheet provides relatively simple interface to add, remove or rearrange the columns (a/k/a "fields"). One can modify the values of a given column/field without disturbing the other columns/fields.

In situations where data is missing or a load file corrupted, the technician can make modifications to the data through the spreadsheet format. Viewing the load file in a spreadsheet program also makes it very easy to get an overview of the data.

When the technician finishes making alterations, the spreadsheet program will save the columns and rows as an ASCII delimited text file ready for loading into your program.

2. Batch File and Folder Renaming Program

Your Litigation Support Department will inevitably receive CDs where the filenames are formatted incorrectly. Maybe they don't have the Bates prefix or aren't zero-padded. An example utility, "Bulk Rename Utility", allows you to easily rename files and directories, based upon flexible criteria. Add date-stamps, replace numbers, insert strings, convert case, and add auto-numbers and more, including a "roll-back" feature!

Bulk Rename Utility is found at: http://www.bulkrenameutility.co.uk/Main_Intro.php

The Litigation Support Department needs a tool to perform this type of function. Bulk Rename Utility is one example title. It does have the decided advantage that this application is free.

3. Text Editor

The majority of the time, a text editor is the Litigation Support technician's favorite tool. The text editors that come standard on one's computer are probably not sufficient to handle the multi-megabyte text files Litigation Support encounters.

My personal favorite text editor is UltraEdit: http://www.UltraEdit.com.

It can open giant text files, and perform search and replace functions on the same files, all in seconds. It can also open multiple text files and perform the same editing functions across all text files at the same time. This is extremely handy when the vendor provides 20 load files that all need the same modifications. The program only costs around 30 dollars.

4. File-Folder Comparison

QC (Quality Control) is very important in Litigation Support. The technician cannot assume that a CD copied correctly to the network. An example utility is called "Beyond Compare" and is available at http://www.ScooterSoftware.com.

Beyond Compare is a Windows utility for detecting and reconciling differences between folders and files. It also compares the contents of files. This is great when you need to compare an original load file and a modified load file.

Litigation Support frequently has the need to compare media and the contents of load files. This type of software addresses this business need. The technician will use this software to verify that a duplicate CD of original discovery actually matches the original on all technical levels. Example: Litigation Support has 2 sets of DVDs. They mostly contain the same documents the legal team needs to find those docs that are on 1 DVD but not the other.

5. File Viewer

Litigation Support gets all sorts of files that no one has seen before. They might be from some program that was used in a niche industry four years ago or some modern software that the Firm does not own. This genre of software allows the user to view and print hundreds of file formats.

Quick View Plus by Avanstar provides the viewing of virtually any business document in more than 225 Windows, UNIX, Macintosh, DOS and Internet file formats. With a simple mouse click on the desktop, in a browser or in an email application, Quick View Plus enables users to view the contents of a document; print, copy and paste the document view; and instantly compress a file or add a file to an existing archive.

When electronic discovery arrives at the firm, the user can browse the contents and make initial determinations as to the character and content of the files. As native file review becomes a greater reality, the legal team is requiring the ability to review the actual Word file in addition to the "petrified" .TIFF image. Instead of installing hundreds of applications, a single application, such as Avanstar's QuickView Plus, makes life much simpler for all.

Website: http://www.Avanstar.com

6. Database Programs

For the more advanced technicians, there are a myriad of database programs available. For example, when a firm inherits a database, there may be some historical problems that require a lot of data manipulation to fix. Examples of problems that require more finesse than a text editor affords are:

1. Inconsistent date format (4/4/01, 2001/4/4, 2001/04/04, 2001/04/4); and
2. Inconsistent Bates format (A1, A0002, A0002.01, A002.A).

Programs such as Concordance and Summation offer users the ability to write their own custom code to fix these types of problems. I strongly urge that every Litigation Support technician learn how to program if only well enough to get past the aforementioned types of hurdles.

Once written, the Litigation Support Department can then reuse the code when the same types of problems manifest themselves in future cases.

Microsoft's Access program is an example of a database program.

7. IPRO IConvert

IConvert converts cross-reference files to one or more of the popular Litigation Support file formats. IConvert also features a verification function to help you ensure the integrity of the files. For example, Summation DII files can be converted to Opticon cross-reference files, and vice versa. As of the writing of this document, IConvert is a free download from IPRO.

Website: http://www.IproCorp.com

8. Password Cracking

Prepare to receive electronic discovery that requires a password the client may not have. Litigation Support can run software that will recover the password.

Passware Kit Enterprise is a recognized leader in cracking passwords. It recovers passwords for files including: Word, Excel, Access, Outlook keys, Lotus Notes, 1-2-3 Key, Acrobat Key, ACT Key, Backup Key, FileMaker Key, Internet Explorer Key, Mail Key, Money Key, MYOB Key, Organizer Key, Outlook Express Key, Paradox Key, Peachtree Key, Quattro Pro Key, QuickBooks Key, Quicken Key, RAR Key, Schedule Key, WordPerfect Key, WordPro Key and Zip Key.

Website: http://wrww.LostPassword.com
Website: http://www.Decryptum.com

9. Macintosh Emulator

Some day a Mac OS CD will arrive, or the legal team will need to create one for a case. Do not bother spending the money for a whole Macintosh machine. Instead buy and install an emulator.

With a utility like MacDisk and MacImage (neither tested nor endorsed by Ad Litem) a Windows PC can read, write and format Apple Macintosh disks, CDs and DVDs. There is no need for any new hardware. Search any major engine for "Mac emulator software" for alternative titles.

Website: http://www.MacDisk.com

10. Email

When dealing with email, the Litigation Support Department's need for software and resources extends beyond the ability to simply send and receive correspondence. The following subsections discuss how the department can take advantage of this tool.

a. Email Readers

Litigation Support will receive discovery files for use with Outlook, GroupWise, Eudora, Netscape and others. One would not want to convert GroupWise email into Outlook, as this will change the files and dates. It may even cause loss of GroupWise metadata while introducing new Outlook metadata. The result can be a court sanction. The Litigation Support Department may need to view the contents, prior to processing into a database. The IT Department can install the most popular email software programs onto the Administrative Server, in the test environment. (See "Administrative Server" and "Production v. Staging" sections.)

Email is also a tool that the department will use on a daily basis to collaborate with team members and create a communications history for each client-matter. Email contains folders. There are also "public folders". Whereas folders are normally private, visible only to the individual, an email administrator can establish a public folder for access by a team.

Team Use

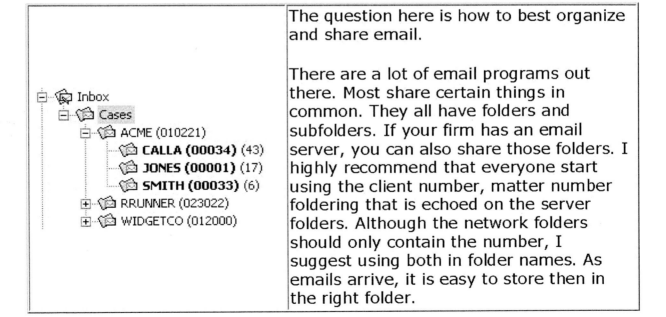

Inbox
 Cases
  ACME (010221)
   CALLA (00034) (43)
   JONES (00001) (17)
   SMITH (00033) (6)
  RRUNNER (023022)
  WIDGETCO (012000)
	The question here is how to best organize and share email.
	
	There are a lot of email programs out there. Most share certain things in common. They all have folders and subfolders. If your firm has an email server, you can also share those folders. I highly recommend that everyone start using the client number, matter number foldering that is echoed on the server folders. Although the network folders should only contain the number, I suggest using both in folder names. As emails arrive, it is easy to store then in the right folder.

As one can see from the example, it would be very easy to provide access to the entire email history for anyone in the Litigation Support Department.

As all work, even internal, relates to a given client-matter, it should be very simple for everyone on the litigation team and in the Litigation Support Department to file and retrieve emails.

b. Email Resources

Listservs

A listserv is an email tool. Every time someone sends an email to the listserv address, all subscribers receive an email copy. All day and every day, Litigation Support persons, vendors and almost every part of the industry pose and answer questions and discuss litigation technology, services and strategies. Depending on various factors, the listserv can be more helpful than contacting the actual software companies.

Have a technical issue? Want to know how others handled a given situation? The participants on the listserv will provide answers and suggestions and caveats. If you want to ask hundreds of other people a question, this is the route. Just remember not to give any case specifics. These emails also provide on-the-job training. You can either participate or simply read the discussions you find interesting.

There are many Yahoo groups, http://groups.yahoo.com, that cover Litigation Support topics. The reader should visit Yahoo groups and search for "Litigation Support". The following are examples of good resources.

Litigation Support

"The Litigation Support Listserv Message Board; The ultimate Litigation Support Group Listserv - Imaging and Coding, Electronic Discovery, Trial Presentation, etc. Questions and Answers. Summation / Concordance / iCONECT / Sanction / Trial Director / IPRO / JFS / Discovery Cracker This message board is the Official Message Board of the LSVA (Litigation Support Vendors Association)."

LitSupport-Announce

This is an opt-in list for members of the LitSupport group who wish to receive vendor announcements from those companies providing Litigation Support technical goods and services. This is also a place for job listings relevant to the field.

LitSupport

This list is intended for the use of those employed in the field of Litigation Support, such as NALSM members, affiliated chapter members, and other Litigation Support Professionals. The purpose of this listserv is to provide a forum for Litigation Support Professionals to exchange ideas, thoughts, questions, and other issues with other professionals.

LawNet

LawNet, http://www.PeerToPeer.org, has a series of listservs that are restricted to law firms. This means one can ask and answer questions without the involvement of any vendors.

About LawNet –

> No staff, let alone individual, has the bandwidth or resources to keep up with and learn all there is to know about the ever-changing technical, strategic and management issues related to the use of technology; and so, networking with one's peers to exchange ideas with those who have "been there, done that," has never been more essential. That is the purpose of LawNet, Inc., the premier peer networking organization in the legal market. For over two decades LawNet has led the way in sharing knowledge and experience for those faced with challenges in their firms and legal departments by providing its members information resources in order to make technology work for the legal profession.

> LawNet members come from firms of all sizes and all areas of practice, each sharing a common need to have access to the latest information about products and support services that impact the legal profession. The dues are reasonable and the benefits tremendous. Membership in LawNet is by entity, so that any interested parties within your firm or legal department can participate in LawNet activities at no additional cost.
>
> -LawNet (©peertopeer.org, 2005)

Vendor Specific and Other Listservs

There are also listservs for almost every software title. Some listservs require the individual be a Firm employee, others are free for all to join. Either way, join all of them, even competing products you do not own. While this industry is high dollar, it is also relatively small in players. One never knows when the Firm may need to switch toward or away from a technology or software title. Reading the listservs is a simple and quick way to keep on top of a lot of chatter.

B. Legal Team

There are a lot of choices these days for most types of software. That being said, the firm needs to pick one title for a given category and then exclude use of all others. It is enough work to support one document review system, so why support more? The advantages range from better user support to better technical work.

1. Case Fact Management

CaseSoft has built a great product. There are huge lists of facts, names, dates, issues and similar information associated with each case. The legal team uses CaseMap to build relationships among the lists. Litigation Support uses the lists to aid both bibliographic coding and court reporters. The software also helps to connect facts and issues. This type of software replaces fact and issue tables the paralegals may have traditionally created in a word processor.

This software integrates with popular document review, transcript management and exhibit software titles, making it useful through the entire case lifecycle.

Website: http://www.CaseSoft.com

2. Document Review Software

Document review software allows the team to review, produce, issue code, and perform reports regarding the demographics of all the above. Whether the firm hosts all document review or uses a hosted solution, Litigation Support can make certain the solution will work with other firm software and in the case technology plan. A hosted solution that doesn't interface with other litigation software may cause delays and extra expenses due to technical considerations.

For firms that host their own discovery databases, there is still the need to have a relationship with a qualified hosting provider. For reasons of storage, scale of project or multi-firm database, the Litigation Support Department may recommend a hosted solution.

The firm can use a hosted solution as a way to try software with special functions, such as document relationship mapping or native file review, without adversely impacting support for other cases or firm operations as a whole.

Although Litigation Support should limit the legal team to a single document review system, the department should own copies of multiple competing titles. Not all software titles can import the load or database files for competing titles. The technician may need to export the data from one software package before he can subsequently load said data into the preferred application.

3. Transcripts

The Litigation Support Department requires a current version of all major transcript software titles. Fortunately, this means LiveNote, RealLegal, Summation and Concordance. The department should already own a copy of the latter two titles.

As with deposition software, the Litigation Support Department needs to select a single title for use by all litigators and paralegals. Through the use of the Litigation Support Technical Standards, the firm requires court reporters to provide their work product, formatted for import by the firm's transcript software. When the court reporter delivers the transcript in odd formats, the Litigation Support Department technician may spend countless hours editing it. Only then can the technician load the transcript into the transcript software.

4. Depoware / Exhibitware

The legal team will need to move their key documents from the document review system to the exhibit software. Documents form the foundation for the attorney as he, or she, deposes or crosses a person. Because issues change based upon testimony, the legal team requires the ability to quickly identify new documents and load them into the exhibit software. The challenge for Litigation Support is to provide a software solution that minimizes turnaround time both finding and then using documents as exhibits.

Note: The need to transition images from the document review software to exhibit software is a prime example of an issue every firm and team faces when the case reaches this stage. The job of Litigation Support is to make certain the software the legal team uses will not adversely impact their ability to move materials from one litigation application to another as the case progresses.

Both Sanction 2 and Trial Director are programs that do this well. As Sanction 2 and Trial Director are direct competitors, the firm should select one application to use and support. PowerPoint, while a good presentation application, does not offer the industry specific functions that the other software titles do. The Litigation Support Department should encourage the team to become comfortable in their use.

Depoware is any software one may use during a deposition. This includes exhibit software, but also extends to applications such as the CaseSoft Suite, including TimeMap.

As Americans are in love with crime drama shows, they watch TV versions of the courtroom experience and expect the same in real life. Reading would indicate that the team that shows video with captions, animations, and timelines has an easier time making its case.

The real advantage is that the exhibits and timelines are now generated dynamically. Should a new critical date appear during testimony, the attorney can instantly update their timeline on a laptop. The results can then appear instantly for the jury, via projector.

Today, there are companies that provide a "courtroom of tomorrow" experience. It behooves the litigator to know what types of options they have when it comes to depositions and trial. That same attorney should always include Litigation Support in any purchase decisions.

2. Hardware

The following discussion addresses the hardware that the Litigation Support Department and legal team can use to achieve goals, such as, expediting review, making DVDs, and reading materials from a wide array of hardware platforms.

A. Litigation Support

The following types of hardware are very useful to the efforts of Litigation Support Department. Mostly, the hardware centers on storage. The first type of storage is the external hard drive.

1. External Hard Drives

Litigation Support can use these inexpensive drives to migrate data from the network server to "near-line" storage, thereby freeing space for other materials. Unlike "off-line" storage, it is very easy to access and copy a large volume of information in one location, the drive, versus dozens of CDs or DVDs.

An external drive is sufficiently small enough and quiet enough to sit on a table, next to the laptop, while storing the entire discovery collection. If using complementary software, the team can actually find a new document on the drive and transfer it to the exhibit software during testimony.

If you are going to receive 10 CDs from the vendor, the media will cost you $250-350 on average. For the same price, you can get an external hard drive. Instead of individually loading each CD to the server, Litigation Support can simply copy the hard drive once. The technician should affix a client-matter number and volume name on the drive and store it in a secure location.

2. Hub

Whereas a laptop may only have 1 USB connection, a hub provides extra connections. If the attorney wishes to connect multiple devices (e.g., printer, projector, hard drive, bar code reader) to one machine, at an average price of $20 - $60, this is a cheap investment for such convenience.

3. Smart Media Hub

These days memory sticks and flash drives for laptops and cameras are everywhere. The day will come when someone sends important photos or video or discovery on this media format. There are hubs for sale that will accommodate multiple types of portable media. As it is a small investment, i.e., $30, the firm should purchase one for the Litigation Support Department.

4. iOmega Zip Drive

One day soon, a client is going to provide you with a zip disk. A vendor will open it for you, but sometimes it is nicer to know what is on the disk first. Zip disks are being replaced by CDs and other portable media, but you will certainly have the need to open old disks from your clients.

5. Administrative Server

In technical circles, administrators talk about "test" and "production" environments. Technicians perform tasks in the test environment that could provide devastating to individual cases or the firm. Once the technician generates the required results, he or she moves it to the production environment for access by the legal team. All legal teams run their software and access their data in the production environment. An administrative server is designed to match the production server used by the legal team, but it exists in the test environment.

The test environment and administrative server provide a safe place for the technician to massage data, create productions and open native files. A virus on the client's electronic discovery could infect and crash this server without any impact on the legal team. A virus on the production environment could infect all servers and workstations, causing serious damage to all data stored on the firm network.

This type of threat is a prime reason the firm must require all litigators and paralegals to route all media through the Litigation Support Department. To limit the exposure, the firm should employ a separate network, relatively free, and a separate "administrative" server.

If the Firm is not ready for a Litigation Support Department administrative server, external hard drives can provide an appropriate staging area. Litigation Support Department should work with the IT Department to minimize impact and risk for the production server, and thereby provide a safe area for data analysis.

Depending upon how the firm operates, the document review software may reside on the local PC, or a network server that is either shared with all departments or is used solely for litigation. The databases and associated images may also reside on either a shared or private server. Regardless of where the software resides, there are organizational rules everyone should follow. The Network Folders section of the book covers these rules.

Technical Works-in-Progress

The database that the legal team reviews may be the grandchild of several earlier versions. When the vendor delivers new data for the discovery review system, there is a chance that the structure and organization of the data may not match the firm technical standard. The use of prequalified vendors helps to alleviate this concern. Nevertheless, the Litigation Support Department should not perform database administration on the same database the legal team uses for review.

Litigation Support will make a backup copy of each database before working on it. There are occasions when the Litigation Support technician will need to spend hours correcting technical problems. Sometimes the database has to go through several steps before the finished product is ready for the Firm. As a precaution, the Litigation Support Department technician should keep multiple versions, as a way to backtrack in the future due to new issues.

Hardware & Software Requirements

The amount of technical work the department performs will help the department VP of Operations determine the type of hardware and software most appropriate for the test environment. It may be possible to use older servers and equipment for this purpose. In this fashion the Litigation Support Department may get this *used* hardware for free or nominal cost. This approach has a second advantage as the firm IT Department will continue to perform administration on these familiar machines.

The Litigation Support Department will need to purchase licenses for the software tools most appropriate for the services offered. This book advocates the business approach to running the Litigation Support Department. Accordingly, the department should be able to generate revenues through billed goods and services. The department can then use this money to buy the appropriate resources: servers, software, storage, training and so forth.

Shared versus private servers

While many people have heard of a "file server", many are unaware of the "application server." Certain litigation software titles require a private application server, regardless of where the technician stores the associated databases, native files and images. The data may reside on the application server, a shared or private file server. If the firm storage needs and geography results in the need for multiple servers, the need for consistent folder organization and backup routines become significant.

Remember: If you receive a hard drive instead of CDs from a vendor, don't use this hard drive for any work. Save this data to CDs or DVDs. As a hard drive may represent hundreds of CDs, one needs an automated way to create and label the media, the "robotic media burner."

Disaster Recovery

In the disaster recovery section, the reader is directed to identify each repository of litigation data and calculate the cost to provide an appropriate level of support. This section asks the reader to address the potential need for a separate administrative storage area.

6. Robotic Media Burners

Robotic CD/DVD burners and autoloaders perform the grunt-work, including the act of labeling, thereby freeing technicians to work on other tasks. Start counting how many CDs and DVDs your Litigation Support Department creates or receives. The numbers may surprise you, unless you are a Litigation Support professional. It can take from 15 to 30 minutes to create and label a full DVD.

A robotic burner is superior to a simple CD copier in that one can load a stack of 1 set of CDs and the copier can create three new sets, with labels. A CD copier can copy a single CD multiple times, but may still require a person to manually load the next original for copying.

The manufacturer can equip the burner to make CDs or CDs and DVDs. While the DVD burners are a little more expensive, it is worth the cost because it will provide for a quicker turnaround time, and more legal teams are using the format due to the increased storage over CDs.

If you receive your deliveries on an external hard drive instead of CDs, the robot burner can make a set of CDs for you overnight. If the department can spend 10 cents per CD instead of $35 per CD, and bill clients for media, this will pay for a robot burner.

Example Hardware
The following examples are simply examples to help the reader begin their own research into an appropriate solution for their environment.

Brands   Picture

    1. Rimage
    2. Primera
    3. MicroTech
    4. MFDigital

Printer Option

An upgrade to the standard robot burner is a label printer. If one gets a robot, one should also get the printer. The machine will label the media. Again, this is a tremendous time saver. After manually printing and applying labels to a few hundred CDs, you'll be glad you opted for the upgrade.

Thermal printers provide the best quality. If, however, you are just printing text, as with most labels, then an ink jet might suffice. Be sure to take a look at a label printed both ways to determine your preference.

7. Robot Loaders

While Litigation Support uses the robotic burner to create media for sending to third parties, or storing internally, the department uses a robot loader to copy optical media to the network.

A robot loader can copy a set of 100 CDs to the Firm file server without the constant attention of a person. This is a great time saver for Litigation Support staff, who would rather spend their time on technical work than babysitting a PC while it copies each CD to the network. As vendors and legal staff deliver CDs on a regular basis, the stack of media to load can get very tall. A robotic loader loads all these CDs. I believe a better use of the technician's time is spent on database administration than loading CDs.

This robotic loading really comes in handy when copying those 50 CDs to the network happens overnight. The technicians, fresh from home, can then concentrate on loading the new images and data to the database - a much better use of technician time. Also the data becomes available to the review team much more quickly.

8. Nylon Binders

Nylon binders are idea for storing large quantities of CDs and DVDs. As the Litigation Support Department should be the central library, or inventory, for all discovery media, it will need many binders. They take up a lot less space than the jewel cases, and weigh less too.

Litigation Support should keep a copy of every CD in their inventory. If there is an emergency, it is much easier for Litigation Support to find the original CD in a binder 10 feet away than if the CD is with one of three paralegals. This being said, Litigation Support has to keep a good inventory list, for looking through a 1,000 CDs is a pain no matter where they are stored.

One may use separate binders for every client and client-matter, or simply just keep adding new media to the next available slot (chronologically ordered instead of case ordered).

9. Projector

If the attorney or paralegal wants people to see what is on a screen, they should really project it onto the wall. A projector of at least 1,200 lumens is suggested.

10. Thumb Drives

A thumb drive is a small piece of hardware around the size of a thumb. These drives hold anywhere from 128MB to 1GB and more. Plug it into the USB port and it appears as a new drive letter on the laptop. If one needs to copy or transfer documents, PowerPoint presentations, or other files, this is a great way to transport data.

11. Monitors

The monitor is the single easiest way to provide a better work environment and increase review speed for all cases. Please reference the section on Monitors for full information.

B. Legal Team

The firm should provide the legal team with the most appropriate hardware for the work they must perform. At court, this may mean a projector. During the discovery phases, it means multiple monitors for each document review station.

1. Trial and Deposition Hardware

There is a wide array of hardware the legal team may use at trial and this topic is easily a book unto itself. This text, therefore, only provides suggestions about trial and deposition hardware.

Whether the Litigation Support Department provides trial support services or not, it should offer the hardware. The firm can either pay to rent the same types of hardware such as a projector and screen, or charge enough to pay for the investment by the Department. If, as example, the Accounting Department will depreciate a $2,000 projector over 36 months, the cost to each client will be nominal. As every attorney in every group will use this type of equipment, it may be in the best interest of the firm to have the IT Department purchase this hardware for use by all. The responsible department can assign the hardware to case teams at no charge. Should the requirements by the team exceed internal hardware abilities, such as higher resolution or more Lumens (brightness), the Department should consider purchasing or renting.

If the Litigation Support Department handles actual support, such as set-up and tear-down, the charge to the client should be for their time. This is in addition to billing for project management work.

2. Scanners

This book in no way advocates having anyone from the legal team perform any major scanning. It does, however, recommend that the legal team employ and have access to scanning hardware. As any document arrives, such as a pleading, the team should scan these materials for use in the cases. The attorney, paralegal or administrative assistant should send copies, via email, to the Litigation Support Department.

3. Fax Server

Technically, everyone, lawyer, paralegal and support staff can enjoy the benefits of this hardware. For organizational purposes, however, the fax server appears here in the text. The legal team, and everyone else at a firm, can use a fax server to both send and receive faxes through their word processor and email programs. This eliminates the need to print and manually fax. Eliminate the need for a person to stand next to a fax machine, make copies and otherwise route paper to people within the firm. An attorney can send and receive faxes from any location on Earth, without printing or the involvement of other people.

4. Monitors

The person performing document review needs to simultaneously view both the database information and the image of the document. This means providing the person with either a very large screen or more than one screen. The goal for Litigation Support is to make certain that the screen(s) are large enough for the reviewer to easily read a document and database information simultaneously.

Monitors are inexpensive and can significantly boost productivity, quality, speed and morale. Service bureaus providing manual coding services understand this and, consequently, many shops provide their document reviewers with multiple monitors.

Today, the flat panel, LCD, screen is inexpensive and takes up very little space on the desktop. By switching from a traditional tube monitor to an LCD screen, the user can even hang it on the cubical or office wall. The user regains real desk space, previously occupied by the monitor.

A second monitor increases the number of documents an attorney can review per hour. It also aids the Litigation Support technician who works closely with all document review databases.

a. Single Monitor Review Station

One person, one monitor is what most firms employ today. Some people actually squint at 15" laptop screen while others use 19" monitors. If only afforded a single screen, the smallest monitor that any document review person should use is 19". When employing multiple screens, smaller screens can suffice.

The firm may be hesitant to deploy multiple monitors for fear everyone will want one; however this may not be a bad thing, considering the advantages detailed below. Although one could argue the second monitor is a requirement for a proper document review workstation, the firm needs to provide the appropriate resources to all persons, Litigation Support or litigator in order to generate the best results.

Switching to a dual monitor

When your firm looks at upgrading monitors, it is also wondering what to do with the old ones. The answer is to have people performing document reviewer use both. Instead of buying a big monitor, buy a monitor that pivots and a graphics card.

b. Dual Monitor Review Station

There are many products in the marketplace that offer multiple screen configurations, such as 2 LCD screens on a single stand. They are great, and I highly recommend them for accounting people who want to see 20 columns at one time instead of 10.

Spreadsheets are made for the landscape orientation. Your current monitor is probably in landscape orientation (i.e. wider than tall). A landscape oriented screen is not ideal for viewing portrait orientation documents. An estimated 95% of all documents use the portrait orientation. Therefore the second monitor should accommodate the portrait orientation.

The second monitor that we are after here is the type monitor that pivots. Users can physically rotate the screen to the portrait orientation for viewing the document images. A scanned page fits perfectly full-screen on a portrait mode monitor. If the reviewer can view the entire page without moving the mouse or hitting a keystroke, review moves faster. A 17" screen is an ideal size.

Note: A 17" screen, in portrait mode, will almost perfectly fit the paper and display the entire page at a time. Even a 21" monitor, in landscape mode, does not display the page as well.

Monitor 1 - Data Screen - 15" or Greater: The document review database, bibliographic coding, searches and all work product reside on this screen. Because the data window fills the full screen, everything is easier to read and there is less scrolling.

Monitor 2 - Image Screen - 17" of Greater and Pivot: This monitor, pivoted 90 degrees, displays the corresponding .TIF image full screen. At 17", the image approximates life size. As a standalone monitor, it can be repurposed for other reviews and moved to other reviewer desktops.

A good example is the ViewSonic VP201s. This monitor is 20", hangs on the wall or sits on a stand and pivots. This monitor is $1,000. You can get a 17" for much less. If you are going to have people in cubicles performing review, the ability to hang the monitor on the wall pays for itself in terms of desk space.

The big secret to getting the most from your second monitor is the pivot feature. Not all monitors can pivot, so expect to pay a little more. It is absolutely worth it. In fact, a 17" pivoted monitor can display the entire page of a document where a 19" non-pivoted monitor can either display part of the image or displays a much shrunken "full-page" view. Associates have told me they would refuse to perform future reviews without that second monitor, due to the benefits.

For a one-time cost of less than $1,000 per document reviewer, the Firm speeds doc review time for all cases. Because the document review will end sooner, the team gets more time to prepare. It is also demoralizing to the other side when the productions come fast and furious.

Be certain the IT Department is able to install and support the extra hardware. Litigation Support shouldn't be responsible for the monitors.

c. Triple Monitor Review Station

Picture ©2004 Chris Hedlund

The triple monitor station is really a dual screen along with the image monitor. The advantage here is the ability to use the third screen for email, legal research, Internet browsing or other functions. These incidental tasks do not need to interrupt the review process because all work takes place on another screen.

Gallery of Multiple Monitor Configurations

Hobbyists, NORAD, stock traders and other people have been taking advantage of multiple monitor sets for years. There is a great gallery of multiple monitor systems available at RealTimeSoft.

Visit the site at http://www.realtimesoft.com/multimon/

This site is great for learning all about multiple monitors. It details what hardware and software is required. It has reviews of various graphics cards and more. A multiple monitor configuration can be the single greatest aid the firm can provide to reviewers in their efforts to provide expedited and top quality results.

V. Litigation Case Lifecycle

A consistent case lifecycle provides the Litigation Support Department with the ability to offer a consistent technology plan, applicable to all cases. The following sections trace the case lifecycle from the perspectives of software, project management, and discovery, from collection to trial.

For the purposes of this book, there are nine phases to the case lifecycle. Phases 1 through Phases 3 are concerned with the creation and execution of a discovery plan for the case. Phase 4 and Phase 5 begin and end the review processes. Phase 6 is depositions, Phase 7, pre-trial preparation, Phase 8, trial and, finally, Phase 9, case "tear down."

1. Software Lifecycle

The firm should evaluate each software application based upon individual merits: consider ease of use, level of utility in achieving case goals, special capabilities, security and so forth. One consideration that must precede all others is how each application complements the other applications in the software lifecycle. The legal team should be able to transfer facts and images from one application to another without involving technical support. The Software Lifecycle outlines each phase of the case lifecycle and explains how the team and the Litigation Support Department can use software tools to achieve phase goals.

Best practices, as regards the software lifecycle, means limiting the amount of training, effort and cost to transfer information from application to application and phase to phase throughout the entire case lifecycle. Each tool must be able to seamlessly share information with the other tools and between team members during each phase. The tools in one phase must be able to share information with the tools in each subsequent phase. Each person's work in any application should be synchronized with that of the other team members. Access to the most up-to-date information by the whole team is vital to successful litigation.

A. Phase 1 through Phase 3

Preliminary through Finalize and Execute Discovery Plan

Results: The VP of Operations aids the attorney in constructing a litigation technology budget. This task requires a list of every potential discovery cache. The identification of key names, key terms, and culling preferences helps lower the cost estimate, by limiting the amount of discovery processed for review. The attorney's production agreement with opposing counsel includes technical considerations the Litigation Support Department can accommodate. Finally, the qualified vendor begins processing discovery, per the list of collections and schedule.

Software:

Case Fact Management Software – The legal team uses the "CFMS" to organize all case details, through all phases. Any person can get up to speed very quickly even on complex cases by reviewing the fact management software. Subsequent efforts will use the key names, terms and dates as identified in the software.

Litigation Budget Spreadsheet – Both Litigation Support and the legal team share this spreadsheet. Both groups use the spreadsheet for estimating the technology budget as well as tracking case related litigation technology goods, services and contact information. The spreadsheet also helps the team identify all client information repositories, as well as key names and terms.

B. Phase 4 through Phase 5

Ongoing Review through Production

Results: After the legal team carefully reviews the preproduction collections, the VP of Operations creates production sets, along with stamps and required redactions. The VP of Operations loads the productions from opposing counsel, which is subsequently reviewed by the team.

Software:

Document Management System - The legal team uses the "DMS" to review for production and then for issues. Many documents become exhibits presented at depositions and trial. It is vitally important that the team be able to easily move information between the DMS, CFMS and exhibit software.

Case Fact Management Software - The team uses the "CFMS" to organize key facts learned during review. All the key names appear inside the CFMS. The team uses facts and documents they identify in the DMS to build chronologies and gain special insights into the case as a whole.

Exhibit Software - The legal team uses presentation software to display key documents and video during depositions. As the case matures, the team looks for documents according to issues. The ability to find and transfer documents from the DMS to the exhibit software provides an especially potent tool when the attorney can perform these tasks in response to live testimony.

Litigation Budget Spreadsheet – During these phases, the Litigation Support Department can track the difference between estimated and actual cost. The VP of Operations can update the spreadsheet to include subsequent projects, such as stamping. In this fashion, the VP of Operations creates a complete treatment history, along with total cost. The VP of Operations updates the spreadsheet to reflect the production media received from opposing counsel.

C. Phase 6

Depositions

Results: At the end of this phase, the team will have reviewed all transcripts, identified key "Q&A" pairs, new essential documents, issues and facts which now reside in the CFMS and exhibit software.

Software:

Document Management System - As a case matures, the issues change. The team uses the DMS to find new documents and add them to CFMS and exhibit software.

Case Fact Management Software - The team links key "Q&A Pairs" from transcripts to case facts, issues, people and dates. Among other reasons, the team uses this software to show relationships and build chronologies.

Exhibit Software - The team transfers new transcript and video exhibits to the list of available exhibits.

Transcript Software - The team identifies important Q&A pairs and issues in transcripts. The team creates annotations and otherwise organizes the content for use in the case.

Litigation Budget Spreadsheet – After this phase, the Litigation Support Department can track the difference between estimated and actual cost for deposition related costs, such as a court reporter and videographer.

D. Phase 7

Final Pre-Trial Preparation

Results: The team has all the necessary hardware and software support necessary for trial. During trial they can search the entire collection and project new exhibits for the jury to view. They can also create custom chronologies in response to issues raised during testimony. The team is comfortable with the tools and is ready for trial.

Software:

Case Fact Management Software - Every case fact and figure, quote, document and video clip is available for use as an exhibit. The team can create exhibits from any of this information to support their arguments.

Document Management System - The team performs final issue searching for documents to use as exhibits at trial. All documents now reside in folders or are otherwise grouped for easy retrieval at a later point.

Exhibit Software - The team loads all potential exhibits into the exhibit software. This includes newly discovered documents and transcript Q&A pairs. The team will continue to transfer exhibits from the CFMS and DMS throughout the trial.

Transcript Software - The team searches for any further quotes that relate to any given issue. The attorney then transfers this information to the CFMS and exhibit software for use at trial.

E. Phase 8

Trial

Results: On a daily basis, the team finds new exhibits from existing collections as well as new transcripts. As this process happens during the length of the trial, the ability of the team to identify and create new exhibits with minimal time and effort is critical to the success of the case.

Software:

Document Management System - The team finds documents relating to issues. These become exhibits in the exhibit software application.

Case Fact Management Software - As the case progresses, testimony will raise issues and the need to find the type of information stored in this software.

Exhibit Software - Attorneys display exhibits at trial during cross-examinations, opening and closing. Exhibits are added and modified during each stage of the trial itself.

Transcript Software - The team adds new testimony into transcript software. The team then exports facts and Q&A pairs to the CFMS and Exhibit software packages.

F. Phase 9

Case "Tear Down"

Results: The VP of Operations updates the firm copy of CFMS, DMS, exhibits and transcripts software files to reflect any changes made during trial. All case materials are retired to offline storage, or otherwise treated, according to attorney direction. The attorney receives a final, updated, budget spreadsheet showing the actual cost to litigate versus the estimated cost or in an appeal.

Aside from providing the VP of Operations with the updated files, the legal team is done with the matter. This is not to say that the team is done with the materials. The team may use exhibits from this matter for a related case.

The VP of Operations will work with the attorney to determine what information can stay and what can go to backup tape. An order to destroy certain materials is also a possibility. The VP of Operations and attorney can use the Budget Spreadsheet to identify the various collections, databases and their treatment.

Software:

Document Management System - If the team used a satellite copy of the DMS databases and images, the VP of Operations should update the firm's copies to reflect changes made in the field. The team needs to make certain the Litigation Support Department gets all materials: software files, external hard drives and so forth.

Case Fact Management Software -The team should synchronize their CFMS files with the shared copy on the network server.

Exhibit Software - The legal team should submit the latest version of their exhibit software files to the Litigation Support Department for inventory and updating the network version.

Transcript Software - The team should synchronize their transcript software files with the shared copy on the network server.

Litigation Budget Spreadsheet – The VP of Operations and attorney can review the budget spreadsheet, updated to show the total actual cost for litigation technology. The VP of Operations and attorney can compare the estimated costs against the actual costs in order to provide a better estimate on the next matter.

2. Case Lifecycle Task List

This task list walks the Litigation Support Department through the entire case lifecycle. By following this lifecycle, the Litigation Support Department provides all parties with a consistent experience for every case. This lifecycle meshes with the flowchart, budget spreadsheet, and technical standards. While the task list assumes the Litigation Support Department has achieved a complete and successful implementation of the principles outlined in the book, use of this list does not require it.

This lifecycle matches the discovery lifecycle flowchart (included here). Whereas the flowchart provides an understanding of how discovery flows as the case matures, this task list details the actual project management steps. As the flowchart illustrates, there are steps that may repeat, such as rolling productions. Each of these steps may require certain persons to repeat their associated tasks accordingly.

Litigation Support does not always begin work during the pleading phase. As such, the department's first task is to begin handling the case, and data, according to the task list. Only then can both the Litigation Support Department and legal team be certain they are following a proven technology plan that minimizes the chance of future technical problems.

The reader should only use the lifecycle task list in the book for reference purposes. For actual case work, the VP of Operations should create a fresh copy of the included Microsoft Project file, as included on the CD, named for the client matter number. The Litigation Support Department technician or project manager will update this file as the case progresses.

Throughout the case lifecycle, the Litigation Support Department will need to perform standard tasks, e.g., generating blow-backs, dealing with legacy databases, incoming media, and generating productions to opposing. These tasks are too involved and occur too sporadically to place in the lifecycle. Therefore the lifecycle references these "supporting" tasks. These tasks actually reference each other. To learn more about the tasks, please read the section, "Litigation Support Tasks."

Although the flowchart only covers up through the production phase, through the following lifecycle sections, one can understand how the department and legal team use the document review software for exhibit purposes.

The following is a rough overview of the phases as they relate to the technology plan and task list.

A. Phase 1 through Phase 3

Plan and Execute Discovery Plan

Phase 1: Preliminary

Results:

The Litigation Support Department and attorney create an estimated litigation technology budget, preliminary list of discovery caches, list of key names, and key terms.

Strategy:

Use this information throughout the case. Put the important names, dates and collection information into the Case Fact Management Software. Use this information to identify, cull and create the preproduction discovery databases. Court reporters use these names and terms to provide a better transcript. Bibliographic coding companies, manual and automated, use these words to provide better products, as well. These strategies should work for every case.

Phase 2: Discovery Planning

Results:

Litigation Support and the attorney update the technology budget, list of collections, and agreements regarding production format and ways to limit discovery formalized with opposing counsel.

Strategy:

If both sides can agree to limit all potentially productive discovery to those documents which were authored or received by key individuals, that contain a key word and also falls within a date range, it may be possible to dramatically reduce the size of the database, the number of hours of review, and the cost to the clients of both firms. The attorney can now be confident that his team will be technically capable of producing to the required format of opposing counsel. Additionally, the legal team knows that they will receive productions in a format their Litigation Support Department prefers. Again, this saves time and cost to all parties.

Phase 3: Finalize and Execute Discovery Plan

Results:

A qualified technician, employed by firm or vendor, begins collecting and processing discovery per the matrix, schedule and culling preferences. As the Litigation Support

Department has prequalified the vendor, the technical aspect of their goods and services will match the department needs.

Strategy:

This minimizes turnaround times on the parts of both the vendor and the department. The strategy is to get all materials in front of the review team in the least amount of time. On a large project with a rolling production, the Litigation Support Department can update the budget to reflect actual costs and deadlines as pertain to each collection. In this manner, the Litigation Support Department can keep the legal team informed as to total cost and schedule.

B. Phase 4 through Phase 5

Ongoing Review through Production

Phase 4: Ongoing Review - Ongoing Issues

Results:

The team and Litigation Support Department can produce all non-privileged documents, including required Bates stamp, text stamp, annotations and redactions.

Strategy:

The Litigation Support Department should be able to produce documents in the appropriate format, per agreement, with a minimum of cost and time.

Phase 5: Production

Results:

The legal team produces all documents, in the appropriate format. The legal team, in turn, receives and reviews those documents produced by opposing counsel. The Litigation Support Department updates the budget spreadsheet to reflect the total cost to review and produce the discovery materials. The legal team continues a case-long effort to find potential exhibits in the discovery database.

Strategy:

The production agreement from Phase 2 now takes effect. The cost and time for a technician to administrate the databases is kept to a minimum when both sides keep to the agreed format. If the other side is unable to meet their commitment, the attorney can use this to advantage.

C. Phase 6

Depositions

Results:

With all transcripts reviewed, the Case Fact Management Software is updated to reflect new facts, issues and "Q&A" pairs. The legal team continues to find additional potential exhibits in the discovery database as the testimony effects which issues are most important.

Strategy:

Improve the quality of the transcripts by providing the names and terms from the case fact management software to the court reporters. The Litigation Support Department can also load these words into the transcript software. Most transcript software uses the same words to provide additional functionality to aid the attorney, such as highlighting terms.

D. Phase 7

Final Pre-Trial Preparation

Results:

All exhibits, hardware and support are ready for trial. The legal team continues to find additional potential exhibits in the discovery database as the testimony affects which issues are most important.

Strategy:

The Litigation Support Department makes certain that the legal team will have access to all case materials from any location, such as the war, deposition and trial rooms. The department also makes certain that the team has the equipment and trial support they require.

E. Phase 8

Trial

Results:

On a daily basis, Litigation Support Department works to make certain the team has access to updated exhibits and transcripts.

Strategy:

During depositions and trial, it is urgent that the legal team be able to use today's transcripts as exhibits tomorrow. The team can update information in the case fact management software to understand how new facts relate to established facts and issues and people.

F. Phase 9

Case "Tear Down"

As some cases settle, this phase may actually occur earlier. It is certainly the final phase. The Litigation Support Department updates the Budget Spreadsheet to reflect the actual cost for litigation technology goods and services. The VP of Operations can now move all electronic materials, databases, images, case fact management files and so forth to near-line or off-line storage, as the attorney requires.

Results:

It is common for the attorney to use materials from one matter in another or in an appeal. It is also possible to have a destruct order. At the end of this phase, the Litigation Support Department provides the final treatments, per attorney requirements.

Strategy:

The Litigation Support Department must always be ready to produce a copy of media, or access to materials in the future. The Litigation Support Department media inventory addresses the first concern. The department can address the second concern by making DVDs of all databases, less the images, and case files, such as transcripts. No matter how the electronic materials change over time, the Litigation Support Department should always be able to provide all materials as they existed at the completion of a matter. The clerk can label and put these DVDs into the inventory.

3. Discovery Lifecycle

This section covers how to handle discovery from an administrative and analysis level. To gain a high-level view of the lifecycle, please reference the lifecycle flowchart in the Support Documents section and on the CD. Litigation Support Department should provide the flowchart to every legal team at the start of a case.

This lifecycle matches the lifecycles illustrated in the diagram as well as outlined in the Case Lifecycle Task List, in the Supporting Files section.

A. Phase 1 through Phase 3

Preliminary through Finalize and Execute Discovery Plan

Results:

The lifecycle begins with technical specifications. All technical specifications surrounding the collection and conversion to a reviewable and inevitably producible database occur during Phase 1 through Phase 3. Litigation Support and the legal team list all discovery caches in the Litigation Budget Spreadsheet. During these phases, the vendor, or whomever, collects all potentially discoverable materials and begins the conversion process for review. The vendor will process the materials to the specifications of the firm. This includes matching the firm technical standards as well as any culling preferences.

Strategy:

Together, Litigation Support and the attorney can create a simple discovery matrix, identifying every possible cache of information, estimating quantities and the proper manner for collection, according to the law. The Litigation Support Department provides the Litigation Budget Spreadsheet for this purpose.

In the world of electronic discovery there could be a dozen caches of information for each deponent. The spreadsheet is the ideal location to identify them. After this point, the attorney can determine which information warrants extraction for the legal team to review.

Locations:

Preproduction discovery resides with at least three parties at this point in the case: client, vendor and firm. One goal is to find everything potentially relevant and move it into a database the attorneys can use for review, production and exhibits. Another is to make certain the collection and conversion process addresses all risk management concerns.

Please review the disaster recovery plan to determine which back-up tapes contain client-matter materials.

- Client
- Vendor
- Firm
- Back-Up Tapes
- Printed Paper

Subsections:

- Discovery Specifications
- Database Strategies
- Pre-Discovery
- Discovery QC Strategies
- Case "Tear Down"

Discovery Specifications

When a technician creates a database and processes discovery, use of the firm's technical specifications is critical to success of the project. The specifications require technical and strategic knowledge. If an attorney or paralegal makes an independent decision, the results can mean losing the case due to technical obstacles.

Discovery has changed. Email, databases and voice mail require different technical specifications than paper, and each other. The hard part is to keep treatment consistent across cases irrespective of the character of discovery. The end result needs to be such that the firm can use the results without any problems. The answer is to create a single document that addresses every type of discovery, associated processing, and product requirements.

The Firm's Litigation Support Technical Standards document gives everyone a point-of-reference for addressing any problems or questions. When the vendor asks the paralegals how they want their data, the answer is always "refer to the Standards document and Litigation Support." The Technical Standards document and the requirement to use prequalified vendors are addressed elsewhere, so I will move on.

As the Standard answers all the major technical issues, this part of the course concentrates on strategy and how to move the resulting database and images from pleading through to trial. Litigation Support needs to understand case lifecycle to understand the strategies. If the VP of Marketing is an attorney, this is a chance for him, or her, to gain a special understanding of the Litigation Support perspective.

Litigation Support needs to work with the legal team to understand that these Standards benefit the firm. These specifications positively impact the team's ability to access and use discovery. The Standards help future vendors and Litigation Support minimize the amount of time needed for discovery to reach attorney eyes. It also then helps when transitioning work product and data from a document review system to deposition and trial exhibit software. When technical specifications are not well planned, the different software requirements may mean a trip to the vendor, increased costs, and longer turnaround time.

Database Strategies

Each pre-production database needs eight fields for production purposes. Remember to stay consistent with your choice of field names for all preproduction databases at the firm. This is because the reviewers are going to grow to recognize them, and there should be no need to make the reviewers learn new field names for each database, pre-production, or production.

The "pre-production" fields end in "PP".

Field Name	Status	Purpose
BEGBATESPP	*Pre*-Production	Internal control number, starting page number. This image key "links" to an unstamped image.
ENDBATESPP	*Pre*-Production	Internal control number, ending page number.
BEGATTPP	*Pre*-Production	Internal control number, starting attachment range page number
ENDATTPP	*Pre*-Production	Internal control number, ending attachment range page number.
BEGBATES	Production	Every production Bates number, starting page numbers for each production created.
ENDBATES	Production	Every production Bates number, ending page numbers for each production done.
BEGATT	Production	Every production Bates number, starting page numbers for each production attachment range.
ENDATT	Production	Every production Bates number, ending page numbers for each production attachment range.

The prefix identifies the source. Be sure to keep track of what each one represents. The Litigation Budget Spreadsheet provides a central location for team and department to do this.

Images

To view the produced version images, one must open that production database. If another production set is required, a copy is available in inventory and on the image server.

Pre-Discovery

This is the best time for Litigation Support and the attorney to talk about the nature of the incoming discovery. Litigation Support needs to know how many GBs or TBs of information the matter may contain. Depending on capacity, a firm that traditionally hosts discovery internally may use a hosted solution. The Litigation Support Department technicians may only have time to play a project management role. As one can tell, there are more considerations around this point, too, such as hiring and which services to offer. Depending upon the type of discovery, the Litigation Support Department may need the IT Department to set up new hardware or install new software for use by either the legal team or Litigation Support. Installation may be on the staging or production environment, per the "Production v. Staging" and "Disaster Recovery" sections.

Your firm may have a specific approach that it prefers to use rather than an idea or strategy in the book. Evaluate the merits of each way and use what works best. If the answer disrupts the Software Lifecycle, it may not be worth using.

Litigation Support starts handling discovery by estimating total volume of discovery in boxes and GBs, potential data caches, such as file cabinets and file servers, and then working with the legal team to determine how best to limit what reaches the review team through filtering (or "culling") and extraction strategies.

Total Volume of Discovery

This is the time to outline every potential data cache, type and quantity. Are there 10 deponents? Do they all have paper and electronic discovery for team review? Where do they store their data? If the people no longer work for the client, what happened to their paper and electronic files? Did their PC or laptop hard drive get reformatted for use by other employees? Is forensics help required? What is the exposure to the case and firm for internal versus vendor involvement in the collection and conversion of source materials to a reviewable database?

For our purposes here, the attorney can provide a good ballpark estimate using the Litigation Budget Spreadsheet. The attorney will want an estimate of price at this point for the client. The ability to provide a spreadsheet that lets everyone play with the numbers has great value.

Types of Discovery

Discovery comes in two main formats: paper and electronic. Considerations around paper include bindings and boxes. Electronic discovery can mean text files. It also includes email for every possible software title and operating system. It can also mean a relational database that requires the team or expert to review in native format.

The legal team can not always review all electronic file types with the same software. While the goal is to move all file types into a single software title for review, this is not always possible. When the VP of Operations understands the various types of files associated with each collection, he, or she, can take the appropriate steps to ensure a smooth review for the team and production by the technician.

If the discovery contains spreadsheets, consider a native file review. Spreadsheets are not printer friendly and may contain thousands of blank pages in even a small file. Further, it is easier on the attorney to review it in this fashion. When it is time to produce the spreadsheet, the attorney can do so as a spreadsheet or in paper or image form.

Culling vs. Extracting

At this stage, the team has access to the greatest possible amount of discovery, ranging from the single, proverbial "smoking gun" document to the 1,000 emails about getting lunch. The goal is to exclude as much of the collection as possible by first eliminating for factors such as date ranges, and then extracting, or processing, only those documents that meet the team's key words and search criteria. "Extraction" is the process of turning native files into a reviewable database with images. "Culling" is excluding documents based on factors such as a duplicate document or document date range.

Unfortunately the paper discovery vendor would need to scan and code the documents in order to make most culling determinations. The firm must pay for processing of documents they will never review. Such is the case for paper discovery. For electronic discovery, however, it is possible to extract and convert into a reviewable database only those native files which contain key terms. It is also possible to extract these documents before any others. One of the greatest things about electronic discovery is the ability to identify and process the most important documents first. The most important documents are those which contain key words and names, per the case fact management software.

Eliminating Duplicates

Let's say a Word file gets emailed to 500 people in the company. If the vendor eliminates duplicate documents *by source*, the database will have 500 copies, one file for each person. If the vendor removes duplicates *across sources*, the database will have a total of one copy. Is it only important to know that the company had the Word file? Is it more important to know whose copy of the Word file is at issue? Make sure the attorneys know the ramifications of their choices.

Extraction Sequencing

1. Create three lists: key terms, privileged and non-privileged key names.
   On a large collection where the vendor will provide the database on a "rolling" production (e.g., weekly) basis, the following strategy can help get the team reviewing the most important materials first.
2. Extract Privileged: create your privilege database.
3. Extract keywords, not privileged: create the non-privileged database.
4. Extract key names from what is left: add to the non-privileged database.

Date Ranges

For cases that only require client materials that fall within a specific date range, the vendor can automatically exclude any discovery that falls outside of this range. The database will not contain excluded materials. Subsequently, the team need never review them.

Perhaps one of the single greatest ways to trim down the size of review is to have both sides agree to a list of sources, names, terms and dates. In this fashion, a million pages of discovery can become 100,000 pages. This represents significant savings to the client for both EDD services and attorney time.

Litigation Support can use the Collection to Production PowerPoint presentation to explain this whole process.

Discovery QC Strategies

Although the discovery may be paper, video or spreadsheets in another language, it all gets turned into something that is stored on DVD or hard drive. Therefore, one must adhere to an organization strategy for all of these materials. As example, by storing all data for all programs under the client matter number, we always know what the path values are for all our load files. This means we can require it in our Firm Standard. It also means we can track storage, thereby giving the Firm the ability to bill for hosting. It also means we can "back track" administratively to figure out where to find historical files.

This unified approach also means the ability to have a technical standard. What a relief it will be for the Litigation Support Department when vendor deliveries are loaded into the firm system with minimal effort. The elimination of the most common technical problems should allow people to concentrate on the incoming materials that do require hours of work by a department or vendor technician. No system is going to solve all your ailments, but the unified approach will at least reduce the number of "surprises" that kill weekends and cause delays of hours, days or weeks.

Vendor Deliveries

Ten CDs arrive in an overnight package. They contain the database and images: results of processing native files. Litigation Support works to minimize the time it will take the technician to load these materials for use by the legal team.

Litigation Support should add this information to the labels as necessary: client-matter number, volume name, volume date. Based on actual experience, one may need to add the vendor name and phone number to the label as well.

Alert the vendor and the attorney regarding any discrepancy between vendor product and the firm's technical standard. If the vendor can not meet firm needs, another vendor will. Loyalty to a "bad" vendor can result in unnecessary work for the Litigation Support Department, slower turnaround time for the legal team, and higher bills to the client. In the meanwhile, Litigation Support should document everything. The department can use this documentation to make arguments for firmwide standards, qualified vendors and other initiatives outlined in the Implementing Best Practices section.

Evaluating Quality

The following section presents the most common quality checks the Litigation Support Department can employ to analyze litigation technology goods and services. The following text contains strategies and analysis. To access task lists, please see the Supporting Files, Litigation Support QC Tasks section.

Paper Discovery

When the vendor or firm converts paper collections into a database with images, as always, require inclusion and adherence to the firm Litigation Support Technical Standards document. If the vendor, or department, must subcontract or outsource, make certain the final responsibility for all work lands solidly on your primary vendor.

The following are considerations for the technician evaluating the final product.

1. Did the vendor match Bates?

Productions from opposing counsel and collections from third parties may already have a Bates scheme. When scanning paper, it is best to have the vendor match the existing Bates numbers when naming files and populating the BEGBATES and ENDBATES fields. Vendors, in an effort to save time and cost, may create a new Bates prefix and rely upon the old prefix being caught in the OCR field. One problem with this approach is the file names reflect this artificial document control number instead of the real Bates number.

2. Are there unintentional gaps and overlaps?

Run a gap check utility. Most document review systems provide a way for the administrator to check for gaps and overlaps. The utility should create a log file showing gaps in the Bates range or whenever the Bates numbers of two documents overlap. Both of these types of errors can be legitimate. Due to legal or historical issues, a collection may not include one or more Bates ranges of varying sizes. This will create gaps. In practice, the database administrator really should create a place-holder record what fills this gap. It should also explain the gap for future visitors. The VP of Operations should alert the legal team as to any gaps or overlaps on incoming media.

3. How does the OCR look?

Even without looking at the corresponding image, it is possible to judge the quality level. OCR text runs the range from nicely formatted and 90% of the words are spelled correctly to what looks like computer code garbage.

The quality of the OCR is a factor of the image (straight, clean, at least 300 DPI) and the OCR software. If the OCR looks sub par, first look at the image. You may be able to determine the garbled word is "contract" but the computer might not. On the other hand, if you notice the document image is rotated on the screen and contains any easy to read text, you may have an issue with auto-rotate.

Top quality OCR software programs offer an option called "auto-rotate." If the option is enabled, each image gets OCR'ed 4 times; once with the image rotated all four directions. The software keeps the OCR with the best results. The cost to the vendor is an OCR job that takes four times longer than when auto rotate is disabled. As 95% of all documents use portrait orientation, not using auto-rotate can be a pretty safe move. That is until the client asks why 5% of the OCR is all garbage.

4. Are the document breaks appropriate?

In a database, there should be a ratio of one document per record. The review team will designate a record as privileged. If there are two documents in a record, both are treated as privileged. Incorrect document breaks can cause the unintentional production of a privileged document. Correcting this problem can disrupt or halt production. It can also cause the team to review prior productions.

The technician should view images and text to make sure there are no obvious document break issues. If there are, then note the document control number or Bates number in your email to both the attorney and the vendor. The legal team should always note this type of problem to the Litigation Support Department. The legal team may not litigation support, however, unless told to do so.

In the technical standards, there is a specification for a one page to one image ratio. There are several reasons for this. The possibility of a problem with document breaks is one reason. The technician will not need to touch the images to correct the problem, if using the 1:1 ratio for images.

5. Orientation

Are all of the images upright ("portrait")? There should not be any upside-down pages. The only exceptions to this are documents such as charts and some spreadsheets. These documents were designed to be viewed sideways ("landscape"). Nonetheless, they should all face the same way on the screen. The ability to physically rotate the screen can dramatically increase the size of the image and speed of review. The section on monitors details the advantages to a second monitor that pivots.

Electronic Discovery

Litigation Support should be the Firm's central hub for electronic discovery. Make sure the Litigation Department and all staff route materials directly to Litigation Support along with a cover sheet indicating the client-matter number. So long as the client-matter number and name of the sender are on the paper, Litigation Support can give a budget estimate and manage any discovery projects.

When the client sends electronic discovery, Litigation Support should make a copy and label it with the client matter number, volume name and volume date (not today's date). Original media should never leave the law firm. Litigation Support should always send a copy. In the case of an emergency, it is Litigation Support Department who will need access to the media. Litigation Support Department should keep a copy of everything in the media inventory.

The following are considerations for the technician evaluating the final product.

1. Inbound Vendor Product - Quality Checks

Look at the contents of the media to determine whether the content meets the basic technical requirements, such as whether the file names include the full Bates prefix and number, or if there are obvious gaps in the image. One can determine if there are gaps by looking in the images folders. As the file name and Bates name are the same, it is simple to spot missing files. If everything looks in order, the technician should load the database into a "test" database.

Once the data looks right, check it for gaps and overlapping Bates numbers. Check that the attachments appear right after the emails.

Perform quality checks, per the QC Task list, under the Supporting Files section.

2. Spreadsheets

If your vendor converted spreadsheets to .TIF or .PDF, make sure the numbers in the columns appear as numbers and not #####. When a column is too narrow to display the entire number, spreadsheets will replace the entire number with #. Vendors are supposed to tell their software to expand every column.

3. OCR

Some electronic discovery requires OCR. Graphics, as example, may contain text. OCR software will extract this text.

4. Bibliographic Coding

Some electronic discovery requires bibliographic coding. While files such as email contain fields that translate nicely to "author," "recipient," "document date" and "subject," other files contain no such metadata. These files require bibliographic coding, just like paper documents.

Overall Strategy

Do not load new data directly into the production database. If you are loading data, do your work in a second database that is empty. This way you can delete or modify data and do other administrative things in a relatively small database while not worrying about affecting existing data. Never perform administrative work on the same database the legal team uses for its work.

Leave "breadcrumbs." As example, when you produce, you will update your database with the Bates numbers for certain records. No matter how this update occurs (automatic function or load file), you first will want to make a backup copy of the database for safe keeping.

When it is time to do more work, do not overwrite the first backup when making the new backup. The technician should make a second backup. In this manner, one can access any version for reference or other purposes. These are breadcrumbs. The same idea applies to working with load files, merging database or exporting materials.

The same idea applies to images and annotations. Always get a version of the .TIF where there is no annotation, redaction or Bates stamping. The reason for this is that the team will not appreciate having the internal control number on their production along with the production Bates numbers. You can only go to the version with the least amount of adulteration, stamped or not.

Data loaded, it is time for the review team to cast eyes upon every page from the client. Hopefully, the Litigation Support Department was able to cull and filter as outlined elsewhere in this book. Ideally, the review team is enjoying the lack of eye strain and improved speed afforded by the pivoted second monitor.

Case "Tear Down"

Now is the time for the attorney and Litigation Support Department and firm to decide how to handle each repository at the end of the case: leave it alone, shred or delete it, or migrate it to near-line or off-line storage. It is vital to include these answers in your agreement with opposing counsel along with issues such as production technical requirements.

B. Phase 4 through Phase 5

Ongoing Review through Production

Results:

The Litigation Support Department isolates those documents designated, or "tagged," for production by the legal team. The department then applies the appropriate stamps and generates new production databases.

Strategy:

The Litigation Support Department identifies the resources, hardware, software and experts necessary for the team to be able to review their various collections. The Litigation Support Department now uses those resources to create a production based upon the team tagging. Each production contains only the minimally required information, per the Phase 1 production agreement with opposing. Each production image only bears those stamps and annotations relevant to the specific production. Because any preproduction stamps will appear on subsequent production images, pre-production images bear no stamps. The pre-production database is, however, amended to reflect all Bates designations, pre-production and production.

Locations:

At this point, discovery resides almost everywhere. Depending upon the amount of potential discovery, the collection process may continue for quite a while. As discovery arrives, Litigation Support makes a copy for the vendor and keeps the original in the media inventory. As vendors deliver new media, the Litigation Support Department will copy the contents to a staging environment. The vendor media goes into the media inventory. After performing any preparation, the technician moves the discovery to the production environment. After the legal team reviews the new materials, Litigation Support sends productive discovery to the opposing firm.

Depending upon the need for experts, portions of the discovery may also reside with them. As one can see, during these phases, discovery can reside in many places. It is always moving toward the same predictable goal, the next phase. The Litigation Budget Spreadsheet provides a worksheet to track all collections throughout the case lifecycle.

The following is a short list of places where discovery materials may reside. Litigation Support, in conjunction with the client, legal team and IT Department should be able to identify caches, accessibility and how the disaster recovery plan addresses each one.

- Client
- Production Environment
- Opposing Counsel
- Media Inventory
- Vendor
- Back-Up Tapes
- Staging Environment
- Experts
- Printed Paper

Review for Production

There are two types of review: production and issue. The first type of review is the first type performed in a case. This is a linear review of every page of every document in the discovery database. The reviewer may be less interested in the content of the documents as it relates to issues than whether the document is privileged or productive. The goal here is speed.

Our Productions

The attorney needs to make an agreement at the start of the case as to the production formats which both sides will use. You want to make certain that the other side produces the right kinds of images and load files. You also want to make certain that your firm can produce in the right format to the other firm.

Remember, these are binding agreements that can get either firm into trouble if they do not comply. The Litigation Support Department will make certain the attorney does not offer more than is necessary, in terms of content, e.g., fields, and achievable, in terms of technology, e.g., CDs, DVDs. If your attorney wishes to produce paper, do not be surprised if the other side does the same. Offer your Standard to the other side. If they have not yet adopted a Standard, perhaps they will adopt yours. Remember, the Standard creates a technical template, so it does not reveal legal ideas or strategies. If they accept your Standard, the technical aspects of handling discovery should pose no major problem for the support staff on both sides. This in turn benefits both legal teams.

Every production results in a new database. This may mean generating CDs, DVDs or boxes of paper, as the aforementioned production agreement stipulates. At this point, Litigation Support should update the pre-production database to reflect the additional Bates numbers. Never replace the original internal document control number. The idea here is to have one database in which anyone can search for a document by any pre-production or production name, and another database which only contains the single production name.

The only way to see the production image is to open the production database and call up that image. The pre-production image will never show any image stamps. Any pre-production stamps will appear on subsequent production images. Only the stamps and redactions relating to a specific production should appear on the production image.

At a minimum, each case will have the following four databases:

Pre-production Database

- The database contains full metadata and text for all records.
- Images are neither stamped nor redacted.
- All pre-production Bates values are included.
- All production Bates values associated with a pre-production document are included.
- No documents contain a "privileged term."

Privileged Term Database

- The database contains full metadata and text for all records.
- Images are neither stamped nor redacted.
- All pre-production Bates values are included.
- All production Bates values associated with a pre-production document are included.
- All documents contain a "privileged term."

Our Production Database

- Unless part of an explicit agreement, no metadata or text is included.
- The database contains production BEGBATES and ENDBATES.
- Images are stamped and redacted.

Their Production Database

- Unless part of an explicit agreement, no metadata or text is included.
- The database contains production BEGBATES and ENDBATES.
- Images are stamped and redacted.

Any subsequent productions result in "Our Production Database #N." These databases follow the same course as the first production. Each should be easy to identify through folders or separate databases as the situation warrants. For example, a large case may mean weekly productions. There is no need to have 15 databases. The team will still want to have a single location to look for this staggered production.

Note - Watch out and make sure you don't produce the same document twice. Remember to add a production tag or field and update it every time you produce.

Production Strategies

The strategy is simple: provide the bare minimum required to the other side. This generally means providing the basics: a database load file containing Bates ranges, an imagebase load file (correlating Bates to image file), and the production stamped images.

Some attorneys like to produce in paper form. While this is easy to do, it may also mean the opposing firm will also produce paper. If our firm is going to review opposing counsel's production on the computer, we will need the vendor to scan all these new documents. Save the time and cost by agreeing to a production format during the pleading phase. The review team does not have to wait to review if materials arrive properly formatted, per agreement.

Production means at least two sets of CDs: one for your firm, one for theirs. Do not have the vendor send the production set to opposing counsel. The Litigation Support Department wants that last chance to QC the work. Litigation Support should use the same Incoming Media check lists as with any other vendor product. Once satisfied with the results, provide the attorney with the details, including shipping numbers and production size (CDs, docs, pages, Bates ranges).

Production dates are extremely important. The other side can argue your missing dates caused some hardship to their case and client. As such the department should keep track of both outgoing and incoming productions. If a production is flawed in any way, make sure the attorney knows the explicit details as soon as possible. The lawyer may be able to use it to advantage. The lawyer should always know, as far ahead as possible, when dates are in jeopardy for any reason.

C. Phase 6

Depositions

Results:

The legal team searches in earnest for documents relating to various issues. These documents become exhibits used during depositions. As the depositions progress, the legal team or VP of Operations will update the transcript software with the latest deliveries from the court reporter and videographer. The team identifies Q&A pairs, or video clips, which can become exhibits. To aid the court reporter, the Litigation Support Department can offer the key names and terms from the case fact management software.

Strategy:

The Litigation Support Department wants to train the review team how to find documents relating to various issues. Whereas the review for privilege was linear, the review for issues is totally dynamic. Issues may gain and lose relevance on a daily basis. Therefore the goal is to use software and training to expedite the process of finding new exhibits from within discovery and testimony. Ideally the attorney can perform this entire process during the deposition.

Locations:

By this phase of the case, all collections (production or otherwise) should be with opposing counsel, the firm, or an agent of the firm, such as a vendor or expert. Some materials may also reside on the staging environment, as well as the production environment. All production media, from both sides, along with client originals, reside in the media inventory.

At this stage, however, the team may require "off-line access," or access without connecting to a remote storage location such as the firm servers. Off-line storage includes items such as external hard drives, "thumb" drives and optical media.

The other type of off-line storage is the back-up tape. Depending upon the disaster recovery plan, client-matter materials also exist on multiple firm tapes. At this time, discovery materials may reside in any of the following locations:

- Firm
- Media Inventory
- Back-up Media
- Expert
- Production Environment
- Staging Environment
- Vendor
- Off-Line Storage
- Opposing Counsel
- Printed Paper

Review for Issue

The second type of review deals with finding all the documents that relate to a concept or match search criteria, such as a document date and author. Today the software companies are employing new conceptual searches and databases that automatically group contextually similar documents. The quest for documents relating to issues will occur throughout the case lifecycle. After the production phase, instead of the team producing thousands of documents, they need to find dozens, or even a handful, of key documents to use as exhibits.

The VP of Operations should train the legal team to understand how to search for issues. The team also needs to be able to easily transfer new exhibits to the exhibit software. To learn more about this ability, please reference the Software Lifecycle section.

Deposition Exhibits

Now that the reviewers have had a chance to look at the documents from all sides of the case, they are ready to show their best stuff. These are documents that help during a deposition. Because a deposition may be held at a conference table with a limited number of attendees, printing multiple copies of various documents can be a good solution. At trial, documents may need to be blown up to several feet for a physical exhibit or appear on a video screen as a "trial graphic." The big advantage of the physical exhibit is that it is visible even while the next exhibits are being shown. A graphic only appears on the screen until something else appears there.

Deposition Exhibit Books

At the start of depositions, the team has identified the majority of exhibits they wish to use. The document review database should have a main folder for Deposition Exhibits and then subdirectories for each person or issue. When the team needs to see all exhibits that relate to a given person or issue, they can simply "click" on the folder to see the associated documents. Many teams prefer to print the exhibits and store them in 3-ring binders. The Litigation Support Department should work with the paralegals and team to understand how they can best take advantage of the electronic folders, in lieu of binders, or as a way to help create and print them.

D. Phase 7

Final Pre-Trial Preparation

Results:

The Litigation Support Department makes certain all client-matter materials are available to the legal team, based upon the war room and trial room requirements. If the attorney or team will be unable to access the Internet, the Department can provide materials on external hard drives.

Strategy:

Identification of all client-matter materials should be a simple task for the Litigation Support Department.

Locations:

The discovery materials continue to reside in the same traditional locations, e.g., firm, vendor, inventory. At this stage, however, the team may require "off-line access", or access without connecting to a remote storage location such as the firm servers. Off-line storage includes items such as external hard drives, "thumb" drives and optical media.

The other type off off-line storage is the back-up tape. Depending upon the disaster recovery plan, client-matter materials also exist on multiple firm tapes.

- Media Inventory
- Production Environment
- Off-Line Storage
- Opposing Counsel

- Firm
- Vendor
- Expert

- Printed Paper
- Staging Environment
- Back-up Media

E. Phase 8

Trial

Results:

As in Phase 6, Depositions, during the trial phase the legal team searches in earnest for documents relating to various issues. These documents become exhibits used during testimony. As the trial progresses, either the legal team or VP of Operations will update the transcript software with the latest deliveries from the court reporter and videographer. The team identifies Q&A pairs, or video clips, which can, in turn, become exhibits. To aid the court reporter, the Litigation Support Department can offer the key names and terms from the case fact management software.

Strategy:

Continuing the strategy from Phase 6, the Litigation Support Department should train the review team how to find documents relating to various issues. The issues may gain and lose relevance on a daily basis. Therefore, the Department continues to use software and training to help expedite the process of finding new exhibits from within discovery and testimony. Ideally the attorney can perform this entire process during testimony.

Locations:

All materials continue to reside in the same locations as the prior phase.

- Opposing Counsel
- Production Environment
- Off-Line Storage
- Media Inventory

- Firm
- Vendor
- Expert

- Printed Paper
- Staging Environment
- Back-up Media

Trial Exhibits

As with deposition exhibits, the majority of exhibits come from the document review system and transcript software. The final destination of an exhibit could be foam board, color print-outs or presentation software such as Sanction 2 or Trial Director. CaseSoft's case fact management software makes it easy to create timelines and factual digests in minutes. This can be a very important tool during testimony.

Trial Exhibit Books

If this text seems duplicative, this is because, during trial, the strategy for organizing and printing exhibit books, or binders, is the same as the "Deposition Exhibit Books" text.

At the start of trial, the team has identified the majority of exhibits for the case. The document review database should have a main folder for Trial Exhibits and then subdirectories for each person or issue. When the team needs to see all exhibits that relate to a given person or issue, they can simply "click" on the folder to see the associated documents. Many teams prefer to print the exhibits and store them in 3-ring binders. The Litigation Support Department should work with the paralegals and team to understand how they can take advantage of the electronic folders, in lieu of binders, or as a way to help create and print them.

F. Phase 9

Case "Tear Down"

In this phase, the VP of Operations moves all electronic materials, databases, images, case fact management files and so forth to near-line or off-line storage, as the attorney requires.

Results:

By treating all electronic materials the same from an organizational and processing perspective, the technician can use materials in subsequent matters or appeals. The databases all use the same field names and order, so transferring information should not pose any problem.

Strategy:

All information, whether stored in the document review software, case fact management or exhibit software, should be able to transfer seamlessly to other matters. This is because all matters use the same tools. It is also because discovery is organized and processed in the same manner for all litigation matters.

Locations:

Unless there is an order to destroy all materials, the attorney, the Litigation Support Department and the firm must decide how to handle each repository: leave it alone, shred or delete it, or migrate it to near-line or off-line storage. Fortunately, the attorney and Litigation Support Department predetermined the answers during Phase 1.

- Opposing Counsel
- Production Environment
- Off-Line Storage
- Media Inventory

- Firm
- Vendor
- Expert

- Printed Paper
- Staging Environment
- Back-up Media

VI. Supporting Files

Thank you for your purchase of the Litigation Support Department by Mark Lieb. The following files are protected by copyright, Ad Litem Consulting, Inc. Please feel free to update generic information on these files, such as firm name and firm contact information. The Ad Litem copyright must be kept in tact.

Files

- Case Lifecycle Task List
- Collection to Production
- Department Status Reports
- Deposition and Trial Resource Sheet
- Discovery Lifecycle Flowchart
- Litigation Budget Spreadsheet
- Litigation Support QC Tasks
- New Matter Assessment Email
- Server Organization Email
- Vendor Compliance Email
- Technical Standards

1. Case Lifecycle Task List

This Microsoft Project file guides the Litigation Support Department through the entire case lifecycle. By following this lifecycle, the Litigation Support Department provides a consistent experience for every case. This lifecycle meshes with the flowchart, budget spreadsheet, and standards. The task list assumes the Department has achieved success in the firm level initiatives, as well as adherence by the firm to the principles outlined in the book as a whole.

A. Phases and Tasks

ID	Task Name
1	**Phase 1: Preliminary**
2	Attorney sends pleading to lit support as PDF, w/ CM#
3	LS OCRs document if necessary
4	LS selects server home based on team location and storage considerations
5	LS creates CM# folders
6	LS saves pleading into \admin folder
7	LS saves CaseMap file into \casesoft folder
8	LS saves new matter kit into \admin\kit folder
9	Paralegal enters key facts, dates, etc. from pleading into CaseMap
10	Paralegal enters names into the Roles & Responsibilities worksheet
11	LS schedules new matter meeting for legal team
12	LS emails team with "New Matter Assessment Email"
13	**Results: Estimated budget, preliminary discovery matrix, CaseMap facts**
14	
15	**Phase 2: Discovery Planning**
16	LS creates a discovery flow-chart for case
17	LS checks availability and price of prequalified vendors
18	Paralegal schedules the Discovery Planning Meeting w/ Team & Client
19	30 Minutes Before Discovery Planning Meeting
20	Review and update discovery matrix
21	Review and update budget if necessary
22	LS finalizes collection names and doc control number prefixes
23	Review of discovery flow-chart
24	LS makes recommendation on database treatment
25	LS recommends in-house versus vendor involvement levels
26	LS recommends firm DRS or ASP solution
27	LS approves technical considerations in doc requests to client and opposing counsel
28	Discovery Planning Meeting
29	LS, team and client formalize matrix, ability to produce and schedule
30	Production method (by Client, by Vendor) to Firm noted per collection
31	Identification of native review only collections such as a relational database
32	Client designates a point of contact for each collection and ongoing issues.
33	Attorney and Client agree on budget
34	LS enters client roles in the Roles & Responsibilities worksheet
35	If client has vendor choice unknown to the firm, LS must prequalify

36	Team member updates CaseMap with all case names, terms, dates, etc.
37	Attorney formalizes the request for production by opposing counsel
38	Attorney uses kit strategies to limit discovery
39	Attorney gets formal agreement about production technical specifications
40	Attorney gets formal agreement about end-of-case destruct orders
41	**Results: Budget, discovery matrix/request, production format, CaseMap**
42	
43	**Phase 3: Finalize and Execute Discovery Plan**
44	LS schedules vendor, team meeting
45	LS provides Vendor Kit to vendor (incl. R&R worksheet, discovery matrix)
46	Use discovery matrix to formalize vendor deadlines, collection and project names
47	Culling Strategies formalized (Including CaseMap data)
48	LS and vendor formalize on delivery media and any technical details
49	Vendor provides estimated minimum turnaround time to create productions
50	LS provides team with total minimum turnaround time (incl. LS) to create productions
51	LS schedules weekly status meeting re: deadlines, QC, invoice, issues.
52	LS and attorney review and accept vendor contract
53	LS saves copy of contract in \admin folder
54	**Results: Qualified vendor begins processing per matrix & schedule**
55	
56	**Phase 4: Ongoing Review - Ongoing Issues**
57	LS generates the latest Privilege Review Progress Report
58	LS reviews all issues mentioned in Vendor Pre-Meeting
59	Weekly Vendor Pre-Meeting
60	LS provides Privilege Review Progress Report
61	Any review issues, such as creating new batches for reviewers
62	Any internal people issues and how to help
63	Any internal technical issues, requirements, deadlines for correction
64	Any client related issues
65	Any collection issues, per matrix
66	Any vendor related issues
67	Discussion of Opposing Counsel's Production
68	Any review issues
69	Any technical issues
70	Any schedule issues
71	Weekly Vendor Meeting
72	Current Invoice, Estimated Total Reviewed
73	Discussion of any collection issues by Vendor
74	Discussion of any processing issues by Vendor
75	Discussion of any loading issues by LS
76	Discussion of any review issues by Team
77	Discussion of any production issues by anyone
78	Update of matrix and schedule
79	LS Database Administration
80	LS performs Incoming Media Checklist
81	LS creates review batches, per meeting
82	LS alerts team about new batches
83	Relational Databases Review
84	Attorney provides Expert contact information to LS and Client
85	LS project manages provision of access to data by Firm (copy, VPN, etc.)
86	Schedule time and place for expert to review system
87	Expert prints reports

88	Paralegal provides copy of reports to vendor with associated collection name
89	Privilege Review
90	Team assigns batches to associates for review
91	Training
92	LS shows Associates how to find their batch and assign designations
93	LS shows Associates how to identify and report problems
94	Team reviews documents, updating folders / tags in DRS
95	Team reports any problems to LS
96	**Results: Able To Produce All Non-Privileged Documents**
97	
98	**Phase 5: Production**
99	Firm Productions
100	Attorney gives completed Production Request Form to LS
101	LS performs Production Checklist
102	LS calculates turnaround time
103	LS reports turnaround time and any identified issues vis-à-vis the checklist
104	LS project manages production
105	Preproduction database updated to include production Bates numbers
106	LS sets up separate production database w/ stamped images for team to view
107	LS provides production sets to internal inventory and parties per checklist
108	Opposing Counsel's Productions
109	All media should be forwarded to LS by Team
110	LS performs Incoming Media Checklist
111	LS creates review batch folders, per meeting
112	LS alerts team about new batches and QC test results
113	LS notes any issues (technical, person, schedule)
114	LS updates Budget Spreadsheet
115	LS provides Discovery Feedback Questionnaire to Team
116	**Result: All Collections Produced and Opposing Counsel's Productions Reviewed**
117	
118	**Phase 6: Depositions**
119	Finding Exhibits
120	LS trains Team Searching and Foldering
121	LS creates folders based on CaseMap keywords and names
122	Team identifies important docs and applies Exhibit Candidate tag
123	Attorney reviews exhibit candidates and removes undesirables
124	LS trains paralegal while copying docs and metadata to CaseMap
125	LS trains paralegal to create timelines with TimeMap
126	Using Exhibits
127	Team may use printed exhibits instead of presentation software
128	Paralegal enters exhibit number into CaseMap and DRS
129	If printing, LS should refer to the Blow-Backs checklist
130	If using Presentation Software:
131	LS trains paralegal by setting up exhibits in software together
132	Copy of exhibit installed on a deposition laptop (attorney's, paralegal's)
133	Paralegal successfully uses exhibit software
134	LS provides copy on CD(s) or DVD(s) or Hard Drive(s) to paralegal
135	Transcript Setup
136	LS preloads names, keywords and issues from CaseMap into transcript software
137	LS trains team on issue coding in real-time, marking Q&A pairs
138	LS explains about the preloaded names, keywords and issues
139	Team identifies important Q&A pairs and issues in transcript software

140	LS assists Attorney in copying pairs and issues to CaseMap
141	Court Reporter
142	Paralegal schedules court reporters and adds to R&R Worksheet
143	LS provides Technical Standards to court reporter, noting key sections
144	LS provides list of key names and terms from CaseMap to reporter
145	Court Reporter sends transcripts to LS (Team forwards, too)
146	Video
147	LS performs QC on video, quality, synchronization of audio and subtitles
148	LS stores video clips in \client#\matter#\video network folder
149	LS alerts team and vendor of any issues and availability to Team
150	LS shows Team how to view video and create Exhibits
151	LS updates Budget Spreadsheet
152	**Results: All transcripts reviewed, CaseMap updated, Q&A Exhibits created**
153	
154	**Phase 7: Final Pretrial Preparation**
155	Exhibits
156	LS works with team to find new exhibits and documents in DRS
157	LS and Team find key Q&A pairs in transcript software
158	LS and Team identify video exhibits
159	LS and Team create TimeMap timelines from CaseMap
160	LS and Team update CaseMap with all new findings, video and timelines
161	LS and Team add all exhibits to trial exhibit software
162	Team identifies exhibits for printing to LS
163	LS helps Team send exhibits to vendor for printing (8.5x11, foam board, color)
164	LS updates Budget Spreadsheet
165	Team selects Trial Tech Team ("TTT")
166	Team updates the Roles & Responsibilities Worksheet
167	LS schedules Requirements Meeting
168	Requirements Meeting
169	TTT, Team and LS determine trial hardware needs
170	TTT provides Team and LS with required hardware list
171	LS decides to rent or buy TTT listed hardware (e.g., video or printing equipment)
172	LS provides cost to put entire case on portable hard drives
173	LS updates Budget Spreadsheet for new costs
174	Hardware Setup
175	LS reserves appropriate Firm hardware
176	LS orders necessary hardware
177	TTT rents necessary hardware
178	LS updates Budget Spreadsheet
179	If required, LS transfers all case data, exhibits, etc. to drives for court room
180	LS updates software to accommodate external drive letter on laptop
181	**Results: All exhibits, hardware and support ready for Trial**
182	
183	**Phase 8: Trial**
184	Transcripts
185	LS helps Paralegal input daily transcripts into transcript software
186	LS helps Paralegal copy Q&A pairs, notes to CaseSoft and Trial Exhibit software
187	Exhibits
188	LS helps team find new exhibits
189	LS helps team add new exhibits to Trial Exhibit Software or Printer
190	LS updates Budget Spreadsheet after trial is over
191	**Results: Team has all daily updated exhibits, transcripts and final budget**

2. Collection to Production

The following pages are from a short PowerPoint presentation which Litigation Support can use to illustrate how multiple collections turn into preproduction and production databases. The following presentation appears on the included CD.

A. Mass Collection

All potential discovery gathered for evaluation, culling, extraction and conversion into a reviewable and producible format.

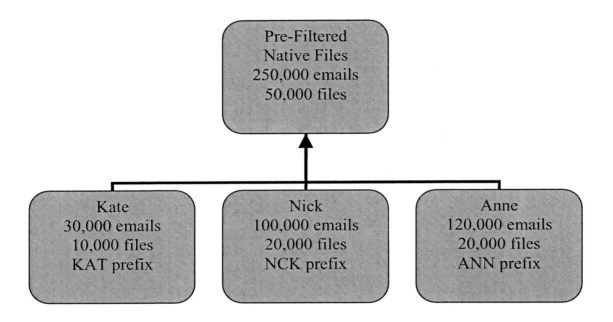

B. Filter for Extraction

The vendor extracts those documents that contains key names, terms and exist within a specific date range. In this manner, one may eliminate the need for the legal team to review a large amount of documents.

Note: It may not be possible to eliminate paper discovery from the review process until the vendor has created OCR and bibliographic coding. The vendor may eliminate electronic discovery before processing it. This eliminates wasted time and money inherent to the paper discovery culling process.

Start With

- 250,000 Emails

- 50,000 Files

End With

- 12,000 Emails

- 5,000 Files

Key Names
(Kate, Nick, Anne)

Key Words
(Cake, Milk, Presents)

Date Ranges
1996-

C. Pre Production Database

In the preproduction database stage, the images do not include any stamping. If the legal team wishes to have the preproduction document control numbers appear on blow-backs or on the image, the Litigation Support Department must reserve a non-stamped version for use in production databases.

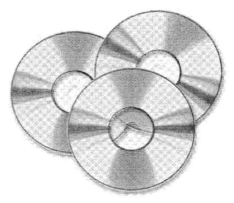

ANN000001 - ANN031942

The images have no stamps, no redactions and no annotations.

Blow-Backs can include the preproduction Bates numbers.

Any stamps here will appear on subsequent productions.

D. Pre-Production Review

The preproduction review process is a linear review for production. This sample document is privileged. The Litigation Support Department, or vendor, will not include this document in productions to opposing counsel.

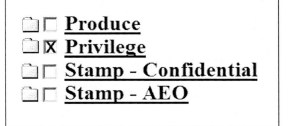

Preproduction Review

The legal team reviews every preproduction document and designates which ones to produce, produce and stamp, or keep.

E. Create Production

Although each collection, "KAT," "NCK" and "ANN," may contain both productive and privileged documents, for the purpose of the presentation, the Litigation Support Department will produce KAT and NCK collections, while retaining ANN documents. The produced documents become the "GMP" production database.

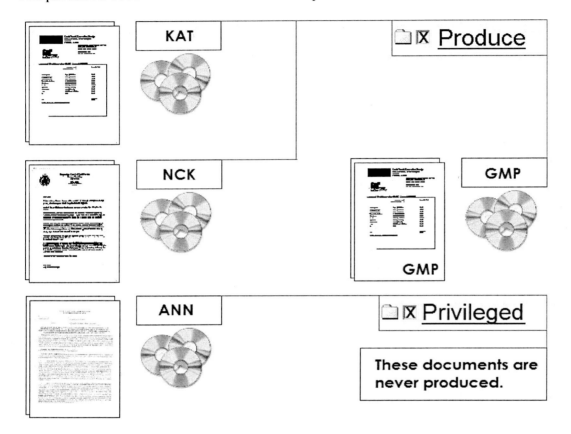

F. Production Database

The "GMP" database is the result of the legal team review.

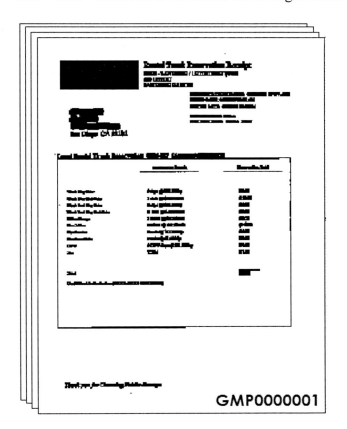

GMP0000001

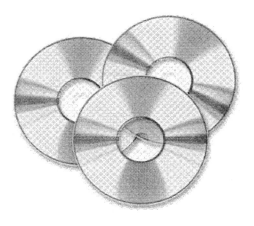

GMP Production Database

3. Department Status Reports

A major responsibility of the Department COO is tracking the financial and operational aspects of the Department. The COO should have a good idea when the Department will require additional capacity, licenses or people. The COO should also know of potential projects and their impact upon the Department. The included status report considerations help the Department COO construct its own status reports. The COO can use these reports when arguing for additional resources.

A. Marketing Report

Considerations:

Perception of Department by firm
Potential projects

> Client-Matter Number
> Size / Hours / Quantity
> Start Date
> % Chance of happening

B. Operations Report

Considerations:

Worker Capacity Report

> Total Hours Billed Per Person
> % month change
> % 3-month change
> Hours billed this month
> Hours billed YTD (Year-to-Date)
> Target total hours billed per year

Storage Capacity Report

> Server capacity (each individual repository)
> % Month Change
> % 3-Month Change
> % 1 Year Ago
> Total used / % used
> Estimated full date
>
> Firm grand total used / % used
> % month change
> % 3-month change

% 1 year ago
Estimated full date

Software Report, license issues:

Software Title
Total Licenses Available
Total Licenses Used
Cost to Increase

C. Financial Report

Considerations:

Billable Hours:

Hours by Worker
% technical
% project management
% month change
% 3-month change
% 1 Year Ago

Department Total Hours
% technical
% project management
% month change
% 3-month change
% 1 year ago

Spending by Cost Code:

Cost Code:
$ spent this month
% month change
% 3-month change
% 1 year ago

4. Deposition and Trial Resource Sheet

The legal team should already have remote access to all of their materials, so long as they have Internet access. In those rare occasions when the team will not have access, the Litigation Support Department should make alternative plans, such as external hard drives.

Deposition and trial support are services your Litigation Support Department may or may not provide. As such, the Department outlines for the legal team whom to contact for support.

Ideally, the Litigation Support Department should be able to identify all materials related to any client matter, and make those materials available to the legal team, from any location, even when not connected to the Internet.

While this book does not actually include a complete resource sheet template, it does contain one critical advisory: make certain that Litigation Support's interests and client-matter numbers are reflected in any resource sheet used by firm or outside vendor, as shown by the following table with sample content:

Software Title	Materials Relating To Client-Matter #s
Transcript Software	201022-00023, 34, 35
Document Management Database	201022-00023
Exhibit Software	201022-00023

5. *Discovery Lifecycle Flowchart*

Discovery Lifecycle Flowchart: People understand certain ideas and concepts when presented as flowcharts and diagrams more easily than simple text. This is especially true when the ideas are very complex. That is why every case needs a copy of the Discovery Flowchart diagram. The following illustration is meant as a book reference. Please see the actual flowchart, as included on the CD, for a legible version.

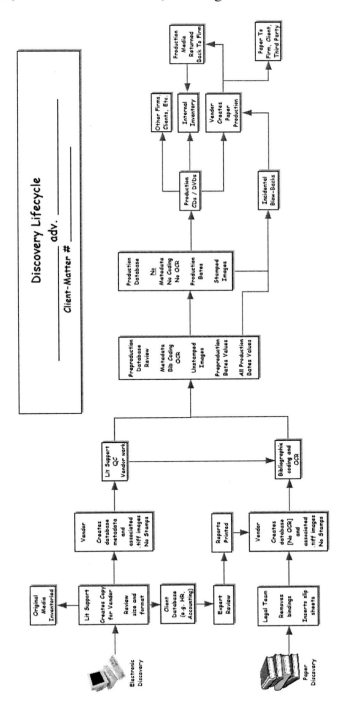

6. Litigation Budget Spreadsheet

Litigation Support can use the Litigation Budget Spreadsheet to explain potential costs to the attorney, and how the attorney can explain potential costs to the client. The spreadsheet is good for tracking collections, projects and contact information. When a case becomes "hot" again after six months of dormancy, this spreadsheet (one per client-matter) proves invaluable.

The spreadsheet is set up to make certain broad assumptions and fill in the numbers according. It also contains multiple worksheets that the team and Litigation Support Department can use to track discovery, key terms and so forth.

For example, if you enter a paper quantity of one box, the spreadsheet will assume 2,500 pages. Please note that there is a side box where one can change quantity and ratio assumptions. It also assumes certain percentages of paper will be light, medium and heavy. This can help give a better estimate.

The same types of assumptions hold true for electronic discovery. Because electronic discovery makes page and document count impossible to truly estimate by the GB, these numbers are notoriously unpredictable. All who cast eyes upon this estimate should know this up front.

At the very least, the spreadsheet format gives the attorney the opportunity to change discovery quantities and get a fresh idea of the new potential cost.

The spreadsheet contains several worksheets:

- A. Budget Worksheet
- B. Discovery Matrix Worksheet
- C. Limiting Discovery Worksheet
- D. Roles & Responsibilities Worksheet

A. Budget Worksheet

This worksheet is the summation of the discovery collection and processing effort. The attorney can use this worksheet to explain costs to the client. As the case progresses, one can track the total cost here.

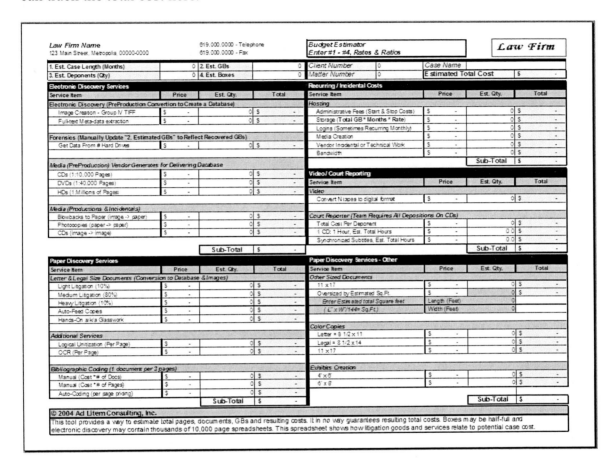

B. Discovery Matrix Worksheet

This worksheet shows the current total pages and storage as entered on the budget worksheet. Now you can track collections that became projects and finally ended up on a vendor bill.

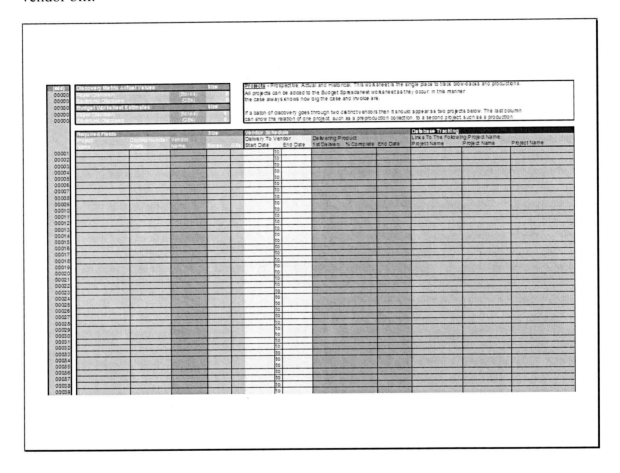

C. Limiting Discovery Worksheet

Use this worksheet in the spreadsheet to limit and cull discovery by key words and terms.

D. Roles and Responsibilities Worksheet

Only update this as is necessary. The worksheet lets the reader know who filled a given role. The role defines the responsibilities. If you need to know who the Lead Attorney is on a given case, then consult the worksheet.

Roles & Responsibilities Worksheet			
Client #	_____	Client Name	_____
Matter #	_____	Versus Name	_____
Role	**Name**	**Phone**	**Email**
Our Firm			
Lead Attorney	_____	_____	_____
Lead Paralegal	_____	_____	_____
LS Project Manager	_____	_____	_____
Outside Firm	Name	Phone	Email
Lead Attorney	_____	_____	_____
Lead Paralegal	_____	_____	_____
LS Project Manager	_____	_____	_____
Vendor	Name	Phone	Email
Sales	_____	_____	_____
Project Manager	_____	_____	_____
Technician	_____	_____	_____
Client	Name	Phone	Email
Lead Attorney	_____	_____	_____
Lead Paralegal	_____	_____	_____
Lead Technician	_____	_____	_____

7. Litigation Support QC Tasks

The following files are included with the book. They provide the technician with steps to take when performing a task. The following is a listing of the task lists and a description as to their content or purpose. The list is hardly all inclusive, but does touch upon some of the most common and important tasks for any Litigation Support Department technician and project manager to understand.

A. Discovery - Blow-Back Steps

Technicians use standard questions in this task list to isolate key documents. The questions cover routine issues such as annotations, new Bates ranges and attachment options. Steps for outsourcing and in-house blow-backs are also included.

B. Discovery - New Media

Incoming Databases from vendors and third parties require appropriate treatment by the technician. This includes evaluation of the label and content, along with taking inventory of the media and loading the database.

C. Discovery - Production Steps

This outline steps the technician through the isolation of documents, generation of the production and finally how to complete the task. This includes quality checks, such as looking for documents marked as productive and privileged, or documents mistakenly tagged for production twice. This lengthy task list finishes by outlining for the technician the pre-production, production and inventory quality checks. The outline references other tasks, such as performing a "new media" check before delivering production CDs to the attorney or opposing counsel.

A. Discovery - Blow-Back Steps

Discovery - Blow-Back Steps

  A. **Isolate the documents in the database.**

      1. **Attorney identifies tags or folders for printing.**

         a. **How many sets:** _____

         b. **Print order: Bates, Date (most recent in front, most recent in back)**

         c. **Sub-groupings (such as author, document type or other such characteristic)**

            (1) **Describe:**

              _____

            (2) **Describe:**

              _____

            (3) **Describe:**

              _____

         d. **Due Date:** _____ **(MM/DD/YYYY)**

         e. **Destination:** _____

         f. **Requesting Attorney (phone):** _____

         g. **Attorney provides an explicit search description in writing / email**

         h. **Include parent/child/sibling documents?** _____
            (If an email attachment is printed, include the email, too?)

         i. **Does attorney want to print the docno / BegBates?** _____

         j. **Print the following text, per attorney:**

            _____

         k. **Litigation Support creates a folder / tag named:**

              Print - YYYY-MM-DD

         l. **All documents for printing are added to the new Print folder.**

         m. **Look for missing images and report to attorney the Bates or document numbers. Print bibliographic coding if acceptable.**

         n. **Email document count, page count and cost for blow-backs to attorney.**

       (1)   **If the attorney provides the final approval, ignore the following search adjustment steps.**

       (2)   **Remove all documents from the Print - YYYY-MM-DD folder.**

       (3)   **Adjust search parameters with the attorney and generate a new count and Print folder.**

       (4)   **Email the resulting counts for final approval.**

B.   Generate Blow-Backs

   1.   Out-Sourcing Steps

       a.   **Create CD vendor will use for stamping / blow-backs**

          (1)   **Include:**

             (a)   **Non-stamped images**

             (b)   **Cross reference file**

             (c)   **Database file**

                 (Note: database file may only need the Bates field; confirm with vendor ahead of time.)

             (d)   **Firm Litigation Support Technical Standards document**

             (e)   **Instructions "readme.txt" file**

                 i)   **Starting Bates Number**

                 ii)   **Text stamping requirements (Such as "Attorney Eyes Only" or "Protective Order")**

                 iii)   **Sets required**

                 iv)   **Due Date**

                 v)   **Blow-Back Delivery Address**

                 vi)   **Original CD Return Address**

                 vii)   **Client Number - Matter Number**

                 viii)   **Billing Attorney**

                 ix)   **Lit Support Contact**

                 x)   **Blow-Backs - if required and how many sets**

          (2)   **Label CDs according to Standard**

       b.   **Create a copy of the CDs for Lit Support's inventory.**

       c.   **Call attorney to confirm receipt of the print job.**

    d.   **Confirm print job quality with paralegal. Look for slip sheets and identify any "sub-groupings" within the collection, such as Smith docs and Jones docs.**

    e.   **Report any problems back to the vendor. CC the paralegal.**

        (1)   **If the problem is large enough to warrant a new printing, identify how long it will take before the new blow-backs are ready. Remember, the attorney needs to know deadlines, not the technical details around fixing a problem.**

        (2)   **Compare the print job against the CD to determine the source of the problem.**

        (3)   **If the problem is a document that needs to be excluded, remove it from the collection and provide a new CD to the vendor.**

2.   **In-House Steps**

    a.   **Filter the database to isolate documents for printing.**

    b.   **Enable slip-sheet option for printing through software as possible. Slip sheet should display a centered Bates number in 24 font.**

    c.   **Do a test printing of the first 10 documents.**

        (1)   **Note the speed to estimate project length. Can you meet the deadline?**

            (a)   **If you cannot meet the deadline, estimate how much will be available by the deadline and completion date.**

    d.   **Print all documents in the Print folder in 50 document increments. As confidence in hardware and the quality of the database varies, the increment may increase or decrease. The point is to limit recovery time in case of a printing problem.**

    e.   **Check the documents to make sure the print job was clean.**

    f.   **Deliver documents to the attorney.**

        (1)   **If the print job is large, a rolling production may be in order. This means delivering boxes as completed. If the job is larger than 2 boxes, offer this option.**

B. Discovery - New Media

A. Check labels for key information, add missing information as necessary:

    1. client-matter number

    2. volume name

B. Evaluate Media Content:

(If the delivery does not meet preliminary tests, a new delivery may be necessary)

    1. Folder and file names

        a. Do the names match the image key?

        b. Are there empty folders?

        c. Check content organization: images subfolder, OCR folder, data folder.

    2. Check load files

        a. Open several images to evaluate: orientation, quality, single-page.

        b. Database load file: note delimiters, year format, field order.

    3. Load File Evaluation

C. Copy media to server

    1. As necessary, create the client number folder, matter number folder, database name folder, volume name folder.

    2. Update paths as necessary to reflect Standard.

        a. Copy the full path from the first line and paste into Windows Explorer.

            (1) The associated image of PDF should open, if not, the path is wrong.

            (2) Test last line and a middle load file line.

D. Inventory Media

    1. Add any missing client-matter numbers, volume names and dates to media.

    2. Open the inventory spreadsheet.

    3. Add any new media.

        a. Enter label information, binder number and sleeve number into spreadsheet.

        b. Enter spreadsheet media inventory control number to media label.

E.   Load Database and Images.

    1.   If there is an existing database:

        a.   Create backup database subfolder in database directory.

        b.   Create an empty version of the production database.

        c.   Load database "load file" into empty version.

            (1)   Run gap check to check for gaps and overlapping Bates numbers.

        d.   Check the fields and records.

            (1)   Look for "cropped" data, such as a 10 character name in a field that only holds 8 characters.

            (2)   Check field order

            (3)   Check dates for format validity (i.e. 20/04/1220 versus 12/20/2004).

        e.   Import image "load file" into database (Summation) or Opticon.

        f.   Make sure the correct, associated images appear for several database records (1st, last, middle)

        g.   Create a "tag" or "folder" using the zLS_[volume] format. This lets lit support easily find all records associated with a given volume. The "z" ensures the Lit Support ("LS") tags fall at the end of all the user generated tags.

        h.   Open the "Master" database.

        i.   Load / Merge the new database with the "Master" database.

        j.   As necessary, Load / Merge the new Opticon .DIR/.VOL files with the "Master" database's Opticon files.

        k.   Check Master database for new data and ability to open associated images.

        l.   Reindex the database.

        m.   Look for the documents with the largest page count. There are 13,000 page documents, but they are very rare. Your new database may have four.

        n.   Make certain you can access the database as an end-user, and everything looks appropriate.

C. Discovery - Production Steps

A. **Isolate Docs for Production in Pre-Production Database**

   1. **Check for conflicting folder overlaps.**

      a. **Query the "Produce" folder.**

      b. **Query the "Privileged" folder.**

      c. **Query the "Questions" folder.**

      d. **Query the previously produced folders.**

      e. **Look for overlaps between Produce and other folders.**

         (1) **Overlaps should all reside in the Questions folder.**

         (2) **Remove overlaps from Produce and Privileged folders.**

         (3) **Alert team about overlaps, noting quantity and new addition to the "Questions" folder.**

      f. **Create production folder: Produced - YYYY-MM-DD**

      g. **Add never produced, produce only documents to Produced - YYYY-MM-DD folder**

      h. **Confirm new starting Bates prefix and number with legal team**

      i. **Alert team about production CD results.**

         (1) **Number of documents: _____**

         (2) **Number of pages: _____**

B. **Generate Production**

   1. **Vending Production**

      a. **Create CD vendor will use for stamping / blow-backs.**

         (1) **Include:**

            (a) **Non-stamped images.**

            (b) **Cross reference file.**

            (c) **Database file (Note: database file may only need the Bates field, confirm with vendor ahead of time.)**

            (d) **Firm Litigation Support Technical Standards document**

            (e) **Instructions "readme.txt" file**

               i) **Starting Bates Number: _____**

    ii)   **Text stamping requirements (e.g. "Attorney Eyes Only" or "Protective Order")**

_____

    iii)   **Sets required: _____**
(copy for lit support, legal team, client, opposing, co-counsel, etc.)

    iv)   **Client Number - Matter Number: _____**

    v)   **Deliver vendor product to:**

_____

    vi)   **Return original media to:**

_____

    vii)   **Billing Attorney:**

_____

    viii)   **Lit Support Contact:**

_____

    ix)   **Blow-Backs - if required and how many sets:**

_____

   (2)   **Label CDs according to Standard.**

  b. **Create a copy of the CDs for Lit Support's inventory.**

2. **In-House Production**

  a. **Generate new images with appropriate stamps (Bates, et al.)**

  b. **Update pre-production database to include new production numbers.**

C. **Results**

1. **Pre-Production database**

  a. **Pre-production document control number is in tact and still the image key.**

  b. **New production Bates numbers added to BegBates / EndBates fields.**

  c. **Pre-Production images not altered.**

2. **Production database**

  a. **Only includes BegBates, EndBates coding.**

  b. **Perform "New Media Checklist."**

    c.   **Images include Bates and confidentiality stamps for this production only**

3.   **Inventory**

    a.   **Pre-Production CD(s)**

    b.   **Production CD(s)**

    c.   **Interim CD(s)**

    d.   **All inventory should include the required label information, per "New Media Checklist"**

8. New Matter Assessment Email

This is a sample text the firm may use to accompany other new matter materials.

To: Lead Attorney, Lead Paralegal, Assistants

Subject: [Client Number]-[Matter Number] - Litigation Technology Goods and Services

From: Litigation Support Department

Text:

It has come to our attention that you are working on a new matter, [Client Number]-[Matter Number], otherwise known as, "Company A v. Company B." To provide the best level of Litigation Support, the Department is providing you with materials to help. To access them, please visit:

L:\[Client Number]\[Matter Number]\Case Fact Management Software
L:\[Client Number]\[Matter Number]\Litigation Budget Spreadsheet

To learn how the Litigation Support Department can save you time and your client money, please schedule a 30 minute meeting to discuss the case. If the case is in the "pleading stage," Litigation Support can help identify discovery caches and provide project management skills and technical considerations to aid the collection process. If the case is further along, the Department can still help.

The Litigation Support Department can also help with budgeting for litigation technology goods and services.

Remember, your team must forward all electronic materials that arrive from a third party, such as the client or opposing firm, to the Litigation Support Department.

Thank you,

Litigation Support Department

Phone: (nnn) nnn-nnnn

Email: LitDepartment@ourfirm.com

Intranet: http://litsupport/

9. Server Organization Email

This is the template email your department can use when preparing to organize legacy data.

Work Product and Folder Organization

In the [days, weeks and months] to come, Litigation Support will organize network folders that contain litigation work product. This will not affect the spreadsheets, transcripts or any other data itself. The purpose here is to apply a simple storage strategy. This will be a rolling effort and will happen gradually. We will alert teams when their data is going to be moved, and also leave a "shortcut" in the old folders so that people can find the new folders.

Why are we doing this?

Today, we have multiple folders, in multiple locations for the same client matters. The folder names may not actually reflect the client-matter number. The transcripts, databases and other associated data may or may not be separated by matter. When a person needs to find a spreadsheet for a given client matter, they have to search multiple locations and possibly involve others to help look.

Proper organization of work product also allows us to heighten security. We will be able to limit access to the appropriate team members.

The end result of our efforts will be folders which identify clients by their billing number. Each client folder will contain a folder for each matter, named for the matter number. All data relevant to a given matter will appear inside the matter folder.

The ordered storage of materials also helps when the team needs a copy of everything. Instead of searching and asking team members to help identify folders that may include required files, Litigation Support need simply know the client matter numbers.

This will also help Litigation Support roll out a new tasking system so that you can assign tasks by client-matter and track the successful completion of your requests.

We need your help.

To aid in the preparation for changes, Litigation Support may contact you, the responsible paralegal and/or the responsible attorney to help identify folders, matters, data (including transcripts) and who should be able to access these materials. There will be files that only the team can associate with the correct client matter number.

To help in this transition, we will move the old folders to a folder named "0 - Old Folders." Every moved folder will contain a shortcut to the new folder. No folders will get moved without confirmation and scheduling with the team lead. There will also be a follow-up email sent to the identified persons explaining in detail what happened to their folder(s).

Thank you for your help.

Litigation Support

10. Vendor Compliance Email

The following email explains the law firm's technical standard and how the vendor can meet compliance. The vendor needs to understand that all work done for the firm, regardless of who initiates the project, must comply with the technical standards.

{Firm}

Firm Litigation Support Technical Standards Adoption

As of MM/DD/YYYY, {FIRM} has adopted Technical Standards for Litigation Support. These standards cover requirements around things such as file and folder naming conventions. These requirements apply to all firm cases going forward.

Regardless of who initiates a project, including any current work, these are the defaults we want you to use for our firm.

Any time your product does not meet our technical standard; we will either perform the corrections ourselves or let you know of any compliance issues. Either way we will still require a corrected delivery from you, for our inventory.

We would like to schedule a time to [meet with | have a conference call with] your project manager and any appropriate technical staff to discuss our requirements. We figure there will be a few hiccups and that's OK. We want to work with you.

We know you can meet the Standard and consistently provide us with a compliant product. Going forward, we would prefer to only work with vendors, such as yours, who can meet our needs. With other vendors, we never truly know what they will deliver and if it will require any work on our part in order to use it.

Enclosed, please find a copy of our Litigation Support Technical Standard. Please provide it the appropriate persons so that they may have a chance to study it in preparation for our [meeting | conference call].

We look forward to evaluating a test delivery. We want you to meet the standard in preparation for all the work we send to you in the future. When ready, please use the standards for any currently ongoing work, too.

Any product you provide that does not meet these standards means additional work either you or the Litigation Support must perform. We really appreciate your help eliminating this unnecessary work.

Thank you,
{NAME}
Litigation Support

11. Litigation Support Technical Standards

This standards document is the public piece of the *Litigation Support Department* book. It is a technical summary of how things are organized within the law firm. So long as all vendor products match the specifications then the attorneys should have rapid access to their discovery. When the product does not match the template, Litigation Support or the vendor may have to modify load files or rename thousands of files. The end result is the attorney must wait longer to access materials.

It is through this document that the firm may prequalify and disqualify vendors. Further, when a vendor is familiar with the firm's technical standards, they can process subsequent projects more quickly.

To obtain the latest public version of the Litigation Support Technical Standards document, please visit http://www.eDiscovery.org. To obtain a copy of the firm version, please contact the Litigation Support Department.

The Litigation Support Department should use this document to eliminate discrepancies between firm technical needs and vendor products. Litigation Support routinely modifies the technical character of vendor products before the department can use it. This is a tremendous waste of time. If Litigation Support bills the client, this avoidable work is also a waste of client money. If the firm specifies a preference, the vendor's technicians and business can meet firm expectations. The result is removal of those discrepancies, or "flaws," and a lot of saved time and stress for everyone.

The document covers as many technical requirements as possible for as many types of discovery and software as possible. Litigation Support Department will modify the document to better match their firm requirements. The Department, however, will not remove the © Ad Litem Consulting, Inc. copyright.

Litigation Support

Litigation Support must be diligent in providing the appropriate requirements to the vendors so that they may have the greatest chance of properly quoting and successfully creating their product for the Firm.

The Standard is also how you can prequalify and exclude vendors. The vendors who successfully met the standard are your preferred vendors. Prequalify new vendors with this document. Vendors can take the initiative and deliver a sample production along with the standard to the department.

Legal Team

The lack of a standard when vending discovery means that non-technical people may make technical decisions. In absence of a stated preference by the firm, the vendor will use its own "default" settings. Some of these settings will directly impact the ability to litigate. Seemingly innocuous preferences can mean the difference between a 12 and 36 hour production turnaround time.

As the technical standard is a living document, the version included in this book will slowly become outdated. Therefore, the reader should download a copy of the most recent version for use.

As one can see, the standard covers a large number of considerations, including media labels, folder organization, slip sheets, video and Bates schemes. To provide additional help, the standard also includes a section illustrating "what not to do".

The following subsection is the default text for the public standard. The VP of Operations should update this text to reflect any particulars of their firm. Using the standard, the VP can then qualify vendors for work on current and future projects.

Litigation Support Technical Standards
2.0

Irrespective of who initiates a project, attorney, paralegal or litigation support, the firm will always expect the vendor's goods and services to meet these technical specifications.

Ad Litem Consulting, Inc.

Litigation Support Technical Standards
©2005 Ad Litem Consulting, Inc.

ISBN Number - 0-9774267-1-8

Ad Litem Consulting, Inc.
PO 124873
San Diego, CA 92112-4873
http://www.AdLitem.com

Acknowledgements

Browning Marean, III
Partner
DLA Piper Rudnick Gray Cary US LLP
401 B Street, Suite 2000
San Diego, CA 92101-4240
Phone (619) 699-2700
http://www.DLAPiper.com

Jason Primuth
General Manager
RealLegal - A division of LiveNote Inc.
4600 South Syracuse, 9th Floor
Denver, Colorado 80237-2719
Toll free: 888.584.9988
http://www.RealLegal.com

Table of Contents

License

I. REQUIREMENTS ON BOTH UNMODIFIED AND MODIFIED VERSIONS

The Litigation support Technical Standards ("LSTS") may be reproduced and distributed in whole or in part, in any medium physical or electronic, provided that the terms of this license are adhered to, and that this license or an incorporation of it by reference is displayed in the reproduction.

Proper form for an incorporation by reference is as follows:

Copyright (c) 2004 Ad Litem Consulting, Inc. This material may be distributed only subject to the terms and conditions set forth in the document license.

Distribution of substantively modified versions of this document is prohibited without the explicit permission of the copyright holder.

Distribution of the work or derivative of the work in any standard (paper) book form is prohibited unless prior permission is obtained from the copyright holder.

Any publication in paper or electronic form shall require the citation of the original publisher and author. The publisher and author's name shall appear on all outer surfaces of printed books. On all outer surfaces of the book the original publisher's name shall be as large as the title of the work and cited as possessive with respect to the title. For electronic publications, the reference should appear on those "pages", e.g. .html page or .PDF page, containing author's text.

II. COPYRIGHT

The copyright to this work is owned by Ad Litem Consulting, Inc.

III. SCOPE OF LICENSE

The following license terms apply to all Ad Litem Consulting, Inc. works, unless otherwise explicitly stated in the document.

Mere aggregation of author's works or a portion of an author's work with other works or programs on the same media shall not cause this license to apply to those other works. The aggregate work shall contain a notice specifying the inclusion of the author's material(s) and appropriate copyright notice(s).

SEVERABILITY. If any part of this license is found to be unenforceable in any jurisdiction, the remaining portions of the license remain in force.

NO WARRANTY. Ad Litem Consulting, Inc. works are licensed and provided "as is" without warranty of any kind, express or implied, including, but not limited to, the implied warranties of merchantability and fitness for a particular purpose or a warranty of non-infringement.

IV. REQUIREMENTS ON MODIFIED WORKS

All modified versions of documents covered by this license, including translations, anthologies, compilations and partial documents, must meet the following requirements:

1. The modified version must be labeled as such.
2. The person making the modifications must be identified and the modifications dated.
3. Acknowledgement of the original author and publisher if applicable must be retained according to normal academic citation practices.
4. The location of the original unmodified document must be identified. (www.eDiscovery.org)
5. The original author's name(s) may not be used to assert or imply endorsement of the resulting document without the original author's (or authors') permission.

V. GOOD-PRACTICE RECOMMENDATIONS

In addition to the requirements of this license, it is requested from and strongly recommended of redistributors that:

1. If you are distributing an Ad Litem Consulting, Inc. work on hardcopy or CD-ROM, you provide email notification to the author of your intent to redistribute at least thirty days before your manuscript or media freeze, to give the author time to provide updated materials. This notification should describe modifications, if any, made to the document.
2. All substantive modifications (including deletions) be either clearly marked up in the document or else described in an attachment to the document.
3. Finally, while it is not mandatory under this license, it is considered good form to offer a free copy of any hardcopy, online access or digital expression of an Ad Litem Consulting, Inc. work to its author(s).

Preface

This is a living document. Download the latest version from http://www.eDiscovery.org, for free.

- Aside from the Introduction section, every section should be generic enough that any vendor or firm can adopt it for use.

- Due to history, some examples in this document are Concordance oriented. Even so, all users should benefit from the best practices outlined.

- Please respect the law and the license; include the copyright information. Creating this document has taken more hours than I care to admit.

1.00 Introduction

Use this document to eliminate discrepancies between firm technical needs and vendor product. Litigation Support spends needless hours changing products in order to use it. The firm and client pay for product that, ultimately, is flawed. Litigation Support then faces a dilemma, fix it internally or have the vendor fix it. Expedience favors having Litigation Support do the work.

If the client specifies a preference, the vendor's technicians and business can meet firm expectations. The result is removal of those flaws and a lot of saved time and stress for everyone.

The document covers as many technical requirements as possible for as many types of discovery and software as possible.

To get a good idea of the reason for these explicit directions, please visit the final section of this document entitled, "Things not to do". All of these examples are from real life. All of these examples caused headaches, delaying reviews, productions and more.

I hope that this document is helpful to you.

1.01 For Vendors

Litigation Support strongly encourages you to always contact us about new projects and bids. We can supply you with the latest standards and requirements. We want you to succeed because we want our firm to succeed. This document outlines all of our product preferences.

Let the Litigation Support department know of any issues. If your company can not create BATES0000001.TIF but can create 0000001.TIF, please let the department know. These are issues best addressed sooner rather than later.

To contact the Litigation Support Department:

Name	_____	email	_____
Phone	(____) _____ --- _____	Fax	(____) _____ --- _____
Name	_____	email	_____
Phone	(____) _____ --- _____	Fax	(____) _____ --- _____
Name	_____	email	_____
Phone	(____) _____ --- _____	Fax	(____) _____ --- _____

Delivery of product that does not meet our standards and requirements may result in nonpayment. Depending upon time restrictions or other factors it may be unfair to bill our client for time spent adjusting vendor product to meet published requirements. When possible, product with significant deviations from Firm standards will be returned for correction by the vendor.

As we require client matter number and attorney name on all invoices, make sure you get it up front. Including this information will help expedite payment by the firm.

1.02 For Firms

Litigation Support

Litigation Support must be diligent in providing the appropriate requirements to the vendors so that they may have the greatest chance of proper quoting and successful creation of their product for the Firm. Remember, if Litigation Support doesn't adhere to these standards itself, how can it expect others to do so? As example, the client matter number and attorney name are required on all invoices by vendors. Make sure the vendors have it.

The Standard is also how you can prequalify and exclude vendors. The vendors who successfully met the standard are your preferred vendors. Prequalify new vendors with this document. Vendors can take the initiative and deliver a sample production along with the standard to the department.

Attorneys and Paralegals

The lack of a standard when vending discovery means that non-technical people may make technical decisions. In absence of a stated preference by the firm, the vendor will use their own "default" settings. Some of these settings will directly impact your ability to litigate. These seemingly innocuous preferences can mean the difference between a 12 and 36 hour production turnaround time.

Imagine if all the pens arrived disassembled. One order of pens results in three packages: pen, ink cartridges and caps. Other pens arrive, assembled in such a way as to require disassembly before final reassembly. Some box labels do not include the actual content, so the pen department person needs to write the contents on every box that arrives.

Meanwhile, everyone is waiting for the pen department to provide access to these pens. What if the solution to this snag was as simple as giving the vendor a document outlining assembly and label preferences? The hopeful result is the receipt of pens that are ready for use. Homogenous

If your firm has not adopted standards, I encourage you to work with Litigation Support to formalize one for yourself.

If your firm does not have an internal Litigation Support Department then this document can be especially useful for you. Once your standard is established, you do not need the technician to outline them again for every subsequent matter. Even firms using a hosted solution, or "ASP", will eventually create a production or use the database elsewhere. The requirements outlined in this document can help your firm make certain the vendor product can be used elsewhere.

1.03 How to Use This Document

This document is a template for a unified approach. As example, the information on every label contains the client-matter number, among other things. This is true for video media, discovery media, CDs, DVDs and so forth. If there are load files, the paths always follow the same structure. The firm may change the "example" names; cost codes and department contact information, but please leave the copyright in tact.

To learn more about implementation, please visit Ad Litem Consulting, Inc., at http://www.AdLitem.com.

2.00 Business Standards

This part of the document outlines what information each role (vendor, Litigation Support, paralegal or attorney) should include from a business standpoint. As example, the firm uses "cost codes". This is how the firm tracks how much it spent on a service such as computer forensics for a given case or firmwide for the whole year. This document outlines what information the firm should provide to the vendors.

2.01 Outgoing Media Kit

Every project must include this document. If the vendor follows the technical standards included in this manual, their product should be available to the legal team very quickly. This will also result in a quicker turnaround for paying invoices.

Vendors will do their best to meet the client requirements. It is unfair and difficult to impose these requirements after a project is completed or in process. Therefore, it is the responsibility of the Firm and Litigation Support to present the standards with any request for quote ("RFQs"). The paralegal can include this file for buying any litigation goods and services such as scanning, electronic discovery or video.

2.02 Cost Codes for Litigation Support

In order to facilitate the billing process the accounting department would like to have several pieces of information appear on every vendor invoice.

1. The *client–matter number* must appear on invoices, media labels and business correspondence (including emails) between Firm and vendor.
2. The *attorney's name,* whose signature will authorize the invoice, must appear on the invoice.
3. *Cost code* must appear on every invoice:

Cost Code	Description
001	Litigation Video and Graphics: Video and Graphics used at depositions, arbitration and trial.
002	Litigation Support Data Services: This covers the range of work such as: electronic discovery and database creation, hosting, administration and so forth. Value added services such as OCR, programming, forensics, conversions, and media creation are all "Litigation Support Data Services".
003	Scanning and Printing: Photocopying paper, scanning paper or printing a paper set from electronic source (a/k/a "blow backs").
004	Court Reporting Services – Non-Video Court reporters and their non-video associated costs.

2.03 Request for Quotes ("RFQs")

All RFQs should include several key pieces of information. As a vendor, please make certain these fields are completed. Missing or incorrect information will almost inevitably result in problems as the project matures. Note that some of the fields should appear on media labels, others on the invoices.

Field	Description
Attorney	The attorney who will "sign-off" and authorize payment.
Paralegal	The paralegal handling inventory, coordination with legal team.
Litigation Support	The project manager contact for this project.
Client-Matter Number	A Firm created number, this uniquely ties the project to the case.
Project Name	Each project must have a unique name.
Collection Name	Usually the same as the project name.
Due Date	When the team must have the completed project.
Description of Materials	A description such as boxes, video tapes. The more specific the better.
Services Required	A list of services such as synchronizing text to video or auto-coding.

For certain types of projects, such a computer forensic work, it may be difficult to impossible for the vendor to provide a qualified estimate. Under these circumstances, the Firm may prefer to pay an hourly rate for the vendor to gain a greater understanding of project scope. At the end of this hourly exercise, the Firm would like to then receive a formal RFQ.

2.04 Quotes

On vendor quotes, please reference the fields from the RFQ. We may be required to obtain multiple quotes. Therefore, knowing both the project name and client-matter number are critical. Please note that inclusion of the required fields as outlined in this document will curry favor with Litigation Support.

In order to properly compare one vendor quote to another, line-item pricing is the best format. In this fashion we can compare quotes. To this end, the law firm may include a preferred spreadsheet for quoting goods and services.

Quote File Format
The generally preferred formats for vendor quotes are all electronic. In order of preference, most to least, here are the accepted formats.

1. Litigation Budget Spreadsheet – This document is available from http://Litigation-Support.info.
2. An electronic format that allows for copy, paste and printing functions.
3. Hardcopy
4. Fax

2.05 Weekly Updates

Overview
The legal and support teams need weekly status and invoice updates. The update does not need to be too formal. The attorneys should always have a solid idea about the project progress and total costs. It never

hurts to communicate too much. This information helps everyone to plan and schedule their own efforts. If a project is going to be complete by a new date or the budget is heading away from the quoted target, these reports and forecasts will help all parties involved. These updates are all about zero surprises.

Please keep the firm informed about the following information.

Project Name
Please include this name in your quotes, reports and on your invoices.

Client-Matter Number
This number is required on all communications. This is how the firm tracks all projects and all payments and work relate to this number.

Project Complete %
On a weekly basis, the vendor should provide a report of all open projects and their status. Are there any issues which will cause the project to end more quickly than expected?

Current Bill
Projects, especially electronic discovery projects, can grow to unexpected sizes. This can happen due to various factors. The main concern here is that the attorney understands their current costs and is not surprised by the bill.

Original Bid
What was the original project estimate?

Paid To Date
What has the Firm paid to date for services on a project?

Work-In-Progress (W-I-P)
What the vendor has yet to bill.

Estimated Final Bill
Vendor gives an estimated grand total. This number is critical. It falls under the "told you so" part of the law that helps attorneys sign off on final invoices.

Estimated Completion Date
Please provide an updated completion date in your reports. In this manner, the team can plan their time and efforts accordingly. It is OK for this date to change. It is required to give as much notice as possible. It is better for the attorneys to schedule their time accordingly.

2.06 Color Blindness

A percentage of the population has a varying degree of color blindness. Some people can not distinguish between various shades of red versus green or blue versus yellow. Accommodating this genetic condition is simple.

Seven example scenarios of a problem waiting to happen:

1. Using red and green "sticky notes" to show plaintiff versus defendant or privileged versus confidential;
2. Using red and green slip-sheets, to show plaintiff blow-backs versus defendant blow-backs;
3. Using red and green media labels, such as a light green background with light red letters;
4. Using red and green highlighters on the same paper;
5. Videotaping a red object with a green background, such as a red dress;
6. If you have a green paper notepad with blank ink and red edits;
7. If you have a trial exhibit that uses red versus green to show important distinctions;

This requirement is very simple. When selecting color, avoid red/green or blue/yellow combinations. One never knows when a juror will be color blind. Litigators may present red/green graphs to highlight key relationships. Certain deponents and jurors just won't see the difference.

To learn more about color blindness, please visit:

- http://colorvisiontesting.com/ or
- http://www.toledo-bend.com/colorblind/aboutCB.html

2.07 Quality Control

The firm runs programs, which perform "QC" checks on every delivery. The QC programs evaluate the vendor delivery, looking for missing data or files, gaps and things of this nature.

It is important that the media label and format of the data comply with Firm standards. A CD containing critical data can be lost due to a handwritten label that simply reads "Data". At the same time, if the format of data contained on said CD is unusable, it does no one any good. It is a safe bet that every law firm has CDs in inventory that do not match what is on the server. In order to make the CD look like the server did (in case of deletion or crash) may take hours.

Content

Media labels, invoices and other important correspondence should always include certain information.

Test	Description
Client-Matter Number	Did vendor provide required information?
Responsible Attorney	Did vendor provide required information?
Responsible Paralegal	Did vendor provide required information?
Project Name	Did vendor provide required information?
Description	Did vendor provide required information?
Services Required	Did vendor provide required information?

Format

These tests look at things such as naming conventions and matching up image keys to the physical file.

Test	Description
Image File Count	Number of image files on delivery.
Document Count	Number of documents in the database load file.
Cross Reference Image Count	Number of images referenced in Opticon load file.
Cross Reference Document Count	Number of document breaks in Opticon load file.

Image File – Cross Reference Match	Does every image listed in the Opticon load file exist? Does every image file on the CD exist in the load file?
Document – Cross Reference Match	Do document start and end number have matching entries in the imagebase load file? Are all Opticon load file ranges in the document database?
Database Load File	We are looking at field delimiters, gaps and a field name header line.
Full Text Formatting	Was the format maintained or were there "odd" characters such as semi-colons instead of spaces.
Folder and File Naming	Does the delivery comply with naming standards and use client matter subfolder structure?

3.00 Technical Standards

This section of the document clearly outlines what information to include and how to format the information. As example, what information should appear on every label, from CD to VHS tape. This section also covers how the Bates, file, folder and volume naming conventions work.

The vendor should immediately alert the firm if it is unable to meet these standards. The firm will use this document to identify any deviations from the requirements. The law firm is very serious about consistency of product within each case and across all cases.

3.01 Media Labels

The following information should be visible on the CD, DVD, Tape, or a space provided where the information can be written clearly later. Some vendors forget to write their own contact information on the labels. It is helpful to have the contact information for the media's creator.

Please reference the examples on the following pages.

Required Fields	Sample Values and Examples
Vendor Name	ACME Scanning and Coding
Vendor Address	123 Main Street
Vendor Phone	(555) 555-1212 (voice) / (555) 555-1213 (fax)
Date of Media Creation	12/02/2003
Format Type	CD, DVD
Volume Name	Examples are "FER001, FER002, FER003"
X / Y	Examples are "1 / 3", "2 / 3", "3 / 3"; or just "1 of 1"
Bates Ranges	Examples are "FER000001 – FER001300"
Client-Matter Number	Example, "320123 – 00123"
Image Count	13,000 TIF images

A Note on Handwriting

A hand-written label is not acceptable. Handwritten labels are cryptic and illegible. Further, a pen can damage the media. Vendors should not make the firm re-label media. The purpose of the label is to provide a complete picture of the origin and content. If a label must have handwriting, script is preferred. Cursive handwriting is never acceptable. Bear in mind that other people have to read your writing.

Remember, the firm is making significant investment of the client's money. The media provides the first impression of the vendor's work. Perception is reality. If the delivery looks boiler room, then the Litigation Support persons will view the vendor as boiler room quality. If a vendor is sloppy on their label, chances are they are sloppy in all else they do.

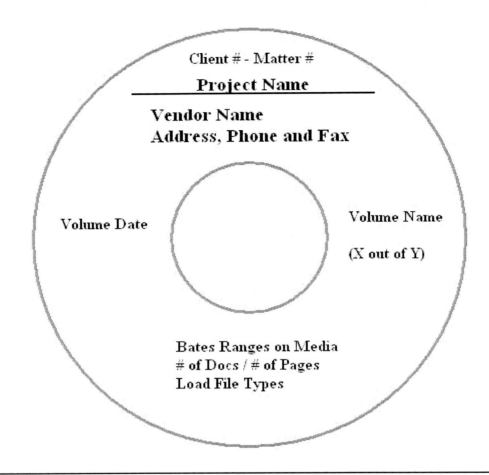

Basic Information – Generic Template

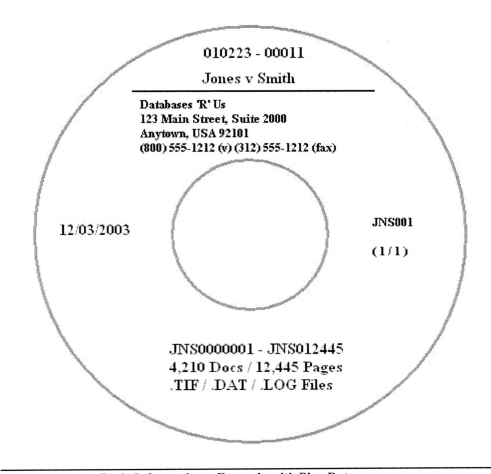

Basic Information – Example with Play Data

3.02 File, Folder and Volume Naming

The following explains how data should be organized on your deliverable to the Firm. Please let us know if you cannot meet this standard, and what standard you are prepared to deliver.

16-Bit vs. 32-Bit

Older computer software could only use filenames and folder names of very limited length. This is known as the 8.3 naming convention. If a filename is wider than 8 characters, 16-Bit programs truncate the name. So suddenly the filename "AMURPHY0000001.TIF" becomes "AMURPH~1.TIF". If the vendor is using older software, they may be restricted to 8.3 filenames. As such, they can create a file named 0000001.TIF but not AMURPHY0000001.TIF. This restriction is a serious problem. The vendor must contact Litigation Support to determine a remedy.

File and Folder Names

1. Only the characters A...Z and the numbers 0...9 are valid
2. Filenames should be unique, matching the image key
3. Image folder names should be zero-padded to 3 wide (i.e. 001, 002, 003, 004...)

NOTE: **The filename _must_ match the image key**. The only exception is where the image key contains additional characters that must be echoed in the .TIF file name. If the vendor cannot provide the full image key, please alert the Litigation Support Department immediately.

While the following is syntax for an Opticon ".LOG" load file, please use the same logic when generating the IPro ".LFP" and Summation ".DII" formats as part of every delivery. For additional examples, please look at the section 4.00 Software Specific Requirements.

Database Image Key	Cross Reference File		Actual Filename
	Image Key	Path To TIFF	
A001	A001	D:\A001\IMAGES\001\A001.TIF	A001.TIF

Volume Names

Each CD should conform to the same standard: [PROJECT NAME][999]. So, if our project is named SMITH, the first three CDs delivered should be named: SMITH001, SMITH002 and SMITH003. Note the zero-padding.

Unless the project name is "VOL", the volume name of the first CD should never be "VOL001". Many applications use the name "VOL" as a default value. This has resulted in many CDs named "VOL001". This can make identification of the related case and content difficult when the Firm has 2,000 CDs named VOL001. Do not use the vendor name as the volume prefix. Use project name as the volume name. The Bates prefix can be an acceptable project name as the volume prefix, but must confirm with the firm as to final decision. Vendors should never use their company name as the prefix. Some firms prefer to use the client-matter number as part of the project name.

3.03 CD Content and Organization

Each CD should contain the same folders each time. This structure is important, as the media is not copied to a single subfolder. Instead, "data" goes under a different folder tree than "images". If not segregated, Litigation Support will have to perform this separation.

D:\[VOLUME NAME]\	Your CD should have a root folder, named the same as the volume name.
D:\[VOLUME NAME]\IMAGES\	All images and image subfolders reside here.
D:\[VOLUME NAME]\OCR\	This folder contains multi-page ASCII text files. The filename matches the "BegBates" key, e.g. A001.TXT, A011.TXT, and A013.TXT.
D:\[VOLUME NAME]\DATA\	All "load", "database", "structure" and technical files reside here.
D:\[VOLUME NAME]\PROJECT\	1. Document coding instructions, 2. Project manuals, 3. Vendor contact information, 4. Source information, 5. Ranges information.
D:\[VOLUME NAME]\ATTACH\	All native files reside here, as applicable.

NOTE: Each CD must be self-contained. This means a CD containing A001...A010 must contain the images, database load file, OCR and cross reference file for A001...A010. A delivery of CD01...CD10 should have the load files for CD01 on CD01. Having load files for CD01...CD10 all reside on CD10 is incorrect. If the firm loses the "load files" CD, the corresponding CDs may not be usable. Further, this means tracking down 2 CDs every time there is a problem.

3.04 Organization of Sub-Folders

We understand that certain applications construct subfolders automatically in different configurations from that listed below. Therefore, this storage convention may not be possible for your organization without unreasonable effort. Do your best.

Standard sub-folders for each delivery: Images, OCR, Data, Project and Attach.

3.04.01 Images Folder

FOLDERS	CONTENT
D:\[VOLUME NAME]\IMAGES\0001\	IMAGE0000001.TIF...IMAGE0001000.TIF
D:\[VOLUME NAME]\IMAGES\0002\	IMAGE0001001.TIF...IMAGE0002000.TIF
D:\[VOLUME NAME]\IMAGES\0003\	IMAGE0002001.TIF...IMAGE0003000.TIF
D:\[VOLUME NAME]\IMAGES\0004\	IMAGE0003001.TIF...IMAGE0004000.TIF
D:\[VOLUME NAME]\IMAGES\0005\	IMAGE0004001.TIF...IMAGE0005000.TIF

NOTE: Zero-Padding is very important. This is especially true if you have 9999 subfolders.

One of the reasons why it is important to have a standard number of images per folder is so that Litigation Support can easily determine where missing images may reside. In this fashion it is also simple to locate the right folder based upon the .TIF filename. Empty or "skipped" subfolders are not acceptable. If there is a folder 1 and 3, there should also be a folder 2.

3.04.02 OCR Folder

This folder contains multi-page ASCII text files named for the image key or the first page of the document.

Different document review systems load OCR in different fashions. As such, this document includes organization and formatting considerations valid for every format. To learn the actual technical syntax, please refer to the software section for examples. Regardless of software title, there are attributes common to each software, such as filenames and organization.

While different OCR programs produce different types of output, the firm requires the vendor's product to match the naming conventions and organizational schemas outlined here.

The OCR filename must match the complete image key. As most programs load the OCR by matching the image key to the text file, all OCR for the entire document should reside in the single image key text file.

IMAGE KEY	BEGBATES	ENDBATES	OCR FILENAME	CONTAINS
A001	A001	A005	A001.TXT	OCR for A001…A005
A006	A006	A006	A006.TXT	OCR for A006
A007	A007	A070	A007.TXT	OCR for A007…A070

All load files and files for loading, regardless of application, should reflect this rule.
Note: The Bates names should be 7 numbers wide. They are limited here due to brevity.

3.04.03 Data Folder

All load files, except OCR, reside in this directory. While many vendors automatically include load file versions formatted for every major application, they all reside in the same folder. For the document review systems, there are basically two main load files: database load file and imagebase cross-reference load file. The first contains the discovery bibliographic coding including Bates. The second file is an index that correlates Bates to .TIF file.

Required files:
The following files should be found in every DATA folder of each delivery:
1. Database Load File
2. Database Structure File
3. Imagebase Load File

Database Load File Format
The database should be an ASCII delimited file. It is preferable to use the delimiters appropriate to the application. If the vendor wishes to include the OCR inside of the database load file, specific step-by-step instructions on how to load this data is required.

The first line of the load file should be the field names. This provides the database administrator a level of confidence upon seeing the field names and values line up perfectly in the database.

Database Structure File
The database structure file is an ordered list of every field name, field type and size. In the case of a date field, the size should show format (e.g. MM/DD/YYYY, DDMMYYYY, YYYYMMDD, etc.).

Imagebase Load File Format(s)
Please provide the image "cross-reference" (a/k/a "xref") load file in the following formats:

- _____; (e.g. Opticon .LOG file)
- _____;
- _____.

All load files, along with paths and technical preferences are contained inside this document.

Naming Convention:
Name the data files to match the CD volume name. In this fashion it is possible to match any load file with the right CD.

3.04.04 Project Folder

These files identify the project, associated information such as attorney name and all the treatments such as stamping or OCR. These files are extremely helpful when identifying an "orphaned" volume. They are also helpful when an old project begins again after a one-year hiatus.

1. **Bibliographic Coding Instructions**:
   This document identifies how the database was codified. This document shows which fields were coded and any rules around the codes themselves, such as valid document types.

2. **Project manuals**:
   As available.

3. **Vendor contact information**:
   A simple text file that tells us which vendor made the CD and their contact information.

4. **Source information**:
   If there was an **intake form**, include it here. What was the source of the project – boxes or electronic discovery? Sometimes we need to backtrack from the produced CD to the originating data.

5. **Ranges information**:
   Show a list of the Bates ranges on the CD.

3.04.05 Attach Folder

This is the home of native files. If there is a movie clip or spreadsheet associated with the collection, this is where is must reside. Of course, once on the folder, the full path will be:

X:\ATTACH\CLIENT#\MATTER#\DATABASE NAME\VOLUME\ATTACH\

FOLDERS	CONTENT
D:\[VOLUME NAME]\ATTACH\0001\	The first 1,000 native files
D:\[VOLUME NAME]\ATTACH\0002\	The next 1,000 native files
D:\[VOLUME NAME]\ATTACH\0003\	And so on…
D:\[VOLUME NAME]\ATTACH\0004\	…and so forth
D:\[VOLUME NAME]\ATTACH\0005\	

NOTE: Zero-Padding is very important. This is especially true if you have 9999 subfolders.

One of the reasons why it is important to have a standard number of native files per folder is so that Litigation Support can easily determine where missing attachments may reside.

3.05 Bates Schemes

While it is helpful to have a "significant" Bates prefix ("ACME" versus "A"), brevity is not without merit. Use the "KISS rule": keep it simple, Simon. Just think how many times you will need to write or enter the prefix. Also, there are computer issues that almost mandate certain syntax. Please use the following conventions when constructing the prefix.

We recommend using the project name for the prefix. In this fashion, each collection, project, Bates and files carry the same name. If you have 5 separate discovery collections, you will have 5 projects, 5 unique Bates prefixes and 5 unique filename prefixes. When it is time to produce, a new Bates scheme can be applied.

Guidelines for creating a correct Bates prefix:
1. No more than 5 characters wide
2. Only use uppercase letters from A to Z
3. Bates prefix should not end in "L", "O", "I" or "D"
4. No spaces or hyphens between the prefix and number

Explanations / Examples:
1. Good Bates prefixes include: A, AA, AAA, AAAA, AAAAA.
2. Bad Bates prefixes include: 9A, 9A9, A9, A9-, A-A-A, 0-A-0, A 0001.
3. OCR may mistake certain letters for the numbers "1" and "0".

Rules for creating a correct Bates suffix:
1. Suffix should be numeric
2. Suffix should be zero-padded to four (4) positions, the ten-thousandths place
3. Suffix should never contain spaces, hyphens, underlines or characters other than 0 through 9.

Good Bates suffixes include: .0001, .9999, .0100
Bad Bates suffixes include: .A, .0A, .A01, .A-1

Examples:
The following two tables will show the identical ranges using proper and incorrect prefixes and suffixes.

Correct Bates ranges:

BegBates	EndBates	Description
A001	A010	Prefix is short. Easy to see where prefix ends and
A011	A011	the next Bates number begins.
A011.0001	A011.0026	Zero-padded and numeric ensures proper sorting and
A011.0027	A015	software friendly format.
A016.0001	A016.0010	

Incorrect Bates ranges:

BegBates	EndBates	Problem
A9001	A9010	Is the document number 1 or 9001?
A9011	A9011	Is the prefix A or A9?
A9011.A	A9011.Z	Suffix is a letter, resulting in sorting issues.
A9011.BA	A9015	Suffix contains letter(s), resulting in sorting issues.
A9016.1	A9016.10	Suffix has no zero-padding resulting in bad sorting. Also, inconsistent suffix naming convention.

3.06 Data Files

The following files must reside in the Data folder on every delivery by the vendor:

1. Database load file,
2. Database structure file, and
3. Imagebase cross-reference load file.

1. Database Load File:

    i.   Delimiters – Although this document does not truly favor one application over another, the Concordance standard delimiter characters have proven reliable time and again. They are:
- Comma (020), Quote (254), Newline (174)
2. The first line of the database load file should be the field names.
3. The name of the database load file should match the volume name.

2. Database Structure File:

The Firm has a standard database structure we use for all databases (electronic and paper). We understand that software restrictions may result in a non-standard product. If the vendor is unable to then post-process their data to match our standard, Litigation Support will have to perform this work as billable time to the firm's clients. As one can imagine, knowing the database structure as relates to the database load file is critical.

This is a text file showing a sample structure file. The following is just for illustration and does not match Firm standards. Please refer to the Bibliographic Coding Manual for this information.

Field Name	Type	Size
Author	Paragraph	-
Date	Date	YYYY/MM/DD
Title	Text	60
Pages	Number	3.0

3. Imagebase Load File.

The following are the rules governing a good load file:

2. The imagebase load file name should match the volume name
3. All images referenced in the load file must be contained on the same volume
4. Document breaks
5. Page counts
6. Image path:

    D:\IMAGES\[CLIENT#]\[MATTER#]\[DATABASE]\[VOLUME]\IMAGES\...

Note: While the path may seem long, it provides everyone with a standard everyone can understand. The database folder may seem redundant at first. That is until there are 12 databases for a given matter number. At that time, one becomes grateful for the database subfolder. The firm uses this structure for many reasons. When the load file does not match this path, the vendor will have to this. If Litigation Support has to fix this, then the client may be paying twice for the same work.

Sample Opticon Load File:
Please note the path, image key matching the file name, doc breaks and page counts. Please refer to Section 4, to see examples for other types of load files.

[Field 1]	[Field 2]	[Field 3]	[Field 4]	[Field 5]	[Field 6]	[Field 7]
A001	[VOLUME]	D:\[VOLUME]\IMAGES\001\A001.TIF	Y			2
A002	[VOLUME]	D:\[VOLUME]\IMAGES\001\A002.TIF				
A003	[VOLUME]	D:\[VOLUME]\IMAGES\001\A003.TIF	Y			1

Here is an explanation of the Opticon load file format:

[Field 1]	Production Number	This is a text field which contains the "Production" or "Control" or Bates number for that page of the document. It is a unique value and is the load file "key".
[Field 2]	Volume ID	This is also a text field. It should contain the Volume ID of the CD on which the images are delivered.
[Field 3]	Full DOS Path	This contains both the path to the image and the actual image filename.
[Field 4]	Document Break	This is a text field. If this particular image is the first page of a document, this field should contain a "Y" (Yes).
[Field 5]	Folder Break	This is a text field. It's fairly rarely used but if used is intended to work just like Document Break, i.e. it would contain a "Y" if this is the first page of a new folder.
[Field 6]	Box Break	This is a text field. Also rarely used but intended to work like Doc and Folder Break...would contain a "Y" if this is the first page of a new box.
[Field 7]	Pages	This is a text field although it contains numeric data. If this is the first page of a new document, "Document Break" will contain a "Y" and this field will show the number of pages for the document.

Each of these fields is "separated", or "delimited", from the others, by a **comma**. When a technician imports a load file into Opticon, the content for each field is divided by the commas. Therefore, one can not have a directory named "\5,312,591 PATENT" since Opticon will view each comma as the start of the next field, per below:

[Field 1]	[Field 2]	[Field 3]	[Field 4]	[Field 5]	[Field 6]	[Field 7]
[Prod Num]	[VOLUME]	\5	312	591 Patent	,	[Pages]

3.07 Database Conventions

There are two main categories of discovery: electronic and paper. Electronic discovery software extracts "metadata" from the file. The metadata contains fields and values ranging from email subject to the last print date of a spreadsheet. Different file types may yield different types metadata.

This means the firm may need to pay for bibliographic coding for certain kinds of electronic discovery to achieve a complete database. If 20% of a database has no author information, this will impact search results and confidence.

All electronic discovery yields "full text". Full text is quite literally all the text inside a word processing or spreadsheet file or any other electronic files. Full text removes the need for OCR. Like OCR, full text does not provide bibliographic coding such as author and recipient. Full text will provide 100% accurate content where paper OCR may be 80% accurate or better, depending on the quality of the paper.

Load File Field Order

To help make life a little simpler for our legal teams, we outline the minimal fields that we require for each document, irrespective of origin, format or file type. This requires a certain amount of bibliographic coding for certain types of electronic discovery and all types of paper discovery.

As possible, the firm attempts to keep field order consistent for like types of databases. As such, the firm appreciates the vendor matching their load file to our field order. Our document reviewers expect to see the same fields in the same order for all databases. Please help us make this happen.

The exclusion of certain fields or their incorrect order may require Litigation Support to bill time to the client for correcting these problems. This is one reason why the Database Structure file (see 3.06) is so important.

While the vendor should provide the Firm with every field possible for electronic discovery, the following list from the law firm includes certain fields that we require at a minimum and in the following sequence. Depending upon the production or pre-production status of a collection, certain fields may contain no data.

Please refer to the *Bibliographic Coding Instructions* for bibliographic coding.

Note: These files, "load file field order" and "bibliographic coding instructions" should reside in the "DATA" and "PROJECT folders", respectively, on the delivery.

3.08 Native Files

There are many types of electronic discovery. This section describes how the firm prefers to handle certain types.

3.08.01 Spreadsheets

Spreadsheets are not printer friendly. Spreadsheets are rarely formatted to accommodate the printed page. As such, when vendors convert a spreadsheet to .TIF file, the results can be hundreds or thousands of pages of almost useless information and lots of blank pages.

The following is the approach the firm wishes to employ in representing spreadsheets in the database, review and production:

In the Database:

For every spreadsheet, there should be a record. Add the appropriate full metadata to the record. Include a hyperlink to launch the spreadsheet as a native file. For the image, put a placeholder explaining that the document is being reviewed as native file. Therefore there is no image of the spreadsheet.

The File:

Files should retain their original filenames and be read-only. These files go under the traditional X:\ATTACH\[client#]\[matter#]\[DB]\

Production Options –

Native: Spreadsheets should be produced natively. The CD label should have a Bates stamp. Included with the CD is a cover-page, bearing the next Bates stamp number. The cover-page should include a list of every native file, along with filename, file date and all other attributes.

Petrified: Spreadsheets should be converted to .TIF, per our technical standards. Any load files you return should reference the internal control number as well as the new production Bates start and end numbers.

Printed: Spreadsheets should be "blown back" to paper with any associated text and production Bates number.

3.08.02 Relational Databases

Certain software stores data in such a way that it will not make sense if printed in linear fashion. A "relational" database presents such a dilemma. A relational database stores related information in multiple tables. Each table therefore only presents part of the actual picture. It is only by matching up records across the tables that the combined data presents useful and complete information.

The best way to present this information is to print a report using the relational database software.

Relational databases should be reviewed in native format. The document review system should include a record that references the relational databases.

In the case of an accounting system, the Firm may decide to employ an expert witness who will review in native format. Production may consist of reports the expert printed. Alternately, the other side may be able to send their own expert to use the accounting system and print their own reports for their review.

Other databases may result in printed pages as a result of review. These pages should be treated per the accounting system example.

3.08.03 Deduplication, Keywords and Culling

The attorney may decide to employ strategies to cull discovery. These include deduplication and use of keywords and date ranges. We also prefer to receive two databases: a privileged and a non-privileged database. The legal team may provide the vendor with privileged keywords, such as attorney names, in order to help the team identify and review documents which do not contain privileged terms but do meet other criteria.

3.09 Project Specifications Document

Every project should include a Project Specifications Document. This document outlines the scale and scope of the project at hand.

This document is one type of project specification document. It specifies things that affect every project. A budget spreadsheet is part of a good specification document. The spreadsheet should show how the quantity of discovery scales along with price.

3.10 Bibliographical Coding Manual

This associated document shows the fields, treatment, valid values (such as document types) and other such standards. This information is not included in this document.

About Bibliographic Coding

The one thing that should always accommodate a coding manual is a list of key words, terms and dates. The more thorough the list the firm provides the vendor, the better the results. There are impressive case fact management tools on the market.

One should code for how they intend to search and retrieve. If it is important to know that "Smith" was the author and not simply a name appearing somewhere in the text, then you need bibliographic coding.

The three types of bibliographic coding include: manual, software and hybrid. Manual coding entails a person who looks at an image of a page and then enters the date, author and other assorted fields into the database. Trust me, this is not a job for the paralegals and associates. Firms pay per document and per page rates for this service. Turnaround times depend on various factors. Ask your vendor.

The second type of coding involves software. The computer will take existing OCR or generate OCR. Using a list of key words and terms (provided by legal team) the computer generates bibliographic coding. Also known as "autocoding" this is a software solution, therefore turnaround time is very short.

The final type of coding is a hybrid approach. Some documents require manual coding. Use autocoding to generate bibliographic coding for the majority of documents. The remaining documents, combined with any electronic discovery that lacked key metadata fields (like author) can then go to the manual coder. Again, certain electronic documents may require bibliographic coding. Otherwise, a search for author="Smith" may omit key documents.

3.11 Image Format

The majority of documents imaged only require black and white. On a less frequent basis, we may need color images. The following are our standards:

1. Black and White images should be 300 DPI, Group IV TIFF;
2. Single page TIFF images;
3. Color images should be discussed on a per image or per document type basis;

Please use the following guidelines, borrowed from Adobe's recommendations when scanning images:

- Choose grayscale for variable contrast pages in the scanning software.
- Increase brightness and contrast by 10% for text on colored paper, or filter out the background if your scanner includes that option in the scanning software.
- Adjust manual brightness control on the scanner if your scanner includes that option (for example, a knob).
- Use 16-bit color or less; 24-bit color images take considerably more system resources in the scanning software.
- Don't use any dithering or half toning options in the scanning software.

Oversized Documents

Every oversized document should result in two pages in the database. The first page shows a legend, Bates or any other identifying marks. The second page should be a full-scale image.

Should the document be a five-foot color map, a full-sized .JPG may be required. In this case, an accompanying first page black and white image of just the map legend is still required.

3.12 OCR

Vendor should use auto-rotate and voting when generating OCR. Most OCR software offers an auto-rotate option. When auto-rotate is enabled, the software will OCR each image four times, rotated 90 degrees each time. It determines the best result and publishes the content to the load file. The majority of documents have the same orientation: portrait. Without auto-rotate, these documents can yield good results. The rest of the documents may be designed for a landscape layout, such as an HR chart. Other documents still may have been scanned "upside-down", resulting in garbage OCR. OCR voting is a process where multiple OCR programs compare results to determine the best results.

Quality Check
The OCR text should best approximate and recreate the formatting found on the original image. The OCR field should never be just the words in one long string.

No text and the top, bottom or either side should be clipped.

Multi-Page Text Files
There should be a one document to one OCR text file ratio. The OCR filename must match the document image key. So, a 10 page document with the image key of AA001 should have a corresponding file AA001.TXT that contains the OCR for AA001 through AA010.

Each page of OCR should have a line identifying the page number, or Bates number. In this fashion, people can search for any Bates number and find the correct document. Please include space between the OCR text and page marker.

The following shows sample OCR:

<< AA001 >>

Text for first page

<< AA002 >>

Text for second page

The following chart shows a sample database and corresponding OCR files:

IMAGE KEY	BEGBATES	ENDBATES	PATH	FILENAME
AA001	AA001	AA0010	D:\[VOLUME NAME]\OCR\	AA001.TXT
AA011	AA011	AA0011	D:\[VOLUME NAME]\OCR\	AA011.TXT
AA012	AA012	AA0038	D:\[VOLUME NAME]\OCR\	AA012.TXT
AA039.0001*	AA039.0001	AA0100	D:\[VOLUME NAME]\OCR\	AA039.0001.TXT

* Please refer to Bates prefix and suffix conventions.

3.13 Slip-Sheets or Unitization Rules

If not already done by the client or the firm, the scanning company should place a slip-sheet between each document before scanning. After the documents are scanned, the vendor needs to provide logical document breaks. The Firm requires a 1 document to one database record ratio. Between slip-sheeting during scanning and the logical document breaks service, this ratio should be guaranteed. Slip sheets should not appear in the database or images.

The resulting database must maintain the parent-child document relationships through the "BegAttach" and "EndAttach" fields.

When the firm requires the vendor to print documents to paper, a non-white slip-sheet must separate every document. Blue and dark green are the preferred colors for slip-sheets. If the slip-sheets use more than one color please refer to the color blindness specifications.

3.14 Video

While the most frequent purpose of video is to capture and replay segments of a deposition in trial, there are other uses and places for video.

Deposition video can be a powerful tool in impeachment by showing contradictions of deposition testimony. Even if a deponent doesn't lie, they can still show powerful non-verbal cues such as nervousness, agitation, fear, or smug satisfaction. If a deponent is unlikely to attend trial for whatever reason, video is a great way to get them into the courtroom.

Beyond depositions, video can also be used as to show construction defects, accident scenes, technical details that demonstrate your case. A "day-in-the-life" video can be a powerful way to illustrate the damage of a real-life situation such as workplace injuries.

Trial isn't the only place to use video; it can also be used in settlement hearings, arbitrations, "markman" hearings and any other place where additional persuasive evidence would help.

If the firm requires the use of a videographer, that vendor must provide the right format, lighting equipment and experience, meeting or exceeding firm standards. These are the details that can help guarantee a quality level that the attorneys will want to use.

One purpose of these standards is to make certain that our legal teams and clients have the best quality and formats. Another purpose is so that our legal team can concentrate on the law and not worry about deciding which formats to use. The final purpose is to make certain the legal team only works with the true professionals who have invested the time and money into their trade and art.

A videographer may have certifications in legal video (such as CLVS or CCV) which demonstrate some level of skill and commitment to legal video. But such credentials do not guarantee perfect quality, nor does the absence of such certifications disqualify them as a committed professional.

Format and Video Gear
If at all possible, all firm-commissioned video must be shot in a digital format. With the recent proliferation of consumer, mid-tier and professional cameras on the market, we would like to request the use of only professional-grade cameras. Sony VX2000 or VX1000, Canon GL1 or GL2 or consumer-grade cameras are not acceptable. Any camera which records on DVCam or full size DV tape is clearly capable of capturing very high quality video.

Additional Gear
Do not rely on what is in the room. A professional videographer will bring the necessary lighting equipment and backdrops to make certain the video quality is good. If your videographer does not have such equipment, you may wish to consider using a different company.

Since good audio is critical in a deposition, make sure that the videographer has good microphones on every person whose voice you want on the tape. Any videographer which relies on the microphone on their camera will not create the quality of video that you will need.

A professional videographer may also use backdrops to minimize distractions behind the deponent. Bookshelves or open windows can cause considerable problems with the video.

Label Information
The following information should appear on every label or package:

1. Vendor Name
2. Vendor Address
3. Vendor Phone
4. Deponent Name (Last name, First name)
5. Dates of appearances (YYYY/MM/DD format)
6. Deposition Date (YYYY/MM/DD format)
7. Case Name
8. Indicate whether synchronized
9. Type of "sync" file (.MDB, .CMS, .PTF)

Note: The sync file may only exist on the last CD or DVD in a set - Clarify with your vendor.

Minimum Video Format Specifications
The Firm requires different encoding based upon the purpose of the video.

Deposition Video
MPEG1 video should be encoded with quality compression hardware to fit two hours on each CD. Video must be adequate for use at trial using Sanction II or Trial Director in full-screen mode.

Non Deposition Video
In occasions like a day-in-the-life video or site tours where picture detail and clarity are the overriding factors, MPEG 2 video may be a good option. (Such video is usually authored on a DVD disk; any video which plays in a DVD player is encoded in MPEG2 format.) But keep in mind that editing or synchronizing MPEG2 video is not nearly as simple as MPEG1 video. Nor is it as simple to use in trial presentation programs such as Sanction II or Trial Director.

Delivery Media
1.   Digital Format (such as CD or DVD) - Preferred
2.   SVHS – 2nd best
3.   VHS – Backup media, only acceptable when provided in conjunction with digital media

3.15 Synchronization

It is best to always get the synchronization done at the time of the deposition to avoid any last-minute expedite fees. Plus, having access to the video will also provide the ability to use your video in pre-trial settings such as mediations. Synchronized text should appear black on a solid white background. The text should be clearly legible no matter the quality or color of the background video. Use a minimum of a 12 point font.

3.16 Transcripts

While there are a wide range of court reporters and companies in the marketplace, every professional should be able to provide their product in one of our accepted formats. The goal is to minimize the amount of time required by law firm staff to make transcripts usable by the legal team.

The vendor should never add their company information to the header or footer.

File Format
The Firm uses [Enter Application Name] for transcript management (e.g. LiveNote, Summation, Sanction, etc.) The following formats are our accepted formats, in order of preferences (most to least):

1. _____ ;   2. _____ ;

3. _____ ;   4. _____ ;

5. _____ ;   6. _____ ;

Many court reporters deliver transcripts as an executable E-Transcript. These are acceptable, so long as the ".exe" file can export to a preferred format, as outlined above.

Media (Delivery Format)

While transcripts are very small in file size, the floppy is slowly disappearing from the PC landscape. In fact, the floppy is an option on some models of computer and laptops. Today, a CD or DVD burner comes standard on the majority of PCs and laptops. An external CD burner costs ~$50. A blank CD costs about $0.10 when bought en masse. Further, no one and no magnet can accidentally modify or delete the court reporter's work.

The following are our accepted formats, in order of preference (most to least):
1. CD or DVD;
2. 3.5" floppy disk;

Delivery via email is acceptable as a stopgap measure for emergencies or for delivery of a draft version before delivery of the final. All transcripts require a final CD, DVD or floppy.

Labels

The Firm has a vast library of transcripts. While every transcript is loaded into software for actual use, it is critical that the delivery media be easy to identify for inventory purposes. The Firm requests that the following information appear on all transcript media deliveries:

1. Vendor name
2. Vendor address
3. Vendor phone
4. Vendor email or web site
5. Names of deponents
6. Dates of depositions
7. Times of depositions

Quality and Production Errors

Errors may result in outright rejection of product, reduction in payment due to internal technical time spent to reformat a transcript for import or a simple request for resubmission of product. The decision may be a factor of time and attorney discretion.

3.17 Delivery Media

As of August 2004, one can buy a 200GB external USB2.0 hard drive for ~$200. As most vendors charge an average of $25 per CD, any delivery of 10 CDs or more should come on a hard drive. Aside from cost savings, loading from a hard drive saves time. It is much easier and expedient for Litigation Support to copy a single hard drive to the server than to copy 10 CDs.

Our firm prefers to receive productions greater than 10 CDs on an external hard drive with a USB2.0 connection. To learn the latest preferences, please contact Litigation Support.

4.00 Software Specific Requirements

As a result of coincidence, Concordance and Opticon are the two applications used for examples in earlier sections of this document. The following subsections identify how to create other load files which are in keeping with the organizational rules already outlined.

If your company would like to be included in this section, please contact Mark Lieb of Ad Litem Consulting, Inc.

4.01 Casesoft Suite

This section provided by CaseSoft.

CaseMap Load Files
1. A comma or tab-delimited text file with no supporting files
2. The first line of the text file should be the field names
3. One document record per line in the text file
4. The first field should have a value for every row. If necessary, this can be a sequentially numbered column that is skipped during the import.
5. No particular sort order is necessary. CaseMap will sort the records automatically.
6. Beginning and ending document numbers are often included, but not required.
7. The Bates – Begin field is a text field; so, Bates numbers should be padded with zeros in order to sort correctly. Example: 0001, 0010, 0100, 1000
8. Since many document databases use the beginning Bates number as the image ID, it is possible to set up links to images without importing any other information.
   a. Set up the appropriate File Viewer for the document database in the target case and make it the default File Viewer.
   b. From the Tools menu, choose Options and click to the Doc. Bates # tab. Check the option for "Use for default Linked File value" under Bates – Begin. (There is also an option here to populate Full Name and Short Name with the beginning number.)
   c. With these settings, your imported documents will be linked to their respective images at the completion of the import.

To learn more about CaseSoft, please visit http://www.casesoft.com.

4.02 IPRO

This section provided by IPRO.

IPRO Tech, Inc. - LFP File Format

LFP files (also called load files) are used to build the image database and to instruct IPRO View how to display a project's images. The image's file location; file type, boundary, and Bates number make up the LFP file.

Here are three methods for creating an .LFP file.

First, the discovery vendor provides an LFP file upon completion of the imaging phase for a project or case.
Second, one can use IPRO's free utility, IConvert.
This is a free download at http://www.IproCorp.com.

The IConvert tool will convert many load file formats to either LFP or other software formats, such as Summation and Opticon. It is a handy tool for people who don't even use any other IPRO products internally.

Third, manually edit or create an LFP file using a text editor.

Each record (or line) in the LFP file begins with a 2-letter code that determines the action the viewer will perform. To load an image, we will start the line with IM.

Commas separate some parts of the record along with semi-colons for the rest of the line. The command in the LFP file takes effect after you load or import the LFP file. (Import > Import LFP File from the IPRO Tech Utility menu).

Here are two examples of an LFP record. In our examples, we use the MSC collection. It contains two documents, two pages each. The volume name is MSC001.

Example 1: Single Page .TIF files
        IM,MSC00014,D,0,@MSC001;IMAGES\ 00\ 00;MSC00014.TIF;2
        IM,MSC00015,,0,@MSC001;IMAGES\ 00\ 00;MSC00015.TIF;2
        IM,MSC00016,D,0,@MSC001;IMAGES\ 00\ 00;MSC00016.TIF;2
        IM,MSC00017,,0,@MSC001;IMAGES\ 00\ 00;MSC00017.TIF;2

Example 2: Multi-Page .TIF files
        IM,MSC00014,D,1,@MSC001;IMAGES\ 00\ 00;MSC00014.TIF;2
        IM,MSC00015,,2,@MSC001;IMAGES\ 00\ 00;MSC00014.TIF;2
        IM,MSC00016,D,1,@MSC001;IMAGES\ 00\ 00;MSC00016.TIF;2
        IM,MSC00017,,2,@MSC001;IMAGES\ 00\ 00;MSC00016.TIF;2

Note: Because the files are multi-page, the entire bates range (or image key range) must point to the same .TIF file. As example, MSC00014 contains both "14" and "15". Therefore, to view page 15, the computer must display MSC00014.TIF.

The following provides a breakdown of the fields:

Value	Description of Purpose
IM	Import code identifier (Importing New Page/Image database record)
MSC00014	The image key/document id number
D	Document designation; only designate the first page of each document.
0	Offset to the Tiff file. Always 0 for single page tiff files. When creating Multi-Page Tiff files, this number will increment for the pages within the file. (If there is an 11 page document, the offset would start at 1 and end at 11 and the next tiff file would start over at 1.
@MDEMO	CD volume name
IMAGES\00\00	Directory path on the CD for the image
MSC00014.TIF	Filename for the image.
;2	Tells IPRO the Types* of image file, e.g. tiff, PDF

*Supported Image Types and their specification in the LFP file are:

1.   Type 1 is for IPRO Tech image from DOS-Based version, still supported (.IMG)
2.   Type 2 is for Standard single and multiple page black & white or color TIFF (.TIF)
3.   Type 3 is for IPRO Tech stacked TIFF (.STF)
4.   Type 4 is for Color image (.BMP, .PCX, .JPEG or .PNG)
5.   Type 5 is for black & white .PDF
6.   Type 6 is for Color .PDF
7.   Type 7 is to Auto-detect the .PDF type, e.g. Color or Black & White

To learn more about IPRO, please visit http://www.iprocorp.com.

4.03 Dataflight's Concordance and Opticon

This section was provided by Dataflight.

Concordance Database Load Files

The most reliable format for Concordance data delivery is a Concordance Database. This will ensure that the vendor has the correct fields, and that the data will load without a hitch. Rolling productions, delivered as Concordance databases, can be merged into the working set utilizing the standard "Import Concordance Database" option. Additional fields of data can be imported into existing records in the same fashion, allowing for initial base level coding to be done, and then more detailed coding for a subset of "Key" documents, identified through initial review. In instances where this is not an option, data can be delivered utilizing standard delimited files for coded data, and TXT or RTF files for OCR data. Refer to the load files section of this document to see the firm's preference.

Delimited Load Files

The first line of the delimited text database load file should be the field names.
Concordance allows users to specify delimiters; however, the best practice is to use the "Concordance Standard Delimiter" characters, which are:

3. Comma (020),
4. Quote (254),
5. Newline (174)

OCR Load Files

OCR is loaded into Concordance through the READOCR CPL (Concordance Programming Language) script, which is designed to import document level OCR (one database record represents one document). Your text files should be on the document level to import properly with this CPL.

The choice of multi-page OCR files, or "Document level" files, means that the full document, including all pages, resides within a single file. If the database has five records, then there are five documents and five OCR text files, each containing however many pages. Most vendors will delineate between OCR pages by adding text such as, << ABC0000001 >>.

The OCR text filename must be unique. Otherwise the READOCR program may import that text into multiple records. The filename, therefore, should match the image key field for the associated document in the database (IMAGEKEY.TXT). The script will scan selected volume directories for the filename that matches the value of the "IMAGEKEY" field.

Example:

Two documents have been OCR'd for import into a Concordance database, with Bates ranges corresponding MSC000001 and contains 3 pages. The second begins at MSC000004 and contains 2 pages. The corresponding OCR text files are named MSC000001.TXT, and MSC000004.TXT.

BEGBATES*	ENDBATES	PATH	FILENAME
MSC000001	MSC000003	D:\[VOLUME_NAME]\OCR\	MSC000001.TXT
MSC000004	MSC000005	D:\[VOLUME_NAME]\OCR\	MSC000004.TXT

* *Image key* - unique value.

Opticon OPT (Load) Files

The Opticon load file details the link between documents in Concordance and their corresponding images. Each line reference defines the image key (the reference from the database), its volume label (for identification purposes), and the associated image (with its full file path). The load file entries also define the document breaks and, optionally, page counts.

The Opticon load file format is a text-delimited file containing all information necessary to link the imagebase with the database. There is one line entry per image file, whether it is a single-page or multi-page image file. The load file consists of seven delimited entries as follows:

ALIAS,VOLUME,PATH,DOC_BREAK,FOLDER_BREAK,BOX_BREAK,PAGES

Example:

The following is a 5-image load file example. It details 2 documents; the first relates to the image key MSC000001 and contains 3 pages. The second begins at MSC000004 and contains 2 pages.

```
MSC000001,MSC001,D:\IMAGES\001\MSC000001.TIF,Y,,,3
MSC000002,MSC001,D:\IMAGES\001\MSC000002.TIF,,,,
MSC000003,MSC001,D:\IMAGES\001\MSC000003.TIF,,,,
MSC000004,MSC001,D:\IMAGES\001\MSC000004.TIF,Y,,,2
MSC000005,MSC001,D:\IMAGES\001\MSC000005.TIF,,,,
```

Value	Description
ALIAS	Should match your image key from the Concordance database. Concordance stores this key in order to reference the image.
VOLUME	This entry is the name of the volume where the image resides. This is typically the volume name of a CD or server. (Optional)
PATH	This is the full path and file name (and extension) of the image.
DOC_PATH	Enter a 'Y' to denote whether this image marks the beginning of a document.
FOLDER_BREAK	Enter a 'Y' to denote whether this image marks the beginning of a folder. (Optional)
BOX_BREAK	Enter a 'Y' to denote whether this image marks the beginning of a box. (Not Currently Supported)
PAGES	This entry is the number of pages associated with the image. (Optional)

Opticon currently supports the following image types:
- TIFF files: (single and multi-page): (.TIF)
- JPEG files (.JPG)
- GIF files (.GIF)
- Bitmap files (.BMP)
- PCX files (.PCX)
- CALS files (.CAL, .MIL)

To learn more about Concordance and Opticon, please visit http://www.dataflight.com.

4.04 Image Capture Engineering

This document does not yet provide any specifics for this software. If you would like to submit content, please contact Ad Litem.

To learn more about ICE, please visit http://www.imagecap.com.

4.05 Summation

Summation provides a wide array of white papers in Adobe PDF format. To download, please visit their website: http://www.summation.com/papers/

One white paper of note is "A Complete List of DII Tokens". This **11 page** document contains a "complete list of DII tokens used in Summation Blaze LG, LG Gold, and iBlaze Version 2.6. It includes, but is not limited to, all recent tokens added to handle the loading of eDiscovery into Summation using a DII file".

If you want to understand that .DII file, then download a copy.

To learn more about Summation, please visit http://www.summation.com.

4.06 iCONECT

iCONECTnxt (from iCONECT Development, LLC)

This section was provided by iCONECT Development, LLC.

iCONECTnxt Data Load Files

iCONECTnxt supports the following load file types:
*   CSV file
*   Delimited text file / Customized load files
    The user can choose from pre-defined templates or specify custom delimiters.
*   OCR text files / Load List files
    If OCR content was not part of the original data import, the OCR text can be loaded later by using an OCR Load List file (your vendor may refer to this as a "Control List"). The OCR Load List file maps the OCR text files to the appropriate record in an iCONECTnxt database by using a cross-referencing field (typically the Bates number field).

    The OCR Load List file from your vendor will have the following structure:

    MSC0010042,J:\[VOLUME]\OCR\MSC001042.txt
    MSC0010046,J:\[VOLUME]\OCR\MSC001046.txt

    The first field (in the example above, a Bates number) identifies the record that requires the OCR text. The second field provides the path to the OCR text file.

    Note: In the example above, the Bates number (e.g., MSC0010042) matches the name of the OCR text file. However, the OCR text file can be named differently (this is up to your vendor).

    Tip: Your vendor should prepare the OCR Load List file to cross-reference at the record (not page) level (i.e., one text file per record regardless of the number of pages in that record). This format will allow the OCR to be loaded when your vendor has placed the text files in subdirectories.

iCONECTnxt Image Load Files

Images are loaded into iCONECTnxt through the use of an Imagelink file that maps the physical location of images to an iCONECTnxt database field. This enables users to launch images directly from an iCONECTnxt database by clicking a link.

The Imagelink file content can imported from one of the following load file types:

- Doculex 5
- Opticon

Note: If the load file is not Doculex 5 or Opticon, you can use a free load file converter (IConvert) available from IPRO at http://www.iprotech.com.

To learn more about iCONECT, please visit http://www.iCONECT.com.

4.07 inData TrialDirector

The following text is reprinted, with permission, from the TrialDirector Help Manual. To learn more about TrialDirector visit their website at http://www.inDataCorp.com.

inData TrialDirector - Object Load List (.oll)

The load file establishes relationships for multiple page documents and determines which tab each item should be associated with.

The Object Load List format is as follows:

Note: Although the text appears on two lines, it is actually one long line.

**"Tab","DocumentID","PageID","Page No",
"Description","Volume","Path","Filename",""**

Sample multiple page document lines in the load file might look like the following:

**"1","TDX00008","TDX00008","1","","","Docs\001","TDX00008.tif",""
"1","TDX00008","TDX00009","2","","","Docs\001","TDX00009.tif",""**

Sample multiple page TIFF lines might look like the following:

"1","EXH001","EXH001","1","","","Docs\001","EXH0000001.tif",""
"1","EXH001","EXH002","2","","","Docs\001","EXH0000002.tif",""
"1","EXH001","EXH003","3","","","Docs\001","EXH0000003.tif",""
"1","EXH001","EXH004","4","","","Docs\001","EXH0000004.tif",""

A sample photograph line might look like the following:

"2","MRE01","MRE01","1","MRE film","","Photo\001","MRE0001.jpg",""

A sample multimedia file line might look like the following:

"4","Gates1","Gates1","1","","","Video\001","gates1.mpg",""

The load file is an ASCII delimited file that contains the following nine fields:

Field	Description
Field 1	**Record Type** - Determines the tab with which the item will be associated. These are the available record types: 1 - B&W Image Documents 2 - Color Photographs 4 - Multimedia Files 5 - OLE Files
Field 2	**Document ID** - if there are multiple pages to an item, all will have the same Document ID, which is the same as the first page of the document. This field is limited to 20 alphanumeric characters and may include spaces.
Field 3	**Item ID** - this indicates the page number in a multiple page item. This number combined with the Document ID must be unique. This field is limited to 20 alphanumeric characters and may include spaces. For Video segment items, DocumentDirector adds four characters to the end of the Item ID. Keep this in mind so you do not exceed the 20-character limit.
Field 4	**Page Number** - the Document ID is the same for each page in the item. The page should be incremented by 1 for each following page. Items with no multiple page association (i.e., OLE links) are always page 1. Videos can have clips and multiple segments, but once a segment is created the number cannot be reused. **Note:** Since long file names create long barcodes, which may not fit the print options, try to keep Item ID between 5 and 12 characters if you plan on printing barcodes.
Field 5	**Description** - this field is not required and is editable within the Case Explorer.
Field 6	**Volume Label** - this field can be blank as long as the load file (.OLL) exists on the same volume as the files and images. The path is relative to the location (path) of the .OLL file. Paths are Volume label based so that on removable drive systems, the drives can change and DocumentDirector will continue to find the items.
Field 7	**Path** - stores the exact location of the item with no leading or trailing backslash.
Field 8	**Filename** - the actual filename of the object (e.g., 001.TIF).
Field 9	**Special Field** - used internally by DocumentDirector only. If you are creating a load file, leave this position empty. If you are editing an existing load file, do not modify this position.

4.nn Additional Titles to Follow

The law firm should add entries as needed for any additional software titles. If a software company wishes to add their sample load file, please submit it to Ad Litem Consulting so that all may benefit. The Litigation Support Technical Standards document is offered to the public for free in an effort to move the industry forward.

5.00 Examples of What Not To Do

The following are examples of bad product. Any of these types of "fouls" will require correction before Firm legal staff can begin their work. Corrections may be performed by Litigation Support or the vendor, as need and time restrictions dictate. All examples are real and taken from deliveries we have received.

5.01 Media Labels

1. Misspellings: Client names, matter names or client-matter numbers are misspelled. This can be especially frustrating when the Firm's client wishes to see or get a copy of the vendor product. If our client's name is SMITH, a CD labeled SITH or SMATH or SMYTHE instantly calls into question the quality of the content of the media.
2. Handwritten: Not only is handwriting hard to read, but it also lends itself to missing information.

5.02 File / Folder / Volume Name Conventions

1. Tilde or otherwise truncated file or folder names. As example, AAA0000001.TIF versus AAA000~1.TIF and D:\PROGRAM FILES\ versus D:\PROGRA~1\. Whenever possible, volume, file and folder names should not be wider than eight (8) characters with a suffix not wider than three (3) characters. In technical circles, this is known as the "16-bit" or "MS-DOS 8.3" naming convention.
2. Use of spaces or any characters in a load file that Windows does not allow in a file or folder name. This seems obvious, but we have received deliveries from vendors who used characters in the database that were not valid in the filename. This resulted in files that would either not copy to the server or would copy with strange naming results. We don't know what kind of software or operating system this vendor used to create their product, but they certainly never tried to load it themselves.
3. I will not name the vendor, but on several separate projects they used VENDOR001 as the volume name. If used, my server could have a dozen VENDOR001 CDs. If the filenames do not have the full image key, e.g. "0000001.TIF", there is no quick way to determine the associated database, client or matter.
4. Missing or empty folders are a big red flag. If your image folder contains 3 subfolders named 012, 014 and 015, your first inclination is to ask what happened to 001-011 and 013. This just isn't right on any level. It leads me to assume there will be problems with the data, specifically missing images.

5.03 Database

1. The date field should only include the date. An example of a valid date is "01/01/2004". An example of an invalid date is "01/01/2004 12:01:01PM".
2. Dates should have 4-digit years. "01/01/2004" is valid where "01/01/04" is not.
3. OCR and full text from electronic discovery should maintain original formatting. Some EDD and OCR applications replace spaces, soft returns and hard returns with characters other than spaces, soft returns and hard returns. If the original text is "Best Practices", then the database OCR field should never contain: "BestPractices", "Best/Practices" or "Best@Practices".

5.04 Media Content

1. Each CD should be "self-contained". If 5 CDs arrive and the load files for all 5 CDs reside on CD #5, then that is wrong. The idea here is to be able to reload any CD as quickly as possible. Sometimes collections become separated over time. It is conceivable that CD #5, with all the database and image

load files, could be lost. This means CD #1 through #4 are now incomplete. Each CD should be self-contained.

2. For a given project, all load files (Concordance .DAT and Opticon .LOG) should use the same field names, ordering and structure as the first delivery.

3. A "synch" file provides the text to go with the video. That term is generic. There are multiple file types to consider. If you are a Sanction user, you want an .MDB. The vendor cannot tell what formats the Litigation Support person uses unless they are told or request that information.

5.05 Load Files

Concordance Load Files

1. A .DAT load file without a supporting file showing: field structure, field size and field sequence.

2. The first line of the .DAT file should be the field names. When loading a .DAT file, this is the simplest way to see if the data loaded correctly.

3. Badly formatted body Meta-Data. The spaces and returns must match the original text. No odd characters, such as a semi-colon, should appear in lieu of a soft-return or a space. These kinds of problems not only make the text hard to read, but they also interfere with searching.

4. More than one document per database record. This kind of error can cost the Firm hours and days or a case. When the review team identifies all the documents to produce, a ratio other than 1:1 will result in the wrong documents getting produced along with the right documents.

5. Databases and load files should open sorted by "Bates" or "docno". Concordance displays records in the same order that they were loaded. Therefore a disordered load file results in a disordered database.

6. Duplicate, overlapping or gaps in "Bates" or "docno" fields.

7. Bates / Docno prefix contains characters other than A…Z.

8. Bates / Docno suffix contains letters and is not zero-added to four places (.0001).

9. Bates / Docno contains a space, such as "AA 00001".

5.06 OCR

1. When there is bad OCR, an appropriate error code and warning to the firm is required. Things such as handwriting and graphics will not provide good OCR results. As such the vendor must warn the firm and Litigation Support about these issues and the associated "<<OCR ERROR>>" text. In this fashion, the law firm knows a legitimate error from a missed problem. This can result in a "false positive" in terms of QC looking for errors.

2. Vendor must use **Auto-Rotate** on every image. This ensures the 5 – 10% of images facing sideways or upside-down get quality OCR. Documents such as hierarchical employee charts are almost always designed landscape instead of portrait. All of these names and titles should be easy to OCR, unless auto-rotate is off.

5.07 Opticon Load Files

1. The following is based on an actual subfolder name we received on a production by a vendor:

   \BOX 3 - JOHN DOE & OTHERS DOCS REC'D FROM BOB SMITH; AL SMITH'S NOTEBOOKS, PAPERS\

2. There are several big fouls here. In addition to the "&", ";" and "'" (apostrophe) characters, there really is no purpose in a "significant folder name". This was part of a series of subfolders that literally went eight (8) folders deep. Not only will the end user never see the folder name when reviewing their discovery, but one cannot load the cross-reference file into Opticon. Opticon requires a comma delimited load file.

3. The example below shows problems we have seen historically:

   A. Image key, "A001" and filename "001.TIF" do not match
   A001,[VOLUME],D:\[VOLUME]\IMAGES\001\001.TIF,Y,,,

B. This first page of a document is missing a page count
A001,[VOLUME],D:\[VOLUME]\IMAGES\001\001.TIF,Y,,,
C. This page is missing the ","s and possibly the begin document "Y" and page count
A002,[VOLUME],D:\[VOLUME]\IMAGES\001\A002.TIF

4. Opticon load file extensions should be .LOG, .TXT or .RXF. Some software vendors used to create the log file output with an extension of .OPT. Opticon does not look for .OPT when displaying potential load files.
5. Image Cross-Reference File – Filename Mismatch. The filename inside of the cross-reference file does not match the actual filename. Again, this could be a hiccup in processing. This is caught when we run our QC tests to make sure every file listed is actually on the server.
6. Only images belong in the Opticon load file. Sometimes vendors will put the OCR files into the same folder as the images. This has, on occasion, resulted in a load file that references both the images and the OCR files. In the following example, lines 2 and 4 should not be included:

1. SMI0001,SMI001,D:\IMAGES\SMI0001.tif,Y,,,1
2. SMI0001.TXT,SMI001,D:\IMAGES\SMI0001.TXT,,,,
3. SMI0002,SMI001,D:\IMAGES\SMI0002.tif,Y,,,1
4. SMI0002.TXT,SMI001,D:\IMAGES\SMI0002.TXT,,,,

Every import line for every delivery should be formatted the same, irrespective of the technician who generated the load file. Right or wrong, at least the delivery is wrong in a consistent fashion from CD to CD. If the path information isn't "plug and play", Litigation Support has to modify the associated load files. Did the vendor not know or not care that their CDs contained inconsistent information?

5.08 Image Format

1. Multi-Page TIFFs. There are two major problems with multi-page TIFFs. The main issue is the inability to easily divide one document into two. Selecting the "logical bindings" option in scanning along with use of slip-sheets is a great way to ensure the required one document to one record division in the database.
2. Unless otherwise specified, we do not want Bates stamps or any other type of stamp applied to our images.
3. TIFF images of Excel spreadsheets where columns are too narrow causing cell content to appear as "######" instead of the actual value.
4. TIFF images of Excel spreadsheets where the cells show the formula instead of the resulting value. An example of this would be a summing cell that should show the grand total for a column but instead shows something such as "=sum(A1..A10)".

5.09 Transcripts

1. Transcript is in WordPerfect format or some legacy word processing format such as Wang or Wordstar.
2. Transcript requires manual editing due to extremely irregular formatting.
3. Gaps in text or pages.
4. Control characters in transcript text file.
5. Each line of text has a "line wrap" instead of "hard return". (Note: UltraEdit, text editor can fix this.)
6. Delivery transcripts on floppy instead of CD. (It is safer and the media cheaper.)

5.10 General Errors / Issues

1. Databases and Opticon load files where every document is one page. While possible and quite likely to have 1 single page document, a database comprised entirely of 13,000 one-page documents is highly unlikely.

2. While a document containing 13,000 pages is possible, is it unlikely. A database with several 13,000 page documents is extremely unlikely. This could be a physical versus logical document breaks issue.
3. Do not create a new image sub-folder for each document. A CD with 300 1-page documents should result in 1 folder of 300 images. 300 folders each containing 1 page is incorrect.
4. When generating electronic or paper documents, the vendor should never add their company information to the header or footer.
5. Add your own real life war stories to the growing list. Visit http://www.eDiscovery.org today.

5.11 Real Experiences

All of the examples in the "things not to do" section are, unfortunately, real. These types of problems eat up a lot of billable time. As the document matures, the list will probably get longer. There are a lot of creative people out there working the controls. What they create is what your firm will use for review, productions and exhibits.

People are welcome to submit their experiences at http://www.eDiscovery.org.

These examples are not meant to criticize any product or person. These examples explain the types of problems one may encounter, by product, regardless of product, firm, vendor or persons involved. One goal of this document is to give both good and bad examples that anyone technical person can use to improve their products.

If you use this document, please let me know.